Writing the Future
of Black America

Writing the Future Of Black America

LITERATURE OF THE HIP HOP GENERATION

Daniel Grassian

The University of South Carolina Press

© 2009 University of South Carolina

Published by the University of South Carolina Press
Columbia, South Carolina 29208

www.sc.edu/uscpress

Manufactured in the United States of America

18 17 16 15 14 13 12 11 10 09   10 9 8 7 6 5 4 3 2 1

Library of Congress Cataloging-in-Publication Data

Grassian, Daniel, 1974–
    Writing the future of Black America : literature of the hip-hop generation / Daniel
Grassian.
        p. cm.
    Includes bibliographical references and index.
    ISBN 978-1-57003-781-8 (alk. paper)
    1. American literature—African American authors—History and criticism.
    2. American prose literature—African American authors—History and criticism.
    3. Hip-hop—Influence. I. Title.
    PS153.N5G69 2009
    810.9'896073—dc22

                                                                    2008036718

This book was printed on Glatfelter Natures, a recycled paper with 30 percent
postconsumer waste content.

Contents

In May 2004 comedian and entertainer Bill Cosby, one of the most famous and widely respected African American men alive,[1] gave an electrifying, impassioned, but enraged speech at a gathering in Washington, D.C., that celebrated the fiftieth anniversary of the landmark *Brown v. Board of Education* decision. Instead of praising the racial and social progress made since then, Cosby blamed the members of the black lower class for their own economic, spiritual, and intellectual impoverishment. He insisted that they and only they (not whites or wealthy African Americans) could lessen the still-existing social and economic gulfs between whites and African Americans. "We cannot blame white people," Cosby insisted. "The lower economic people are not holding their end in this deal." Repeatedly referring to poor African Americans as "these people," Cosby seemed to separate himself as well as his generational, economic, and educational class from other less-illustrious and/or less-successful African Americans. His comments identify and reveal a huge gulf that has evolved between many successful, middle- or upper-class African Americans and struggling lower-class African Americans (2004). Yet perhaps more importantly, it illustrates a gulf between the civil rights generation of African Americans, who came of age from the mid-1950s to the early 1970s,[2] and the hip-hop generation, which consists of African Americans born in the 1960s and 1970s.[3]

While never directly naming them, Cosby clearly targets the hip-hop generation in his speech by deploring their outward appearances, claiming in his speech to the NAACP, "People putting their clothes on backwards. Isn't that a sign of something going on wrong?" Cosby continues to berate the hip-hop generation, whom he describes as "people with their hat on backwards, pants down around the crack" and women who wear dresses "all the way up to the crack" with "all kinds of needles and things going through their body." Furthermore, he calls them "knuckleheads" for speaking nonstandard English and for "fighting hard to be ignorant" (2004). Cosby implies that the elder generation, his civil-rights-generation peers, by granting their progeny more freedom, per- haps in response to the freedom they had been denied, growing up as they did in still-segregated America, has helped encourage what he perceives to be the unacceptable and socially detrimental behavior and attitudes of the hip-hop generation. Cosby's speech was not a fly-by-night, aberrant activity, as he has since made many similar speeches in cities across the country, reiterating these claims. For instance, in spring 2006, Cosby conducted a twenty-city U.S. speak- ing tour entitled "A Call Out with Bill Cosby" ("Funnyman's Serious Message" 2006).

Cosby's comments are obviously exaggerated, as comics often do for humor- ous or dramatic effect. People are not really being "shot in the back of the head over a piece of pound cake," as Cosby certainly knows. Furthermore, not all lower-class African Americans speak nonstandard English as Cosby claims, at least not in all circumstances. Are there "football players" and "multimillion- aires" who "can't read," as Cosby claims (2004)? That is possible, but if so, they could be of any ethnicity. Are all lower-class African Americans raising pimps as Cosby claims? Of course not. I am certain Cosby knows that, but he certainly believes that these problems exist in significant proportions and need to be addressed. For him, right now, the hip-hop generation is a lost generation that is not only self-destructing but is taking with them all of the advances and achievements made by previous generations of African Americans, especially those made by the civil rights generation.

The response to Cosby's speech and subsequent claims has been mixed, as one might imagine. Some applaud him for his honesty and generally support his emphasis on personal responsibility, such as Jesse Jackson and NAACP Presi- dent Kweisi Mfume (Jones 2006). Along similar lines, Sam Fulwood III claims, "Cosby was bold enough to say what needs to be said and what many of us say in private" (2005). Likewise, Reverend Al Sharpton responded to Cosby's speech, "I think a lot of what Cosby is saying is good." At the same time, ques- tioning Cosby's nefarious lack of a clear solution, Sharpton asks, "Are we just going to attack young people or are we going to try to constructively get some- thing done?" Similarly, political activist and author Donna Brazile responded to Cosby's speech by saying, "He's saying what people have been talking about for a while. Cosby has done his part, but now it's time for African-American elected leaders to do their part" ("Cosby Cries Foul" 2004). Yet others, mainly younger African Americans, members of the hip-hop generation, found Cosby's com- ments unrealistic, even insulting or demeaning. For instance, after Cosby's initial speech, *Newsweek* magazine spoke to several African American "at-risk youth and ex-cons." One seventeen-year-old ex-con claimed that, contrary to Cosby's claims, he "robbed 'cause I was hungry," while another inner-city youth claimed that the main culprit for problems in her neighborhood was un-employment (Childress, Cose, and Helem 2004, 66).

Cosby's comments sparked not only a significant amount of vocal praise and criticism, as well as essays, but also at least three books, including *Essays in Response to Bill Cosby's Comments about African American Failure* (2006) edited by Theresa A. Mohamed, and *Marriage and Caste in America: Why Bill Cosby Was Right* (2006) by Kay S. Hymowitz. The first published book in response to Cosby's comments, *Is Bill Cosby Right (or Has the Black Middle Class Lost Its Mind)?* (2005), was written by Michael Eric Dyson. Born in 1958, Dyson is a limi-nal figure, technically part of the civil rights generation, even though he would not have been old enough to really participate in the civil rights movement. His allegiances clearly lie with the hip-hop generation, not the civil rights genera-tion. Despite his having written books about Martin Luther King Jr. and Marvin Gaye, among others, he is often referred to as a hip-hop scholar, in large part a result of his book *Holler if You Hear Me: Searching for Tupak Shakur* (2002).

In *Is Bill Cosby Right,* Dyson heavily criticizes Cosby, whom he regards as no expert in racial issues, given Cosby's previous reluctance in his public life to deal with racial matters. For Dyson, Cosby is part of what he calls the "Afristro-cracy," the upper-class black elite who often denigrates lower-class African Americans, whom Dyson calls part of the "Ghettocracy" (2005). This is not just an economic division; it is a generational one. Most younger African Americans (and for that matter, most young Americans regardless of ethnicity) tend to embrace the Ghettocracy over the Afristrocracy, even if they truly belong to the latter because they are part of the upper class. In part they do so because the media tends to equate African Americans with urban impoverishment and vice versa. Hence, the label *the hip-hop generation* has come to hold, for, after all, hip-hop was originally a street music and originated from the ghetto or inner city. Why has there developed such an affinity for ghetto or inner-city life? It is prob-ably a result of several reasons (although Dyson does not directly discuss this). First of all, many hip-hop artists (at least in the early day of hip-hop during the 1980s and early 1990s), grew up in the inner city, and their music reflects their upbringing. Wanting to emulate their passion and toughness, fans, especially young fans who grew up with mainstream hip-hop, in turn embrace the ghetto. Furthermore, their affinity for the ghetto may reflect a desire to take pride in something (extreme poverty) that used to be shameful for African Americans.

For Dyson, Cosby wrongly believes in the egalitarian nature of American society and thereby "slights the economic, social, political and other structural barriers that poor black parents are up against: welfare reform, dwindling re-form, dwindling resources, export of jobs and ongoing racial stigma" (2005, 7). Still, Dyson and Cosby agree on two main things: there has not been enough progress for African Americans since the civil rights movement, and there still exists a wide discrepancy between whites and African Americans. Dyson points out that while black median incomes have increased, they have not kept pace with that of whites. Furthermore, he identifies that not only is African American unemployment twice that of whites but also "the poverty rate of black households is more than 24 percent, compared to 6.1 percent for white households" (2005, 63). Clearly there are significantly problems in the African American community, and there still exists a large gap between whites and African Americans. Why is that, even in early twenty-first-century America?

When I pose that question to my classes in which we read about and discuss racial issues, the typical response (to my recollection, always delivered by a white student) is very similar to that of Bill Cosby: things could be better for African Americans if they tried harder. "I come from a poor family," one white student said. "I work two jobs and go to school full time. So can they." This echoes the sentiment of most classes I have taught, from North Carolina to Pennsylvania to Oklahoma to Nevada. Rare is the student who suggests that we may still live in a racially unequal society; I am often the one who brings up the idea of lingering institutional racism in contemporary America, which usually generates confused and befuddled looks from my predominately white students—at least until something immediate occurs to change their minds.

Such an event occurred in fall 2002 at Oklahoma State University in Stillwater. Aside from a sizable Native American population, OSU is not a particularly ethnically diverse school. Out of about a hundred students in my classes that semester, about four were African American. In my writing classes, we discussed essays by African American and Native American authors who contended that there remained culturewide institutional and implicit racism in America, as well as lingering forms of overt racism. These essays met almost universal rejection from the predominantly white or part–Native American students.[4] However, one semester, one class had a rather one-sided discussion of race in which my students largely concluded that it was a matter of personal responsibility, certainly not institutional racism, that caused any economic disparity between different racial or ethnic groups. The next day, a story broke about two white OSU fraternity members who had dressed up for a Halloween party, one as a Klansman and the other as an African American in blackface: "In the photo that was taken of the two, a noose dangled above the head of the student in blackface" ("Halloween Fallout Continues"). In rather outrageous comments, the fraternity members claimed that they did not know that their actions could be construed as racist, but most of my students did. When we discussed racial issues that next day, they were much more open to at least the possibility of institutional and/or lingering prejudice and racism in America. Although a few students brushed off the act of the fraternity members as aberrant, most no longer possessed the same amount of certainty about personal responsibility that they did before. The point in this is that, sadly, it often takes something directly visible and nearby in order to convince people that as much as we'd like to believe otherwise, America is not yet a racially egalitarian country.

Yet these same students who initially rejected the idea of contemporary institutional racism were also, for the most part, avid consumers of hip-hop music and devotees to the culture. It is ironic that the largest consumers of contemporary hip-hop—young, white, middle- to upper-class Americans—seem to be the most resistant to the idea that there is not yet an equal playing field for minorities, especially African Americans. Hip-hop has changed from being at least in part a medium of social protest, as it was more so in the late 1980s and early 1990s,[5] to more of a big business promoting toughness and hedonism.

The primary focus of the current volume is on young African American writers, writers of the hip-hop generation, born in the 1960s and 1970s. This is essentially black America's Generation X, but while the label *Generation X* is used to describe those persons born in the 1960s and 1970s, African American scholars and critics have not accepted the label, preferring instead *hip-hop generation*. This schism in itself shows that America has not yet become a fully integrated country.

African American scholars and critics want to assert their own generational identity as separate from that of whites and for some compelling reasons, given that some central concerns of young African Americans are not necessarily concerns of most non–African American Generation Xers. The issues of racial authenticity and racial progress (or a lack thereof) are central to many hip-hop-generation writers, whereas they tend to be lesser or nonexistent issues in the writings of white Generation X writers such as David Foster Wallace, Dave Eggers, Aimee Bender, and Douglas Coupland. The two groups have much more in common with one another than in ways they differ. Both groups tend to be cynical, ironic, and uncertain. This is apparent in their literature, the lives of their fictional characters, and in popular culture. In addition both groups tend to be antagonistic towards their parents' generation (baby boomers or the civil rights generation). As with Generation X writers, hip-hop-generation writers sometimes use experimental, modernistic, and postmodernistic techniques in their fiction and poetry, but their work is also reminiscent of the traditional, emotionally affecting fiction and poetry of realist and naturalistic writers. However, the literature written by the hip-hop generation displays little evidence of the literary allusions of an Ishmael Reed or the historical revisionism of Toni Morrison or Charles Johnson. Still, there is great intellectual merit in the work of the writers of the hip-hop generation.

It has become an especially difficult and complex time to be African American in the sense that prejudice, discrimination, and racism have become so often subtle, unclear, and harder to discern. The civil rights generation did not have to encounter much subtlety, at least not in terms of their fight against prejudice, discrimination, and racism. In the 1960s, debate was how best to achieve equality—"by any means necessary," as Malcolm X argued, or through nonviolent protests as advanced by Martin Luther King Jr.—but there was a common fight against a clear enemy. Prominent African American historian and cultural critic Henry Louis Gates Jr., himself a member of the civil rights generation, explains that in the world in which he grew up and during his parents' era, "our purpose and our enemies were clear. We were to get just as much education as we possibly could, to stay the enemies of racism, segregation, and discrimination" (Gates and West 1996, 11). In contrast members of the hip-hop generation often view the educational system as well as any form of governmental bureaucracy with great skepticism, especially given that local and national organizations like the police seem to target rather than help them. Furthermore Gates believes that among his generation, there was a strong consensus on the need to learn the methods of white America in order for African Americans to achieve equal economic footing with whites. In contrast, with the rise in popularity of hip-hop and African American literature in recent years, younger African Americans have come to feel that they can achieve success by virtually ignoring white America. However, in actuality, adhering to hip-hop tropes actually is a form of acquiescence to the white majority that helps set the standards for African American authenticity. For it is the white majority that tends to purchase the music of certain hip-hop-artists-turned-celebrities whom they embrace and who usually exhibit gangster- and/or hedonistic-like qualities.

Subsequent to the civil rights movement of the 1950s and early to mid-1960s, there arose an increasing amount of fragmentation between competing groups of African American intellectuals and leaders. The Black Power movement, which came into being in the 1960s, promoted an almost militant unity amongst African Americans and helped make some important political headway "by electing by electing black officials at an unprecedented rate. By 1969 there were over a 1,000 black elected officials at across the country. By 1975 that number nearly tripled to 3,000 black elected officials" (Ginwright 2004, 12). Meanwhile, "cultural revisionists wanted to re-write history and change dominant conceptions of black history and identity, while revolutionists tended to be Marxists who wanted to 'redistribute the wealth' and establish a separate black nation" (Ginwright 2004, 14). According to Bakari Kitwana, author of the germinal book *The Hip Hop Generation* (2002), "The hip-hop generation has embraced the idea of Blackness in ways that parallel the Black consciousness raising of the late 1960s and early 1970s. The popularization of the Afrocentric movement from the late 1980s through the 1990s, pro-Black lyrics on the contemporary rap scene, as well as traditional hairstyles (dreadlocks and braids, for example) adopted by many hip-hop generationers all speak to this" (2002, 8). This might have been clearer to see during the heyday of political hip-hop in the late 1980s and early 90s, but it is much more difficult to find any current popular hip-hop artists or songs that deal directly with race; rather, they tend to focus on materialism, partying, and sexuality. Popular hip-hop artists such as Jay-Z, Kanye West, and 50 Cent also all do not sport "traditional hairstyles."

Hip-hop is primarily a street music, originating from the impoverished inner city. Whereas R and B, blues, rock 'n' roll, soul, and disco performers through the 1970s tended to be nonthreatening in musical style, lyrical content, and appearance, hip-hop performers (at least those from the 1970s and 1980s) tended to be products of inner-city violence and crime; their gritty lyrics were unadulterated, and they dressed and acted in ways that the white majority often perceived as threatening. Gwendolyn Pough, as do some other critics, believes, "Rappers, with their bold use of language and dress, also use image and spectacle as their initial entry into the public sphere. In this instance spectacle functions dually as both style and a plea to be heard, to be allowed to represent" (2004, 28). According to Pough (2004, 29), "After a legacy of slavery and being labeled as three-fifths human, Blacks had to create a spectacle that allowed them to be seen as respectable citizens." This would be one way of explaining or even defending the use of profanity and violence in hip-hop music as a necessary means to get the attention of others.

As hip-hop grew in popularity in the 1990s, it became a big business, an ethos, and a culture. The extent to which it exerts a power can be seen in the co-option of the label *hip-hop generation* primarily for African Americans born in the 1960s and 1970s. This is not to suggest that there has not been some debate as to the appropriateness or lack thereof of this label. Critic Mark Anthony Neal has chosen instead the label *post-soul generation*. However, such a name suffers from a couple of significant problems. First of all, soul music never really defined a generation of African Americans or whites for that matter, nor did it ever truly dominate the music charts like hip-hop has. In addition, labeling a generation as post-soul has derogatory connotations. While it is not Neal's intention to debase this generation, nevertheless, *post-soul* suggests soulless or vapid; in that sense it is not that dissimilar to the stereotypes that still dog Generation X, such as that they are morose and/or apathetic slackers. For good reason more scholars have accepted the label of *hip-hop generation* instead, but even that label has come with its share of criticism. For instance Brian Gilmore asks the important question, "Are you a hip-hop generationer if you are in the military, are black, were born in Kitwana's time frame, and despise everything about hip-hop music and culture?" (2002, 42). As Gilmore suggests, there are definitely some African Americans who do not wish to be called part of the hip-hop generation for precisely the reasons he mentions.

However, there has always been dispute about generational labels, and a label cannot please everyone all of the time. Not everyone, for instance, is happy about the generational label *baby boomers* or *Generation X*, but these generational labels have stuck. What remains an important question, though, is to what extent is it beneficial to label a generation through racial exclusion or separation? What of the millions of whites, Latinos, and Asian Americans born in the 1960s and 1970s who feel that their lives have been defined by hip-hop but who by dint of their race are not allowed to be part of the hip-hop generation? Does this contribute to racial divisiveness, or is it a necessary response to the remaining institutional prejudice in American society? Would a hip-hop artist such as Eminem be excluded from the hip-hop generation, despite that he has been embraced and included by most African American hip-hop artists? As of now, *hip-hop generation* does refer to African Americans, which would exclude an individual such as Eminem. However, it is not my intention to argue that the label *Generation X* or *hip-hop generation* be used for all Americans born in the 1960s or 1970s, regardless of ethnicity, as both labels have been accepted by both the critics and public at large, hence making that issue a moot point to debate.

As with Generation X, there is some dispute as to the birth ranges of the hip-hop generation. For instance Neal's post-soul generation consists of African Americans born between 1963 and 1978; Kitwana's hip-hop generation spans 1965 to 1984, although he suggests, "Those at the end of the civil rights/black-power generation were essentially the ones who gave birth to the hip-hop movement that came to define the hip-hop generation, even though they are not technically hip-hop generationers. The African Bambaataas, Grandmaster Flashes, Melle Mels, Kool DJ Hercs, as well as hip-hop journalists such as Nelson George and even hip-hop moguls such as Russell Simmons, belong to what writer and activist Lisa Sullivan calls the 'bridge generation'" (2002, xiii–xiv).

Ultimately, it is insignificant whether one picks 1963 or 1965 and 1978 or 1984 as the beginning and end dates for the hip-hop generation, and despite the differences in term, most authors discussing this group or generation see similar characteristics in them. This is a generation that not only did not have to experience segregation first hand but also saw what seemed to be milestones in African American history. These events include, as Neal points out (2002, 101), "Jesse Jackson's two historical presidential campaigns . . . [and] the first black Miss America," as well as the first African American secretary of state, the rise of the African American athlete/celebrity such as Magic Johnson and Michael Jordan, and the renaissance of African American film and literature. This is what Neal calls "the first substantial presence of black images within the mass media" (2002, 102). He also suggests that members of the hip-hop generation are not aware of or do not acknowledge the debt that they owe to the civil rights generation for these advances but are rather "divorced from the nostalgia associated with those successes" (2002, 103). Kitwana has an explanation for Neal's criticism: "For hip-hop generationers, it is difficult to find instances where Black baby boomers in mainstream leadership are collectively making a difference in the lives of young Blacks" (2002, 184). Similarly, Kevin Powell comments (1997, 219), "From my generation's perspective, we believe that many in the civil rights generation are living in an illusionary world, and are foolishly holding on to the nostalgia and memories of an era long gone. That's why there is such a high level of mistrust and miscommunication between the two generations."

According to Shawn A. Ginwright, hip-hop culture is dominated by an "urban youth aesthetic," which includes not only rap music but also clothing, language, and art. In addition he claims that hip-hop culture is also defined by "urban youth experience," which has become synonymous (fairly or unfairly so) with poverty and violence. He also suggests that hip-hop culture places an emphasis on the "struggle to make it out of the trappings of urban ghettos" (2004, 31). Why is it, then, that so many people who identify with hip-hop culture are from middle- or upper-class environments and thereby have no direct experience of impoverishment? In part, this is a result of a rampant sense of entitlement and desire for celebrity especially endemic among adolescents who, even if they grow up in a wealthy environment, can feel deprived or marginalized for an almost infinite number of reasons from getting poor grades to romantic failings to family problems. Hip-hop culture provides instruction, albeit rather misguided instruction to most (except the lucky, famous few) on how to achieve a level of power and success that many have not only come to desire but also feel is their birthright. Literally though, hip-hop has become an avenue for some, a select few, to overcome poverty, to channel their artistic ability, musical ability, and/or force of personality, but its success largely rides upon providing listeners with at least the illusion of power.

In its best form, hip-hop is also a form of social criticism and can also serve as a cultural bridge. For writer and former MTV *Real World* star Powell, the hip-hop generation is incredibly cynical and rightly so because of the contemporary abysmal status of African American community (1997, 219). However, for hip-hop historian Jeff Chang, the hip-hop generation "brings together time and race, place and polyculturalism, hot beats and hybridity. It describes the turn from politics to culture, the process of entropy and reconstruction. It captures the collective hopes and nightmares, ambitions and failures of those who would otherwise be described as 'post-this' or 'post-that'" (2005, 2). Whereas Chang sees the positive developments of the hip-hop generation, Cornel West, a product of the civil rights movement, although praising some aspects of hip-hop culture, mainly sees its darker side: "Hip-hop culture is based in part on the desire to create an artistic expression of rage. It is conceived and conducted by a group of young black Americans rebelling against their marginalization, their invisibility that only became worse during the Reagan and Bush years. They do not have a movement to appeal to for help. Nor do they have institutions or infrastructures with spiritual and moral vision. They are living in a culture void of hope, a culture in which the rapidly decentralizing production of goods and services is making them obsolete" (West 1993, *Prophetic Reflections* 17).

Clearly, the amount of disparate opinions about hip-hop music and hip-hop culture indicate that it is largely a matter of perspective the extent to which one values or debases it. Ironically two hallmarks of hip-hop culture are nearly contradictory: a desire for honesty or realism and a desire for materialism or transcendence. On the one hand, there is a desire for raw, naked, emotional honesty, but in reality, there is much artifice in hip-hop culture whereby individuals feel that they must develop a steely, invulnerable façade in order to achieve economic or individual transcendence. Todd Boyd hints at this near paradox in hip-hop culture: "If there are two things that indicate the cultural politics of hip-hop most, they are the idea of 'keepin' it real,' which is about honesty, and 'not giving a fuck,' which is also about honoring one's convictions whatever they may be, regardless of the circumstances" (2003, 156).

This is one strong difference between Generation X culture and hip-hop culture. Whereas in its beginnings, Generation X became synonymous with disaffected consumers who often tried to remove themselves from the corporate/economic totalitarianism they perceived in contemporary global society, hip-hop culture tends to celebrate materialism and hedonism. One obvious reason for the emphasis on materialism is that hip-hop culture is also associated with the impoverished inner city. The desire for riches is, of course, much stronger in people who grow up in poverty than it is for people from middle- or upper-class environments.

Most scholars of hip-hop culture argue that African Americans are no different from peers of other races in their materialism. There is certainly merit to this argument. The ethos of Generation X tends to apply to a resistant minority, whereas the ethos of the hip-hop generation tends to apply to a much-larger group. In other words more Gen Xers are materialistic than are actively anticorporate or anticonsumerist. For Cornel West, the materialism of the hip-hop generation is mainly a result of a "culture of consumerism" or a market culture "that promotes a market morality" (1993, *Prophetic Thoughts* 17). Similarly, Kitwana argues (2002, 6), "We, like our white peers, are more likely than our parents' generation to be obsessed with our careers and getting rich quick. For us, achieving wealth, by any means necessary, is more important than most anything else, hence our obsession with the materialistic and consumer trappings of financial success."

Yet there is more justification for the hip-hop generation's desire for wealth in that it can help offset the economic disparity between African Americans and whites. However, the problem is that materialism for the hip-hop generation tends to be individual, not collective. That is to say, most seek individual aggrandizement and do not necessarily seek to improve the status of the African American community. Powell tellingly writes, "Hip-hop is and has always been about winning on our own terms. Moreover, hip-hop culture lets us say to society: If y'all don't like us or the way we talk or the way we act, we don't really care" (1997, 210). The problem with this attitude is that it can lead to apathy and a lack of concern for others.

On a broader scope, this apathy can be seen in the hip-hop generation's relative lack of political activism, at least before Barack Obama was a presidential candidate. As with their Generation X counterparts, this political apathy can be attributed to a general cynicism about the government. However, at one time, the late 1980s and early 1990s, hip-hop (even mainstream) was rather politically active. As Yvonne Bynoe explains (2004, ix), "In the 1980s and early 1990s, rap artists like Public Enemy, KRS-One, X-Clan, and Paris, reacting to the negative effects of the economic and political policies of the Reagan-Bush administrations, produced socially conscious songs like, 'The Devil Made Me Do It,' 'Fight the Power,' and 'Who Protects Us from You.' Such songs suggested the emergence of a Hip-Hop inspired political movement."

Still, most critics tend to fault the hip-hop generation for its perceived lack of political engagement. For instance Bynoe claims that the hip-hop generation lacks "gravitas and thus has failed to develop its own political agenda, much less a strategy to execute it" (2004, x), and, furthermore, "what is missing from the Hip Hop generation's political agenda are organizations with national scope that are attempting to radically change the political landscape of America. There are no national organizations representing the Hip Hop generation that are visibly and intelligently addressing crucial issues such as education reform, AIDS, the prison industrial complex, felon disenfranchisement, police brutality, or American foreign policy" (2004, 17).

Still, others point to success stories such as that of Kwame Kilpatrick, the so-called hip-hop mayor of Detroit, who was born in the early 1970s and has a great love for hip-hop music. In his own words, "This is the music that speaks to young people and speaks to me. I am in the hip-hop generation, and it's the music I grew up with" (quoted in Boucher 2003). Similarly there are political rising stars such as Barack Obama, who, born in 1961, is a borderline hip-hop-generation member. The optimistic Chang claims that the hip-hop generation is, "at least as, if not more, politically active than the civil rights generation" (2005, 454). He cites the 2001 University of California Los Angeles freshman survey, which he describes as "the definitive documentation of college-age youth attitudes since 1966." The survey "found that nearly half of the freshman said they had participated in an organized demonstration during the past year. That number was three times greater than in the inaugural survey, conducted at the peak of the civil rights movement" (2005, 454). However, it is unclear how vast a survey this was, and for that matter, "participating in an organized demonstration" might be defined as merely stopping by a demonstration for a few minutes and doing virtually nothing. While it is true that hip-hop moguls such as Russell Simmons have been politically active, as Chang points out, and the 2004 presidential election saw the newfound activism of Sean "Diddy" Combs, with his "Vote or Die" campaign, hip-hop culture is, for the most part, rather politically stagnant and/or apathetic.

One of the reasons for hip-hop's lack of political engagement and relative homogeneity in contemporary times may be because of the media and to corporate culture. As Kai Wright notes (2004, 42), three major corporations (Universal, Viacom, and Clear Channel Communications) hold a virtual monopoly on the distribution of hip-hop. Furthermore pop culture reinforces the connection between realism and poverty or ghetto life. According to Michael Eric Dyson (2005, 174), this creates "ghettocentrists" who "hold that the ghetto, the inner city, the local black neighborhood, is the source, the locus classicus, of authentic black identity and supplies important standards, norms, habits, traits and behavior for black community." At the same time, popular culture (movies, television, music, and other media forms) often presents African Americans in roles in which they seem to exclusively want money and material products, whether it is in MTV shows such as "Pimp My Ride" or "Cribs" or movies such as *All about the Benjamins* (2002). If popular culture does not stereotype African Americans as materially obsessed, then they often stereotype them as violent gangsters: "Aside from rap artists, films released between 1991 and 2001 that depicted gun-toting, ruthless, violent, predatory Blacks killing other Blacks (dubbed 'hood films' by industry insiders) have been the most effective medium for defining and disseminating the new Black youth culture" (Kitwana 2002, 121).

Like the rest of Black America, the world of Hip Hop is not a monolith, yet all too often Hip Hop is only represented by young Black males with gold teeth, wearing baggy pants and shouting obscenities, and libidinous young Black women shakin' their asses. What the Music industry has done through rap music is to frame the "authentic" Black American not as a complex, educated, or even creative individual, but as a "real nigga" who has ducked bullets, worked a triple beam, and done at least one bid in prison. This image, along, with that of scantily clad women, is then transmitted worldwide as a testament of who Black Americans are. This means that corporate entertainment entities have no vested interest in seeing that rap artists advance themselves creatively or intellectually. (Bynoe 2004, 149)

Likewise, television provides aspiring African Americans with a formula through which to achieve success.

For critics such as Darren Ferguson and Marjorie Fields Harris, contemporary hip-hop culture has become a complete sham in which corporate (almost exclusively white) executives capitalize on African Americans while keeping them still intellectually and economically enslaved.

Movies, television and music are now peppered with Black and Brown faces that America has deemed "marketable." This marketability that was once based on looks and talent now uses a measuring stick of outrageous and denigrating behavior. Today, young brothers and sisters coon, clown, preen and grin for a moment of fleeting fame, which in today's market can mean millions of dollars for the proverbial 15 minutes. You don't have to have any real talent. You don't have to sing or dance. Hey, you don't even have to look good. You can be a marginally talented, uncreative high-school dropout if you know how to call your women ho's and roll "nigger" off your tongue on top of an infectious beat. (Ferguson and Harris 2006, 25)

The fact of the matter is that only a small minority of African Americans ever achieve major success, let alone get a good-paying job. Ras Baraka, deputy major of Newark, New Jersey, comments, "It is a lie that young people do not want to work! Presently, I have over 100 employment applications on my desk. Unfortunately, the City cannot employ everybody. . . . The Civil Rights & Black Power Movement created so many African American leaders and Black middle class persons having access to power, yet the overwhelming majority of people in our community have not benefited, resulting in one out of three persons living in poverty in Newark. Many are still dying, still in jail and not getting educated" (quoted in Dais 2004, 6).

Through this emphasis on popular culture, it might be surprising that African American literature is being read at all; however, in some ways there has been a renaissance in contemporary African American literature, not just through the likes of older, critically acclaimed authors such as Toni Morrison and Maya Angelou but also from a new genre of literature called "urban fiction" or "hip hop fiction" (McQuillar, Mingo, and Venable 2004, 24). Popular authors in this genre include Nikki Turner, Omar Tyree, and Sister Souljah.

This book's focus does not include Souljah, Turner, and other similar authors, not because their novels are without merit but because they do tend to lack the intellectual depth I perceive in the work of the writers explored in this book. Typically the novels of these authors are set in the inner-city, contain a tough-talking female protagonist who gets mixed up in the hustling or drug world but who gets double crossed by smooth but callous, drug-running lovers, while maintaining a relationship with a faithful former hustler father or lover in jail. Eventually the female protagonist typically overcomes over her antago-nist(s) (usually male) and becomes financially and/or romantically successful.[6] This kind of fiction "is set in the world of hustlers, pimps, thugs, chickenheads, blinged-out rappers or 'round-the-way baby mamas. The genre displays a street sensibility by using the language of everyday people in the hood. . . . So-called street literature is now enjoying major mainstream success with many of the major publishing houses doling out six-figure deals to the writers who can tell the grimiest tale" (McQuillar, Mingo, and Venable 2004, 24). Many booksellers and critics, though, are critical of urban or hip-hop fiction: "As was the case with the music industry where every major label had to have a 'gansta' act, sud-denly every big publishing house has to have a 'fiction' writer who jacks the dialogue of a beauty salon or barbershop and passes it off as good literature. Toss in a catchy, black vernacular-driven title, a colorful cover, and a blurb or two from a nonliterary 'star' and *Bling! Bling!* Gold is on its way" (Powell 1997, 7–8). Similarly Brett Hewitt, the manager of the African Vibes and Positive Vibes store in Hampton Roads, Virginia, says he sells urban or hip-hop fiction not because he holds it in any esteem but because it sells well. Others are less critical, as is acclaimed author Walter Mosley: "There can be an art to ghetto lit. I would never dismiss it out of hand" (McQuillar, Mingo, and Venable 2004, 24).

Turner, who situates her novels in her hometown of Richmond, Virginia, and who has been dubbed the "princess of hip-hop fiction," wants her books to serve as moral lessons. *A Hustler's Wife* is "not just about drugs—it's about a girl and her struggle. I wanted to warn young girls about street life. They never know the risks that come with it. They listen to the music and see the bling-bling. But nobody ever says what can happen to you—that you can go to jail. . . . I try not to reinforce stereotypes, I try to show a different light." Turner describes her audience as "ages fifteen to twenty-five—people in jail, people that went to college" and points out, "At book signings, I have people from all walks of life—grandmothers, middle-aged men" (quoted in McQuillar, Mingo, and Venable 2004, 24–25).

Turner and Souljah tend to portray the ghetto or inner-city as a dog-eat-dog world in which trust is almost nonexistent, and the individual only cares about his/her family (sometimes) and him- or herself (the only constant). A poetic dedication to Souljah's novel *Coldest Winter Ever* (2000) shows Souljah's cynicism about the modern age.

> This novel is dedicated to the era in which we live.
> The era in which love, loyalty, honor and
> respect died.
> Where humility and appreciation are nonexistent.
> Where families are divided and God reviled,
> The era.
> The Coldest Winter Ever.

On a similar note, Souljah's female protagonist in the novel, Winter, tells us, "Only dumb girls let love get them delirious to the point where they let things that really count go undone" (2000, 4), and "I live for me. I die for me" (2000, 304).

In these novels, there is little or no real sense of community. Friends turn on one another easily, usually for money, which is the only collective desire those in the ghetto have (as portrayed by Turner and Souljah). Living in a corrupt world in which the police and judicial system are perceived to be inherently and explicitly racist and unfair, ghetto residents view drug dealing and/or other criminal activities not only as justified and legitimate but also as the only real way to achieve respect, power, and success. This may be, in part, because of music, television programs, and movies that reinforce the link among African Americans, the ghetto, and crime.

In all fairness, though, Turner and Souljah distinguish among people in the ghetto. Some are shameless hustlers or drug dealers with absolutely no sense of loyalty or compassion, while characters with more sympathy maintain their individual codes of ethics. Still, in this fiction, the ghetto is a dangerous environment in which violence seems possible to erupt at any time, which Turner describes: "It's funny how in the hood everyone can be in the house, but let a fight break out and people come out like roaches do when the lights are cut on" (2005, *Riding Dirty*, 60). Furthermore, in their novels, romantic love rarely appears, as ghetto residents become emotionally hardened or even deadened by their tough lives. These novels also do not tend to showcase truly empowered

African American female characters.[7] Even in the most desperate circumstances, the female protagonist mostly cares about her own appearance above all else. For instance Tressa, the main character in Turner's novel *A Project Chick* (2004), believes "that as long as her hair was right, then everything else would fall in place" (97). Along these lines, the younger female characters desire mainly to be physical attractive and a "real" or "bad bitch," which, according to them, is a woman who is ultratough, who never shows weakness, and is loyal and powerful. For Souljah's Winter, "A bad bitch controlled without the man ever knowing that he was being dominated. A bad bitch was so slick that she made him think he was calling the shots while she planted the seeds and was the owner of all his thoughts" (2000, 41). These novels can also glamorize gangster life and criminal activity at the same time that they show the dark side of both. Turner and Souljah's female protagonists rarely have a problem with people who murder or commit crimes if they feel it is justified (which they often do), and some get away with their crimes.

The literature explored in this book is more academic and intellectually dense than the novels of Souljah and Turner. The writers in the chapters of the current volume do not just focus on the ghetto or inner-city but on almost all aspects of contemporary African American life, the upper class as well as the lower class, the academic as well as the "street." In doing so, they explore a wide cross section of issues, confronting racial questions such as: What does or should it mean to be African American in contemporary society? What role does or should literature play in the African American community? What spaces are opening or closing for multiethnic individuals? What progress has really been made since the civil rights movement? To what extent is popular culture and hip-hop empowering or enslaving African Americans? While a couple of these issues are not specific to the hip-hop generation, most are.

The writings of eight hip-hop generation writers—Trey Ellis, Jake Lamar, Colson Whitehead, Paul Beatty, Danzy Senna, Allison Joseph, Terrence Hayes, and Suzan-Lori Parks—are explored because I feel that their work is not only among the most intellectually, socially, and literarily important of the hip-hop generation but also because their socially and racially charged writings directly, provocatively, and comprehensively address the crucial questions mentioned above about the hip-hop generation as well as the current and future state of the African American community. If academics continue to canonize fiction writers, poets, and playwrights (as I believe we will), then these authors should be considered as among the most promising candidates at this point. Similar to the Harlem Renaissance, the literature of the hip-hop generation (as represented by the authors above) is a new category of related writings that should be considered in a different literary category to that of their postmodern or civil-rights-era forebears Morrison, Alice Walker, and Reed. This is not to suggest that the literature of the hip-hop generation is completely distinct from the literature of the civil rights generation, as there is some common ground between the two groups, but there are also important differences as well.

If as Gates and Cornel West argue (1996, 40), "The rise of a black middle class, a black reading public, has fueled the prominence of the black novel," then, unfortunately, the serious, literary African American writer of the hip-hop generation has been more commercially ignored. I hope that this book will change the minds of readers. Whereas the civil rights-era generation of African Americans tend, Gates and West say (1996, 40), to experiment more with form, then the literary hip-hop generation is more formally traditional. Madhu Dubey claims, "With academic institutionalization, African-American literature seems increasingly remote from generalized notions of 'the black experience' yet continues to be freighted with racially representative value" (2003, *Signs and Cities*, 44). This is indeed a danger for African American literature, yet the writers of the hip-hop generation are very much aware of and a part of the contemporary black experience. It has been said that the hip-hop industry and hip-hop culture are youth dominated. This can be seen in how critically and commercially successful hip-hop artists such as Jay-Z often consider retiring (if not outright retire) when they reach their early or mid-thirties. Along similar lines, the literature of the hip-hop generation provides important insight into the lives and culture of young African Americans, the very future of the community. With the struggle for civil rights seemingly over, these writers focus on one of the most important issues and questions facing the African American community: What, then, should we strive for or aspire towards individually and collectively for the African American community?

Members of the civil rights and earlier generations, like Bill Cosby, often criticize their proverbial offspring for not striving towards what they consider to be personal, social, and racial improvements. They have it so much easier than we did, they think or suggest, so why is it that the members of the hip-hop generation squander the educational and social opportunities that they have, which we did not when we were their age? Still, their logic depends on beliefs that there have been significant racial and social advancements for African Americans in recent years. Have things really improved that dramatically for African Americans since the 1960s? The evidence is not strong that there has been. As Dyson points out, while black median incomes have increased since the mid-1960s, they have not increased at the same rate as that of whites (2005, 62; Kitwana 2002, 20). African American unemployment is double that of whites, and "the poverty rate of black households is more than 24 percent, compared to 6.1 percent for white households" (Dyson 2005, 63), and it has been estimated that "60 percent of America's poor youth are black" (Kit-wana 2002, 20). A good deal of intraracial violence in the African American community remains, and in early twentieth-first-century America, "young Black men are most likely to die at the hands of another young Black male" (Kit-wana 2002, 21). Clearly much advancement needs to be done in the African American community, and by no means is the work of the civil rights move-ment close to completion. This is one important reason for the study of the writers of the hip-hop generation who explore the increasingly complex nature of race, discrimination, and prejudice in contemporary America, as well as the status of African American culture and life. I hope that the reader will perceive the literary works presented here as unified, artistic, and socially important, deserving of both scholarly attention and a larger commercial audience.

1

While hip-hop as a musical form dates back 1970s New York City (specifically the Bronx and Harlem), it did not achieve any level of mainstream popularity until the mid- to late 1980s with Run DMC and the Beastie Boys. Also in this same period, a new generation emerged of independent African American filmmakers such as Robert Townsend and Spike Lee. Lee, who helped reawaken America's awareness about racism and prejudice in his exploration of contemporary African American life in films such as *She's Gotta Have It* (1986), *School Daze* (1988), and *Do the Right Thing* (1989) helped spark a renaissance in African American film.[1] This time period also saw the first publications of the hip-hop generation, and the most appropriate starting point for a study of the writing of this generation is with the writer who positioned himself as its spokesperson, Trey Ellis, whose literary role is similar to that of Lee in sparking a new generation of artists.

Ellis, with his impressive academic background as a graduate of elite Andover College and Stanford University, is the quintessential embodiment of W. E. B. DuBois's talented tenth (DuBois contended that the best hope for African Americans lies in the hands of the African American intellectual elite, the "talented tenth"). Born in 1962, Ellis is a generation removed from established and critically acclaimed African American writers such as Toni Morrison and Ishmael Reed. Like others of the hip-hop generation, he came of age after the civil rights movement and thereby has no direct experience of segregation and presumably less direct experience with racism and prejudice as writers of Morrison and Reed's generation. Instead, Ellis, like his peers, was reared on the blaxploitation films of the 1970s and came of age at the very beginning of rap/hip-hop. Like Douglas Coupland, Trey Ellis became known as the spokesperson of his literary generation. Yet unlike Coupland whose novel itself became known as a generational manifesto (*Generation X*), Ellis made his broad generational claims through an oft-quoted essay, "The New Black Aesthetic," first published in the winter 1989 volume of *Callaloo: A Journal of African American and African Arts and Letters.*[2]

Ellis's first novel, *Platitudes* (1988), portrays a growing schism between the more accepted African American folklore tradition, postmodernist literary experimentation. His writing that followed was new, nearly race-free, and influenced by popular culture. Ellis's next two novels, *Home Repairs* (1994) and *Right Here, Right Now* (1999), indicate that in subsequent years, he chose to navigate a trajectory that was less focused on race. In these novels, on the surface, race takes a back seat to issues of media, adolescence, and sexuality. This, in itself, shows that Ellis believes in the lessening importance of race in contemporary America. However, a closer look at both novels reveals that despite the raceless facades of contemporary America, race still plays a significant role in the lives of these even successful African American protagonists. If these characters are limited or categorized by their race, Ellis suggests, that experience must be nearly ubiquitous among African Americans.

After its publication, "The New Black Aesthetic" sparked divergent reactions from critics. Mark Anthony Neal describes the essay as not only a "generation's manifesto" but also "a profound rearticulation of the sounds and signs of socially reconstructed notions of blackness" (1998, 8). The essay is not without its critics, though. For instance Madhu Dubey sees the essay's main argument as a generalization, and that by focusing on the black bourgeoisie, Ellis thereby ignores the crucial issue of class differences amongst African Americans, a point with which another critic, Eric Lott, concurs (Dubey 2003, "Postmodernism as Postnationalism?" 11; Lott 1989, 245). However, Lott also calls the essay "exciting" in its progressive analysis of African American intellectualism by taking a serious look at influential and intelligent race-conscious comics/entertainers such as Richard Pryor and by suggesting that he should be considered as "one of the major thinkers of the seventies" (Lott 1989, 245). That an essay by a little-known writer came to the attention of many prominent African American critics indicates how original and groundbreaking his theories were about the transformation of African American culture and literature and how a new generation of African Americans was beginning to assert a separate identity from those of their forebears. The essay expresses much of Ellis's theories and philosophies about writing and African American culture in the late 1980s.

Ellis's essay begins with an epigraph from James Baldwin's *Price of a Ticket,* in which Baldwin states that even though the portrayal and account of suffering will not be original, the suffering must be told by each successive generation. That Ellis chose to begin with this epigraph demonstrates that he believes serious, even possibly devastating issues were facing the African American community in the late 1980s and that there has, in some ways, been little progress since the civil rights movement of the 1960s (a common theme in the writings of the hip-hop generation). He also makes it clear that he wants his ideas to be considered as part of a broader cultural and artistic movement. This is not merely a literary discussion but a cultural manifesto, exploring the status of African American social and political life and the way a new generation of African Americans has been asserting its identity and concerns distinct from that of previous generations.

A by-product of the civil rights movement, black nationalism grew in the late 1960s and 1970s and became accepted on a wider scale. African American literary works published during this time frequently focus on celebrating the achievements of African Americans in part to help to counteract decades of physical and mental oppression. This period of ethnic or self-affirmation, Ellis suggests, has some negative consequences in creating greater barriers between African Americans and whites and by setting up frequently unrealizable cultural standards for African Americans. Instead, in the spirit of black nationalism, it could be construed that embracing the dominant white culture in virtually any way contributes to cultural and personal oppression. In contrast Ellis asserts that the new African American artist of his generation should have the freedom to embrace whatever cultural form he/she prefers, regardless of race, without being prejudged or scorned by whites or African Americans. Ellis suggests that this point of view represents his generation as a culturally hybrid group who "all grew up feeling misunderstood by both the black worlds and the white" (1989, 234). The emphasis here is cultural, for Ellis is not only discussing those of mixed ethnicity but also all African Americans of his generation, regardless of whether they are mixed or not.

On the one hand, Ellis suggests that he and his cohorts are breaking away from standards of so-called authentic or legitimate African American life and behavior, such as the cultural or black-nationalist belief that African Americans should consistently and wholeheartedly embrace African American artists over white artists. According to this polarizing schema, if African Americans embrace forms of white culture, they are labeled, primarily by other African Americans, as sellouts or desirous of being white, but, on the other hand, they can never feel fully included in the white world (nor do they want to be a part of it), which holds its own conceptions of African American authenticity, typically as contemporary noble savages, musically and athletically gifted and above all else physical, not intellectual beings. Ellis writes that his generation rejects this black/white dichotomy, which its members find to be harming rather than helping African Americans, taking away their freedom to choose and to define themselves as they so desire.

Ellis praises the African American punk group Fishbone and the African American rock group In Living Color, who are both unafraid to play a white-dominated music and recognize no limitations or criticisms should be placed on what they do.[3] Hence members of this group will "admit liking both Jim and Toni Morrison" (1989, 234). They could be described as transforming a tool of cultural oppression into one of possibility for African Americans in a similar way to how contemporary hip-hop artists sometimes sample other beats and melodies from mainstream, predominately white pop songs.[4] This "minority's minority," as Ellis describes them, does appear similar to W. E. B. DuBois's talented tenth; Indeed Ellis calls them "junior intellectuals" (1989, 234). Their strength, Ellis suggests, is not through their homogeneity but, rather, in their intellectual, economic, and personal diversity. Even though members of Ellis's New Black Aesthetic are all African American, like the members of Fishbone, they come from different backgrounds: military, intellectual, and working class, for instance. Their purpose is not necessarily to preserve African American culture, which Ellis regards as an overwhelming and unfair job to place upon any individual or generation. Besides, what exactly does one define as African American culture, and how does one preserve it? If that is done by continuing in the tradition of previous African American writers/artists or exploring the same themes as them, then it can be limiting to any artist. Rather, Ellis argues that African American artists ought to be able to choose what appeals to them regardless of race. For example Fishbone identifies the all-white, experimental rock bank Pink Floyd and the African American funk/soul band Parliament/Funkadelic as major influences. In a way this makes Fishbone an ideal representation of Martin Luther King Jr.'s colorblind society, but it also opens them up to criticism for supposedly betraying their race or being selfish.

Ellis describes his own background as "bourgie," having grown up in Ann Arbor, Michigan, and New Haven, Connecticut (1989, 235). This is closer to the norm for most writers explored in the current volume, most of whom did not grow up in the ghetto or projects. Ellis anticipated the contention that his was a sheltered existence in which he did not face racism or discrimination, hence invalidating his racial theories: "It was not unusual to be called 'oreo' or 'nigger' on the same day" (1989, 235). Writing at a time when African Americans were reaching unparalleled (up to then) levels in sports and entertainment, Ellis suggests that the decade of the 1980s was a era of the "cultural mulatto" in the ascension of the domestic, middle- to upper-class Cosbys in *The Cosby Show* to the popularity of basketball stars such as Michael Jordan and Magic Johnson, who appear culturally neutral and nonthreatening to whites and are hardly overt supporters of black nationalism or Afrocentrism (at least not in public) (1989, 235). There is a fine line, Ellis suggests, between subverting one's identity to white expectations and being true to one's self or acting "natural," which is what Ellis believes should be the goal of any self-respecting artist, regardless of race (1989, 236). He also distinguishes between "cultural-mulatto, assimilation-ist nightmares," like Whitney Houston and Lionel Ritchie, and thriving hybrids "like Living Colour—the difference being one tries to please one's self instead of the white and/or black worlds" (1989, 242). Still, Ellis does not suggest that young African American artists ignore other white or African American artists who have helped pave the way for them but that they not be forced to shoul-der the heavy, artistically draining burden of having to follow in someone else's footsteps or tradition.

Rather Ellis's vision in "The New Black Aesthetic" is that of a group of artists/intellectuals who do not reject the work of their forebears (Morrison, Reed, and Clarence Major, for instance), but neither do they feel a sense of obli-gation to follow in their footsteps. He praises these civil rights generation writ-ers for helping to free African Americans from "white envy and self-hate" (1989, 237). Ellis acknowledges that his generation does not have to struggle as much to succeed as the previous ones, especially not in the entertainment industry. However, he also emphasizes, "Despite this current buppie artist boom, most black Americans have seldom had it worse" (1989, 239). This is a sentiment repeatedly seen in the work of hip-hop-generation writers: despite commonly held beliefs, virtually all of them suggest that the contemporary state of African Americans is quite poor indeed. In order to wrest readers out of complacency, Ellis claims that he and other African American artists of his generation prac-tice "Disturbatory Art," which he defines as art that "shakes you up" (1989, 239). What Ellis (as well as other writers of the hip-hop generation) wants his readers to realize is that prejudice and racism still exist, albeit often in subtle, muted forms, a full generation after the civil rights movement. This is the dis-turbing part of his art (at least disturbing to the large number of Americans who believe Americans live in an egalitarian society). But, Ellis also says, "For us, racism is a hard and little-changing constant that neither surprises nor enrages" (1989, 239–40). In a way this statement seems to promote apathy, and while it may be that some contemporary African Americans ignore race completely, most address it, but they have forgone conventional methods to do so. Histor-ical revisionism, for instance, seems to be largely passé, as is literature promot-ing the collective unity of African Americans (in the spirit of cultural or black nationalism). Instead, what is done more commonly is an exploration of con-temporary African American life, largely unadorned and free of textual and ver-bal gimmicks.

The ability to express one's self freely and without fear of either whites or African Americans is key to Ellis's argument in the essay, and coming as it did in the late 1980s, he views rap or hip-hop as an important medium through which to achieve these goals. Indeed he describes it as "the most innovative sound since rock n' roll" (1989, 241). Granted, with the rise of groups such as N.W.A. and Public Enemy, rap/hip-hop, at that time, was more socially outspoken, whereas in recent years, it became a big business and arguably has lost a good deal of its social appeal. One suspects that Ellis, had he written his article fifteen years later, would not have been as sympathetic to rap or hip-hop as he was in 1988 and 1989.

Ellis's first novel, *Platitudes,* was published a year before "The New Black Aesthetic" and garnered impressive accolades from critically acclaimed African Americans authors and scholars such as Reed, Major, and Henry Louis Gates Jr. On the surface, the novel is a metafictional account of two writers (Dewayne Washington, a struggling, divorced African American man who writes in a light, playful manner virtually devoid of any racial motifs or connotations, and Isshee Ayam, a critically acclaimed, overly elaborate African American feminist writer who seems racially obsessed). In opposing ways they each write a basic coming-of-age story and clash over choosing the appropriate form and content with which to tell the story. While their argument seems rather picky and academic at first glance, it has broader significance. What they are actually fighting over is the best literary approach for contemporary African American literature through their opposing use of black nationalism and race consciousness (Isshee) and racial obliviousness (Dewayne). Through this literary dichotomy, Ellis suggests African American writers of his generation are caught in a double bind. They are damned if they do focus mostly on race, as that limits the scope of their work and often forces them to adopt stereotypical plot devices and caricatures, and damned if they do not address race, as that suggests that race does not play a role in the lives of African Americans, which is to not be realistic.

While the feminist author Isshee, who writes a somewhat hackneyed imitation of Morrison and Alice Walker, employs (or at least tries to employ) African American folklore and tends to write historical revisionist accounts of empowered slaves and sharecroppers in the South, Dewayne writes more of a contemporary adolescent coming-of-age story, a romantic and sexual bildungsroman. His narrative could be accused of being white infused or transcending race, depending on one's point of view. One's written correspondence, complete with literary criticism and, eventually, literary praise, affects the other's writing (Dewayne is affected more than Isshee because he is more of the struggling writer, and she is an already established, critically acclaimed writer). Through his account of each author, Ellis presents a schism in African American literature; he also suggests that a medium (possibly a happy medium) can be found somewhere between the rather prurient, race-divorced, semi-experimental writings of Dewayne and the traditional, folk-infused, self-important, racially conscious writings of Isshee. The result is a kind of hybrid fiction, characteristic of the literature of the hip-hop generation in that it blends different literary forms and approaches without regard to social or literary conventions.

Although *Platitudes* appears to be a postmodern text in line with that of Reed or John Barth, it actually critiques postmodern fiction as much as it embraces it,[5] just as certain hip-hop artists might berate the seeming sterility of soul, R&B, and disco music in the late 1970s and early 1980s as being overly indulgent and insubstantial while still sampling songs from these eras in their own music. Towards that end, the novel begins with an epigraph from a fictional postmodern literary scholar whom Ellis calls Brian O'Nolan. In a footnote to O'Nolan's name, Ellis indicates that O'Nolan goes by other names such as Flann O'Brien and Myles na gCopaleen. The use of multiple names indicates that Ellis finds this particular scholar to be shady and untrustworthy, and in turn, finds the same qualities in theories of postmodernity. Furthermore he uses two quotes from O'Nolan's invented book, *At Swim-Two-Birds:* "The modern novel should be largely a work of reference" (1988, 2). This sounds reminiscent of John Barth, who suggested in "The Literature of Exhaustion," that because all literary forms have been essentially used up, the new postmodern writer must rely on parody, pastiche, and historical revisionism. The second quote reveals Ellis's hypocritical attitude towards fiction: "It's [the novel composed of references] the sort of queer stuff they look for in a story these days" (1988, 2). With these two contradictory quotes, Ellis suggests that this postmodern author is not much more than a literary parrot, content to follow the dominant trends of the time and without thought, something of which both Dewayne and Isshee are guilty. While each believes he/she is autonomous in his/her own way, in reality, each is easily manipulated by expectations of others, Isshee by the African American folk and slave narratives, and Dewayne by Isshee herself. Through these characters and in the novel, Ellis thereby critiques the often-postmodernist fiction of the civil rights generation, which often lays claim to being more autonomous and honest but actually can be just as derivative and formulaic as any literary form. Writers of the hip-hop generation tend to not be so single-mindedly academic or highbrow in their literary approaches.

The novel begins by focusing on the protagonist of Dewayne/Isshee's story, Earle, who is in many ways the perfect representative of the audience for contemporary, mainstream hip-hop. Earle, a sixteen-year-old high school student, is rather nerdy and largely sexually preoccupied. One of his first activities for the day is to spy upon a woman in an adjoining apartment building from his window as she does her aerobic exercises. At this stage, Washington seems determined to not write about race. The only real indication that Earle is

African American in the first few pages is Dewayne's mentioning that Earle will be attending the B'nai B'rith–NAACP dance that evening and indeed that Dewayne couples Jews with African Americans indicates his willingness to abandon black-nationalistic themes. Furthermore Dewayne pointedly describes Earle's mother in a manner to distinguish her from stereotypes of the African American "mammy" figure: "She is neither fat (her breasts don't swell the lace top of the apron she has never owned), nor has she any gold teeth. She cannot sing, nor is she ever called 'Mama' (though that is what she calls her own mother). She does not, not work in public relations and her two-handed back-hand is not, not envied by her peers" (1988, 4). In a way Dewayne's objective ought to be praised as he is attempting to counteract literary and social stereo-types of African Americans, but he goes too far in the opposite direction to the point of neglecting racial issues, just as mainstream hip-hop tends to do. Aside from that, the first two chapters of Dewayne's story are rather tedious, bogged down by overly drawn details such as a entire paragraph devoted to description of a punchbowl at an evening's dance and Earle's failed attempts to get a girl to dance with him.

If the reader had not already realized that Dewayne's story is rather clumsy and uninspiring, confirmation comes from an unnamed editor or possibly even Ellis himself who states after Dewayne's first two chapters: "Well, Earle's story has degenerated pretty quickly, hasn't it? If you ask me, it's got 'No Sale' writ-ten all over it. But girls, women. Now black women *sell*, according to a friend of mine who works in publishing" (1988, 10). There is indeed a good amount of truth in what this person suggests, for the most renowned African American authors in the mid- to late 1980s, such as Morrison, Walker, and Maya Angelou, were mostly female, and their fiction often details the lives of women. Similarly the most popular contemporary urban or hip-hop fiction, such as the novels of Nikki Turner, also tend to have female protagonists and/or focus on the lives of women. Aside from the fact that women make up a larger percentage of the reading public than men, the popularity of female authors may also have another cause. Because of lingering stereotypes about African American men being violent, when it is women who write about women or even write about men, as Morrison did in *Song of Solomon,* they may be less threatening to the white mainstream. They would thereby be more likely to be commercially suc-cessful.

As if in response to this criticism and commercial advice, Dewayne contin-ues his narrative by focusing on black women, but, as in popular hip-hop music, he objectifies them mainly as sexual objects, describing a few as "deli-cate balls of assorted deliciousness" (1988, 10), and he focuses on their appear-ance rather than making them into substantial, three-dimensional characters.

Even though he does create a reasonable conflict between his new protagonist, Dorothy, and her mother, Darcelle, their minor dispute about homework and Dorothy's plea to be allowed to go to a party are hardly substantial. In all fairness Dewayne's portrayal of Earle is rather flimsy, and when he tries his hand writing from the perspective of a teenage girl, Dorothy, instead of the teenage boy, Earle, he continues to resort to flat generalizations. In Dewayne's story Dorothy is a moody, overworked teenager who wants to have fun instead of working, and Earle is a sexually obsessed but socially lacking teenager. Neither characterization is particularly interesting or important.

Just as the reader's patience begins to wear thin with Dewayne's story, Dewayne himself interrupts the narrative by confessing that he's at a breaking point because he's having difficulty remembering what it was like to be a teenager: "I'm sorry. I don't know what more to write" (1988, 14). This shows Dewayne's lack of imagination. He is writing from only empirical experience, like most hip-hop lyricists do, whereas Isshee, like a postmodernist, civil rights-era writer, is all fanciful imagination and no realism and puts little of herself in her writing. She also lacks sympathy for other people. In response to his plea for help, Isshee writes Dewayne a letter and calls him a "freak," insisting, "We women of color do not need your atavistic brand of representation, thank you" (1988, 15). Indeed Isshee's criticism seems remarkably like the kind of criticism that tends to be leveled at hip-hop performers by certain critics. While it is true that Dewayne objectifies women in his narrative, he is not noticeably atavistic, nor is his narrative sexually explicit at this point. However, Isshee sees everything from the framework of being an African American feminist, and so any female characters that do not possess depth and strength make a story or novel fail to her eyes.

Isshee rewrites Dewayne's story in a heavily descriptive, female-focused manner reminiscent of Morrison. In doing so Ellis lightly mocks the literature of the civil rights generation. Alluding to Morrison, he includes a character called I. Corinthians, who, at least in name, is quite similar to the character First Corinthians, who appeared briefly in *The Bluest Eye* and at greater lengths in *Song of Solomon* as the kindly but repressed daughter of Macon and Ruth Dead. However, Isshee's I. Corinthians is an amoral servant of the landlord/master of Earle's family. Instead of situating the story in contemporary times as Dewayne does, Isshee situates it in the segregation-era South (presumably early twentieth century). This allows her to extol the fortitude of her characters in their struggles against racism, and it allows her to provide a clear distinction between good and evil. Not many critics, after all, could really criticize Isshee's work without at least some fear of being labeled a racist him/herself. Isshee is also able to place her characters in a natural, earthy setting, where she can also display the physical and emotional strength of her female characters, for Isshee is first and foremost a feminist writer (at least she believes herself to be), immediately apparent by the first simile she uses, which compares the morning to "Mama's handstarched and sun-dried petticoat" (1988, 16). Aside from Earle, there are no significant male characters in Isshee's female-dominated tale (Earle's dopey sidekicks Bassmouth and Cornbread are two-dimensional country-boy stereotypes or do-nothing drunkards or traitors such as I. Corinthians); the women are the life and energy of the house.

Yet in her narrative, even Isshee's female characters come off as stereotypically folksy caricatures, and her overdrawn descriptions are contrived. Although she writes in a more literarily accomplished manner than Dewayne does, the content of her story is equally vapid to his own. Dewayne's biting criticism of Isshee in his rebuttal letter to her, in which he describes her revamped version of his story as a formulaic African American "glory" story, has some accuracy to it (1988, 19). The rest of Dewayne's response is juvenile; after reading Isshee's overly wrought descriptions, he becomes more drawn to the real and specific, but unfortunately, that does not improve his writing. There is really no rationale for Dewayne providing Isshee with a list of Earle's supposed favorite things, nearly all nonethnic specific contemporary things such as "sweaters, bikinis, calendars," except to frustrate her and provide further rationale for Dwayne to keep steady in his insistent and stubborn desire not to focus upon race (1988, 20). At this point, the two are engaged in a heated battle with one another, just as a writer of the member of the hip-hop generation might be at war with a member of the civil rights generation. However, their efforts will eventually lead them both towards literary and personal improvement.

Dewayne goes back to narrating his equally contrived story, now describing Earle as part of a nerdish group, along with two other male teenagers who collectively call themselves the Trinary. Still, one can already see that Isshee's letter has affected him to some degree, as he devotes several pages to narrating from the point of view of Earle's mother, who works as a reservation agent at the fictional South African Airlines (SAA). While Dewayne's description of Earle's mother is one of a subservient and not elegant person, it is not deserving of Isshee's categorization as "puerile, misogynistic, disjointed," and "pathetic pornography" (1988, 39). Her violent reactions can only be explained that subconsciously she realizes that Dewayne may be somewhat correct in describing her work as rehashing African American glory stories and that she may be hypersensitive to the portrayal of female characters.

Instead of working together, the two irrationally attack one another. Here Ellis hints at the dark underside of African American life, whereby these two writers become rather vicious and bloodthirsty in their attempt to outdo, defeat, and even destroy each other instead of pooling their energies to help one another. This repeatedly is seen in African American literature and history from the literary and philosophical feud between Richard Wright and Zora Neale Hurston to infighting within the Nation of Islam and, most recently, in the controversy surrounding Bill Cosby's remarks that exposed the hostility between the civil rights and hip-hop generations as well as the conflicts between African Americans of different economic classes. Indeed these characters, despite being similar in age, represent the conflicts between the civil rights and hip-hop generations.

Unlike Dewayne, Isshee is an established, critically acclaimed writer, so at this point she sees no reason to change her literary style because of a literary nobody like Dewayne, whose opinions, at this point, she does not value in the least. So, when Isshee goes back to writing her revised narrative of Earle's story, it continues to be overdrawn, melodramatic, and contrived. Her revised chapter is situated in church, and there Isshee is able to extol the virtues of religion as providing community and solidarity for African Americans. This is a common theme in the writings and lives of the civil rights generation, but religion does not play as significant a role in the lives and writings of the hip-hop generation. Although there is truth to what Isshee suggests, she neglects to show the opposite side: how Christianity kept many African Americans figuratively enslaved long after they were emancipated in the sense that Christianity allowed them to be reconciled to oppression and segregation, to see themselves as Christ-like martyrs, to rationalize discrimination and racism as part of God's plan, or to console themselves with hopes of a perfect afterlife. Her story has much that Bill Cosby might praise because it emphasizes strength in the face of adversity or oppression; still, her characters are not much more than agrarian simpletons.

Above all, Isshee has a typical civil-rights-era message in her writings. She wants to portray African Americans, specifically African American women, as incredibly strong and noble, and she is willing to sacrifice virtually everything to emphasize this message. In part to do that, Isshee describes Earle's family as being incredibly impoverished, barely having enough food to survive, with Earle having to walk fifteen miles to school (one way). The latter is a good example of the extent to which Isshee is willing to sacrifice realism in order to emphasize hardships, for a fifteen-mile walk would take at least four hours. One of the hallmarks of the hip-hop generation is their desire for realism or to "keep it real," and Isshee's work would understandably lose some credibility in the eyes of the hip-hop generation because her writing is overdone for dramatic effect. Furthermore Isshee, in her description of the school, cannot help but interject her own rather melodramatic comments: "All the students pledging allegiance to the flag, but not really to the flag, more to a future flag, not only with more stars but with new, invisible stripes, colored rainbow stripes earned by the blood, sweat, and tears of all those Selma grandmothers firehosed into history" (1988, 49). Were African Americans in the early twentieth century really so prophetic and hopeful as to envision a more-egalitarian America, in which they would be treated as equals by whites? It is doubtful, as they had little to convince them that the attitudes of whites would so dramatically change. No doubt this is an aspect of Isshee's writing that Ellis criticizes, for empty platitudes, which is essentially what Isshee writes, are ultimately meaningless. Indeed it is exactly this that members of the hip-hop generation often criticize about the civil rights generation: that they possess pie-in-the-sky idealism about race relations but fail to see the stark realities of contemporary, everyday life.

Isshee's chapters and vehement criticism of Dewayne's writings end up pushing Dewayne in the opposite direction, just as an aspiring hip-hop generation African American writer like Ellis might be inspired to write less–race-conscious prose after reading the contrived, ultra racially conscious prose of a postmodernist civil-rights-generation writer like Isshee. This is a position arguably that many of the hip-hop generation find themselves in. Although similar in age to Dewayne, Isshee really represents the elder African American generation that came of age in and fought for the civil rights movement and for whom racial issues are tantamount, in addition to fostering positive images of the race. Hearing so much about race from their forebears, the hip-hop generation rebels by demanding there is more to contemporary African American life than the struggle for racial equality. Dewayne's desire to frustrate Isshee appears in his next letter to her, in which he sarcastically thanks her for her "oh-so-generous assistance" and responds by giving her "an even longer and less readable list" (1988, 52). Indeed Dewayne proceeds to describe the Trinary (Earle and his two white, nerdish friends) as they spend an uneventful day at Coney Island, unsuccessfully trying to pick up girls and ending up seeing a soft-core–porn movie. His writings are meandering, light, and lack the depth of Isshee's, but it is more realistic in uncovering the relatively meaningless lives of these teenagers. Both authors are egoists, and their letter writing escalates into a war of egos. Isshee accuses Dewayne of "transparent jealousy," while Dewayne scoffs at her writing (1988, 79). Once again, instead of working together and attempting to help each other become better writers or even offering some encouraging words, thereby supporting African American art, they attack one another rather than metaphorically attacking the system that favors Caucasians over African Americans. Time and time again, this interracial fighting is seen in the works of hip-hop-generation writers, who regard it as one of the greatest, if not the greatest threat to the contemporary African American community.

However, *Platitudes* is a novel about making connections between these two disparate groups. Indeed something about the letter from Isshee or the next part of Isshee's story affects Dewayne enough to change his story and his writing. In part Isshee may have hit close to home when, in her letter, she groups Dewayne with "countless other underachieving middle-aged black 'artists'" (1988, 79). Her comments, though, are insulting rather than constructive. In addition her subsequent rewrite of Earle's story with her attention to how Earle is transformed by reading the poetry of Paul Lawrence Dunbar may have affected Dewayne emotionally in the sense that he realizes that she has some good intentions in stressing the importance of African American literature. Furthermore he recognizes the importance of his cultural and literary heritage, which many members of the hip-hop generation seem to forsake, not seeing its direct utility in their lives. Consequently, when Dewayne picks up the story, his writing style veers closer towards Isshee's. Earlier Dewayne wrote short, declarative sentences: "There she is again, dancing with some girls. The crazy lights darken her hair. Another black young man nears Janey Rosebloom to the beat, groin first. She turns to him to the beat. They dance at each other" (1988, 7). Now, his prose is a little more metaphoric, involved, descriptive, and introverted. For instance, when Earle comes home, Dewayne/Ellis writes, "Kicking the serving tray, the decanters upon it gossip but don't break. The dim reflection of the dark in the glass over the Impressionist print next to his mother's door fools him. He steps into the shimmer and stings his nose" (1988, 93). In addition, after a description of John Coltrane's music, Dewayne switches gears and focuses on his female characters like Isshee does. Instead of treating his female characters as sexual or two-dimensional objects, Dewayne now imbues them with the same three-dimensional qualities as his male characters. His female characters go out shopping, gossip, talk their personal lives, and get involved with some men in a bar in New York City. Thereby, Dewayne breaks away from the misogyny often associated (rightly or wrongly) with hip-hop music.

Isshee responds with some mixed praise to Dewayne, but her praise is mainly because his writing is becoming more like hers, not because he has necessarily improved his story. With this, Ellis equally criticizes the civil rights generation, who purportedly want to help the hip-hop generation, but they may do so for egoistic rather than altruistic reasons. Rather, there continues to be little or no depth to Dewayne's main plot. However, Isshee reads more into Dewayne's story than is actually there, claiming that Dewayne's descriptions of his female characters include a "dialectic between class struggle and cultural assimilation, the mental anguish of rising from a middle-class Harlem household to the rich, white, New York, controlled-substance-abusing elite," that "is almost interestingly handled" (1988, 109). However, that scene had nothing to do with anguish or class differences; rather, the four girls Dewayne portrayed were, according to their own account, merely looking for "the best-looking guys" (1988, 97). Here Isshee is being hypocritical in praising the sexual objectification that she had been consistently criticizing in Dewayne's treatment of women, because to her, there can be no real sexual objectification (or other forms of objectification) of men. Despite her purported commitment to racial equality, Isshee seems more like she's ruthlessly arrogant, narcissistic, and condescending and only really caring about how she's perceived, which again, is how the hip-hop generation can see the civil rights generation in its worst possible light. One gets a sense that Ellis felt this to be a danger of literary success. Along these lines, Isshee not only insists that she made a significant contribution to Dewayne's novel but also claims that her editor is interested in publishing it. Though she offers, in a rather backhanded way, to compensate Dewayne financially, she also insults him by offering to try to help him get a job as a copywriter (1988, 109).

She concludes the letter, in a rather passive-aggressive manner, by telling Dewayne, "Your position on negritude, sir, continues to befuddle me" (1988, 110). For Isshee a socially responsible African American must have a position on race or write racially conscious fiction; anything other than that would be meaningless and/or unrealistic. At this point, the schism between the two is largely to write about race or not to write about race. This is an unfair dichotomy that writers of the hip-hop generation rebel against. However, it is not a new debate but goes all the way back to the debate between Alan Locke and W. E. B. DuBois during the Harlem Renaissance.

Dewayne responds to Isshee's letter, claiming that he has now read and appreciated her works, and they have in turn, influenced his own writings. He does so in part out of flattery, being that he is an egotist almost as much, if not as much, as Isshee. Yet, his interest seems to be rather romantic or sexual, as, in order to see if they can meet, he asks Isshee if she will be attending the BAA conference, and he even requests her picture while including a picture of himself with his letter. This does not suggest that Dewayne has grown a social conscience; rather, he is still as self-involved as before, only now he is trying harder to impress Isshee. In turn Earle, instead of being sexually obsessed, is now more romantic and shy, evident by how Dewayne describes him as being content to just "sit there and look at her smile for days like a dopey goon" (1988, 136). However, Dewayne has not yet evolved from being an egoistic and possibly misogynist member of the hip-hop generation. Furthermore, in his desire to impress Isshee, Dewayne makes Earle politically active, joining and volunteering for the Jean Toomer Democratic Club in order to help a prominent African American mayoral candidate get elected. Dewayne wants to portray Earle as being responsible and racially conscious because he believes that will help spark Isshee's romantic interest. This is also apparent in how, while at the Jean Toomer Club, Earle discovers many of Isshee's books in a small library, and Dewayne not only shamelessly includes a whole page of his story to describing Isshee's books and quoting from positive reviews of her books, he has Earle eagerly take one of Isshee's books home with him. Far from bothering her, she tells him in her next letter that she is "obviously pleased" (1988, 149). This should come as no surprise as, above anything else, Isshee is an egoist, not a devoted feminist or fighter for civil rights.

All of this does have the effect of warming Isshee up to Dewayne. In so doing, Ellis shows that, at heart, both Dewayne and Isshee are quite similar to one another despite how they attempt to distinguish themselves, just as is the case with members of the civil rights and hip-hop generations. In her next let-ter Isshee apologies to Dewayne because she claims she has learned he was just "another heartbroken human being," but it is more likely a result of his flatter-ing comments of her (1988, 148). Despite how Dewayne's story has turned into clichéd melodrama, Isshee praises it: "I believe *Platitudes* is now coming along rather well. The two-completely-different-types-fall-in-love Love Story is a time-honored favorite. If it was good enough for Shakespeare . . ." (1988, 148–49). Yet her comments only address the surface; Dewayne's work is still lightweight and insubstantial. Although Isshee herself comes across as being almost asexual at first, it can be presumed that her comments were influenced by seeing Dewayne's photograph, which she praises. Expecting an unkempt or "over-weight man," Isshee is pleased to find that Dewayne looks more like "an ath-lete" (1988, 150). With this flattery from Isshee, Dewayne, in hopes that it will impress her, continues changing Earle into a more innocent and shyer teenager rather than a hormone-raging adolescent. Indeed it has a positive effect upon Isshee, as noted by her praise for his latest writing, which she describes as "han-dled wonderfully and, above all, sensitively" (1988, 157). These comments are nothing more than the title of the book—platitudes. While the two writers have warmed up to each other personally, they still have not become better writers or surmounted their egoistic tendencies. However, it is finding this common ground that Ellis suggests is the necessary and important first step in helping to bridge the gap between these two authors and, metaphorically, between the two generations they represent.

Up to this point, Dewayne represents the lesser emotionally and socially developed aspects of the hip-hop generation. That Dewayne's objective is purely romantic or sexual becomes clear when we find out that Isshee stood Dewayne up at a writer's conference for another African American writer, Richard Johnson. Although she apologies, Dewayne takes it as a rejection.

Consequently Dewayne not only abandons his more introverted, innocent, descriptive, Isshee-influenced narrative but also abandons his original light-hearted approach. Instead, his story turns dark and angry, mirroring his own feelings. In short Dewayne is writing like an individualist, not for the greater collective good, as is more typical with hip-hop generation. When Dewayne picks up the story, Earle gets rejected by the girl he is most interested in, Dorothy (mirroring Dewayne's own perceived rejection by Isshee). Consequently Earle gives up his political volunteer work, while his mother loses her new, promising job. The extent of Dewayne's anger is apparent in how Earle explains that he discovers Dorothy in flagrante delicto, describing her as "the only love of my life getting fucked up the ass like a pig" (1988, 161). Along similar lines, Dewayne goes back to writing more sexually explicit prose in part to anger Isshee, but this time it is nearly pornographic in his description of a sexual encounter between Earle and Janey. Isshee, in her next letter, this time being basically accurate, sees the changes in his story as a response to her perceived rejection of him. She believes he has "willfully" sabotaged his own work to cause her pain and that her rejection has demolished his "faith in black women and in our people as a whole" (1988, 171). The latter is an overstatement, of course (a result of Isshee's narcissism), but it does seem like they are finally communicating to one another. Isshee does seem genuinely regretful, though, as she tells Dewayne that she is not only "fond" of him, but she has decided not to publish her version of the story. Furthermore she tells him that she will "sign over all rights" to Dewayne and then give his version "to my publisher with the highest possible recommendation" (1988, 172). To confirm her interest in Dewayne, she also invites him to dinner.

However, Ellis makes great efforts to show how racial infighting affects both groups and in this case, Isshee as well as Dewayne. For her own part, Isshee's narrative seems to degenerate as well. Earle and Dorothy kill the evil slave master Wyte and his apprentice, I. Corinthians. Still, her encounter with Dewayne seems to have seems to have made her more humble. While at a conference, a person points out to Isshee that some have criticized her for "being anti-male" (1988, 177). She responds to this criticism in an unexpected manner that demonstrates how she has changed, in large part a result of her interactions with Dewayne: "I think to a large degree they are correct, especially in my very early works. I began writing shortly after some rather disastrous romantic encounters, one with a university professor no less, and my early works reflected this misandry" (1988, 177). Now, both characters are changed in positive ways by one another, and while that is not directly manifested in their writing, it seems like this is the starting point for their social and personal development, for they have begun to see their own faults and limitations while they reach out to one another. In a broader sense we see both generations collaborating with one another, complementing their strengths, and by doing so collectively improving.

The novel ends with Isshee and Dewayne having dinner together and then making love, which, metaphorically, can be seen as a unification of these two generations and literary approaches. However, at first Dewayne has trouble performing, which signifies his own feelings of inadequacy and fear of Isshee. He literally needs to write himself into having more confidence and does so by going back to the story and having Earle act with genuine confidence. The story comes back to Earle and Dorothy, and Dorothy apologizes to Earle for having an affair with someone else. "You're too pure," she tells him. Instead of being overwhelmed by his insecurities, Earle acts, kissing Dorothy, who returns in kind. Dewayne, just like Earle, has overcome his own lack of literary and sexual confidence, and the last sentence indicates this: "Now that it presses the underside of his desk, he will go wake Isshee" (1988, 183).

That Dewayne needed to write the scene with Earle before becoming aroused indicates a symbiotic relationship between fiction and real life for Dewayne. Indeed that is part of Ellis's intentions: to deconstruct the motives of authors. Throughout the novel, Dewayne is clearly motivated by his desire to combat and then connect with Isshee, and although she does not admit it, Isshee is also driven to outperform, rather than to connect with Dewayne. In addition the literal coupling of Dewayne and Isshee at the end of the novel indicates that he believes a middle ground can be forged between what could be described as two extremes of the civil rights and hip-hop generations: the race-conscious writings of the former and race-oblivious writings of the latter. In other words African American writers can address racial issues in a significant way without overwhelming the narrative and ignoring other nonracially specific themes and ideas. This hybridity or at least attempted hybridity is evident in the writings of other members of the hip-hop generation. This is more along the lines of Ellis's trajectory in his next two novels, *Home Repairs* (1994) and *Right Here, Right Now* (1999), in which he focuses on contemporary life. He does so by blending conventions of the civil rights and hip-hop generations. In these novels race is an issue and theme but not the only one and not necessarily the main one either. However, it is important to note that it is Ellis's characters more than Ellis himself who make choose not to focus on race. By doing so, Ellis suggests that they are unable to find a satisfying and complete sense of self.

In *Home Repairs,* Ellis addresses race by counteracting stereotypes of black masculinity and by having his characters defy societal expectations. In that sense the novel challenges contemporary hip-hop's portrayal of masculinity as ultrasexual and ultraconfident. *Home Repairs* is largely a sexual and romantic

bildungsroman of the teenage years and young adulthood of Austin McMillan/
Jones (he changes his last name later in the novel), written in a diary form, span-
ning a nine-year period from 1979 to 1988, in which the narrator is sixteen to
twenty-five. One reviewer of the novel, Darryl Pinckney, suggests that the novel
is "intended as a rebuttal to modern black women's charges that the black man
has sold out and mistreated them" (1993, 33). Indeed Austin is not a stereotypical sexually powerful African American man as often portrayed in hip-hop
music and culture; rather, he is unsure, awkward, and rejected many times
before he achieves any measure of romantic or sexual success. Still, for the most
part, he treats the women in whom he is interested with respect and courtesy.

Although the racial subject matter and implications in *Home Repairs* lie
somewhat submerged in the narrative, they still exist. Austin's difficulties with
women and difficulties establishing a strong sense of self may have a good deal
to do with being an African American man growing up in a mostly white environment. From the beginning of the novel, Austin, who is attending a nearly
all-white school in New Hampshire, is quite self-conscious about his ethnicity.
His subverted, alienated feelings seem to emerge while walking to a school
party; he describes "a white Afro of icy wind," and "Main Street is empty, and
its black is washed white with dried salt" (1994, 10). It is as if he feels white-
washed, and he is projecting those feelings onto the environment. When he
gets to the party, Austin notes, "I'm the only black kid, so a stranger here, too"
(1994, 10). Because of his race, Austin feels he can be nothing but a stranger.
When he goes to Cape Cod with his white friend, Morgan, and they meet a
seemingly interested white girl, Austin immediately gives up on her, presuming
falsely that she will not be interested in him because he's African American:
"You know, I don't think I've ever wanted to be white before tonight," even
though he has no indication or way of knowing if this white girl might be interested in him (1994, 38).

None of this is particularly new or specific to the hip-hop generation, but
that Austin has to navigate the same issues of racial exclusion that his forebears
did indicates that members of the hip-hop generation still have to deal with the
same racial issues that members of the previous generation did, despite the perceived advancements made by the civil rights movement. What makes it even
more difficult for Austin is that the women he pursues often lose interest in him
because he does not express the level of sexual and romantic self-confidence
that they have come to expect from other African American men (quite possibly learned from the common portrayal of male hip-hop generation members as hyperstrong and sexual). In other words they buy into the stereotypical
sexual bravado of African American men and consider such behavior to be
alluring. That part of Austin's difficulties may result from his own conflicted

feelings about being African American is also evident when he goes to Harlem and feels uncomfortable: "I felt awful being afraid of my own people" (1994, 76). But it remains that he never expresses a fear the of white people with whom he has grown up. No one in Harlem does anything to inspire fear; rather, because of the media and hip-hop culture, Austin has come to associate Harlem and the inner city with violence regardless of whether or not it is true.

In order to combat his conflicted racial feelings, Austin decides to live in a black dorm when he begins school at Stanford University, a move that might very well have been praised by more-radical elements of the civil rights generation. He explains, "It will be good for me. I could have had a black roommate at Andover, but I thought it was stupid, reverse racism. Now I'm sick of being on the outside of everything, the black world and the white. That's probably why it's been so hard to get laid. I'm going to be normal, finally, and then we'll see if my life shapes up" (1994, 99). Austin blames his romantic and sexual failings on his feelings of racial exclusion, but although race might have something to do with it, he uses it more as an excuse to absolve himself from personal responsibility. It turns out that merely being around other black people is not enough to reverse Austin's losing streak with women, nor does it give him a more stable sense of identity or confidence. Rather, it is a crutch that Austin uses in order to avoid blaming himself. In that, Ellis rejects as simplistic the belief that race underlies Austin's behavior and failings. He convinces himself that he needs to be surrounded by African Americans in order to feel comfortable and happy. However, neither his time in an African American dorm nor his summer spent amidst a large number of African Americans in Atlanta helps him with his romantic and sexual difficulties.

Austin could be described as representative of the postsegregation/hip-hop generation in that his immediate personal concerns supercede social or racial consciousness; he invokes race only to justify his failings or in times of personal crisis. This is not to suggest that he is necessarily wrong in his assumptions (for he may be right), but he is only concerned with race and the larger African American community when something personal happens to him. Actually Austin is rather egotistical; he is a man on a mission to have a stable, steady, and satisfying romantic and sexual relationship. Even in August 1983 at the twentieth anniversary of Dr. Martin Luther King Jr.'s March on Washington, Austin is more concerned with getting involved with Calista, the woman with whom he attends the event, than anything else. Still, it's not just Austin who seemingly trivializes this important anniversary; it seems to be endemic among Austin's peer group. While on the train to Washington, D.C., Austin notes the "high school and college students masquerading as 1960s–era hippies, nuns, the Red Communist Youth Brigade, and various black Baptist deacons," as well as white ultraliberals there singing John Lennon's "Imagine" and protesting Reagan (1994, 184). Austin and others at the anniversary seem like empty imitators of 1960s idealism, merely mimicking their roles but possessing little or none of the spirit and drive of the original marchers. It would be too easy and unfair to suggest that they are apathetic or vapid, as members of the civil rights generation sometimes do, because racism and prejudice have become so much more nebulous than in the 1950s and 1960s with the end of segregation.

Particular to Austin's situation as a member of the hip-hop generation is the effect of the media, which ends up being, at least initially, a huge asset to him in his personal life and professional career. Austin becomes the host of a home-improvement show for cable television. This is the only clear way that being African American seems to help him. In this case racial stereotyping works to Austin's benefit, for despite that he knows next to nothing about home improvement, Austin is hired, and the audience accepts him as a knowledge-able working man because he is black (unlike a more skilled professional such as a lawyer or doctor). Here is the insidious effect of subtle prejudice and stereotypes brought on by the media. The producers want to capitalize on his race when they ask him to consider changing his last name, which Austin willingly does: "They were concerned that 'Austin McMillan' sounded more like a British prime minister than a home repairs adviser, so I suggested Jones" (1994, 251). No doubt, the producers of the show are happy with Austin's name change because to their ears, and the ears of many people, it sounds more authentically African American.

This stereotyping is reinforced by how successful the program becomes and in how it benefits Austin. Living merely off his looks and apparent charisma does wonders for Austin's social life, which was previously a series of disasters, but it also makes him internally hollow or, by his own account, "a shallow, vapid asshole" (1994, 249). He admits that not only can he not remember the last book he read, he "can't remember a single class from college" (1994, 273). Still, he has never been more popular and pleased to find out that, according to the African American magazine *Chocolate Singles,* he's "the twenty-second of the fifty most eligible black bachelors in New York" (1994, 273). This shows how important the media and entertainment industries have become in the African American community and to the larger world. It also shows how easy it is for Austin, a sham and imposter, to manipulate his audience, who has preconceived notions that an African American man could be an expert at something physical or manual like home improvement. Lastly it shows how the African American community seems to be complicit in rewarding shallow and insubstantial behavior. The result is that Austin's "successes" become hollow. After a couple of years as the television host, Austin finds that despite his growing popularity, he has never felt so isolated and empty. Still, he does not quit his job and continues at it until he is terminated because of the increasing costs of the program and Austin's botched attempt to ask for a raise. This is significant in that the media executives seem to make this decision because they regard Austin as a replaceable commodity, which leads one to wonder how much progress there really has been for African Americans in an area (entertainment) in which they are thought to have the most successes. After he loses his job, Austin decides to turn his life around by applying to graduate programs in African American studies. However, even though he is accepted to Cornell University and plans to begin there in the fall, he is drawn by a more tempting offer: to do his home-repairs show for the Playboy Channel. Although it might seem that this kind of success will only lead Austin into a further emotional downward spiral, it actually has the opposite effect upon him: he no longer enters into unfulfilling sexual and romantic relationships that he began pursuing after he became a television star. Getting what he has dreamt of for so long, being surrounded by a large number of extremely attractive women, shows Austin that he has been living in a dream world all these years because he realizes that what he desired does not produce genuine or lasting fulfillment. This makes him a clear counterpart to many contemporary hip-hop stars who, once they reach the level of Austin's celebrity or greater, become caught up in a whirlwind of sex, violence, and drugs.

The novel ends with Austin asking his African American assistant Michelle to dinner, insisting that he has matured and that he will no longer fall victim to unrequited love. He has grown comfortable in his own skin and no longer feels dominated by a need to prove himself romantically, sexually, or racially. Although that might seem like an uplifting end to the novel, Austin's journey is so improbable (specifically, the Playboy offer) that one cannot generalize his experience to other African Americans. He may have been successful in overcoming his personal and racial problems, but what of the millions of others who do not have the opportunities Austin had? It took failing for Austin to appreciate success, and failing and admitting one's vulnerabilities are not part and parcel of the hip-hop cultural ethos. Indeed this is one of Ellis's critiques of hip-hop: that the machismo it endorses ultimately does more damage than good to the African American community. Ellis leaves it uncertain as to what might happen to Austin after his success at the end of *Home Repairs*. Will he continue to feel comfortable in his own skin? Will he become a better, more sensitive person, or will he become even more narcissistic and oblivious, despite what he says?

In a way, Ellis's next novel, *Right Here, Right Now* (1999), situates an Austin-like character, several years later, who becomes somewhat of a monstrosity, a rather nightmarish end result of the hip-hop generation. The protagonist, a suave motivational speaker named Ashton Robinson, is what Austin McMillan might become ten years later: a rather vapid, fraudulent entertainment entrepreneur/con man with little or no moral concern about cheating his needy "clients" out of money. *Right Here, Right Now* is more of a warning call of what could happen to a person completely devoid of racial or ethnic consciousness as is the case with Ashton. He represents the hip-hop generation run amuck: amoral, scheming, and manipulative and with no allegiance to anyone but himself. The characters in the novel, while often lacking depth, are purposely made to be caricatures, because the book is told from the perspective of Ashton, who is rather shallow himself.

To a large degree, Ashton represents everything that Ellis has come to critique about contemporary society, especially the hip-hop generation. A self-described narcissist and fraud who admits he's "never been formally trained in psychology, theology, anything," Ashton becomes successful by promoting the idea that a person can change his/her behavior by changing his/her self-image (1999, 25). In other words acting in a certain way or as a certain type produces that reality if it is done repeatedly, for long enough, and with sufficient belief. Ashton's typical client is a middle-aged, white man who "stumbled into success early but for some years now has stalled and watched people he had early on competed with and vanquished suddenly overtaken him" (1999, 44). This majority client has no deeper goals other than wanting to appear better or stronger in the eyes of others, just like teenage consumers of hip-hop. Given that Ashton's clients are not that sympathetic, we do not fault him much for duping them. However, Ashton even convinces a much more sympathetic African American minority recruiter to give up his job and pursue something more financially lucrative: insurance. Ashton has no moral center, no ethnic allegiance, and no desire to help the African American community. In short he has no more important desires other than to become wealthy and desirable. Furthermore, in private, Ashton reveals that not only does he not believe in the message he preaches but also that he's still "hiding a fragile, frightened wimp within me" (1999, 26). Similar to Austin in *Home Repairs,* the success that Ashton achieves is ultimately hollow and insignificant.

Ashton can be seen as a nightmarish hip-hop generation–era reincarnation of Ralph Ellison's invisible man (1952), as both lack a stable identity and moral center, a result of implicit and explicit racial reasons. For Ashton (like Austin in *Home Repairs*), it is largely a response to his later youth in which he was often one of the only African Americans around or the only one. After Ashton's parents move from the predominately African American city of Flint, Michigan, to the predominately Caucasian and Chicano, Santa Cruz, California, he becomes a worse student and an empty caricature. He insists that he had to adapt or die, and that in order to be accepted or fit in, he needed to either blend in with others by learning "Spanish and how to surf" or pretend to be a more dangerous, stereotypical African American man because that is what his peers want or expect him to be (no doubt due at least in part to media caricatures). Ashton realizes he can fulfill their stereotypes by inventing "an exotic past for myself of urban bravery, college-aged girlfriends" (1999, 53). Ashton attempts to do both and does so successfully: "In four months I had more friends in Santa Cruz than in my lifetime in Flint" (1999, 53). Realizing, then, that "life is acting," Ashton loses all sense of shame in lying and becomes a living lie, telling people whatever he wants in order to get what he wants (1999, 53). Ellis largely blames racial stereotyping for creating people like Ashton, who, feeling devoid of a stable identity, becomes amoral, and ironically, solipsistic, admitting, "I love me so goddamn much!" (1999, 15).

This is not to suggest that Ellis completely absolves Ashton of blame, for in the novel, Ellis often pokes fun at him for his newfound beliefs in New Age mysticism when he has a vision, hallucination, or religious experience[6] one evening after he drinks an entire bottle of cough syrup. Subsequently Ashton is "visited" by a Brazilian midget who tells he that he needs to find his "ashay," a "Brazilian Portuguese term imported from Africa that roughly translates to 'spirit' or 'power'" (1999, 120). Subsequently Ashton changes his message from self-serving actualization to an emphasis upon spirituality and the search for meaning in what he now sees as a disposable, empty materialistic life.

On the surface, this seems like a perfectly good change for Ashton to make (and possibly for much of the hip-hop generation). However, Ashton's "religious vision" is really a manifestation of a suppressed death wish derived from his years of forced playacting as a tough, African American teenager or would-be surfer in a predominately white community and from his real acting as a motivational speaker. In other words Ashton has become nothing but a hollow façade. He somewhat realizes how empty he has become and wants it all to end. Indeed he later defines his objective as to "leave this world and leave our bodies, our personal histories, and in the truth of the Other Side as the pure essence that all humans understand to be their true nature when they are honest enough to see through their socioreligious acculturation" (1999, 170). Up to this point, the novel is concerned with only Ashton, but the power of his rhetoric is strong enough that he is able to gather a small but devoted following that becomes a cult. Similar to the Heaven's Gate cult, Ashton has them dress identically, although the clothes are from the clothing-store chain the Gap. Ashton's attempt to make everyone look the same indicates his unwillingness to deal with being an Other and his inability to accept racial and ethnic differences. He really wants to look like everyone else so that he does not have to deal with painful feelings of exclusion and the self-consciousness that goes along with being African American in his world (at least as he perceives it). In short he is so blinded by the rhetoric of color blindness that it ends up backfiring upon him.

The extent of Ashton's inner turmoil becomes evident when he attempts suicide by purposely crashing into a building after he had just been devastated by watching an episode of *60 Minutes* in which he was portrayed as a corrupt moneygrubber. Throughout his new spiritual life, Ashton has sought to "disappear," yet he is not aware of how he can do that. Even before his mystical/ religious experience, he had already disappeared into the façade and aura he created as a motivational speaker. The book ends with the reader somewhat uncertain as to whether Ashton has died in the car crash, as he is visited in prison (where he has presumably been put for destroying public property and reckless endangerment) by the Brazilian midget/spirit who claims that Ashton did "disappear," but "we just didn't count on the air bag" (1999, 285).[7] Metaphorically, it makes little difference, as Ashton has been deadened inside for years. He is the possible nightmarish end result of the hip-hop culture, in which, in its worst form, nothing has become valuable except image and perception. Because being African American man is largely a liability in America, Ashton has learned to act in ways that will please others, but he is never able to push himself beyond stereotypical expectations.

What could have helped change Ashton or turn him around? Ellis does seem to suggest that had he remained in his hometown of Flint, Michigan, which is predominately African American, Ashton would have grown up to be relatively stable and content. Or would he? After all, Flint, as portrayed by Michael Moore in his film *Roger and Me* (1989), was economically devastated at the time when Ashton would have come of age. In order to fit in and be successful, Ashton sacrifices his identity, and while it is conceivable that a stronger or better person might have avoided that pitfall, at least part of the blame ought to be placed upon the expectations of whites around him, who have, in turn, been influenced by the media. Had Ashton not been expected to be an urban tough (presumably derived through listening to hip-hop music or hip-hop videos) or not accepted unless he were like his peers in Santa Cruz, he might have been able to develop his own identity and not be pigeonholed because of his race and thereby might not have grown to be as cynical about the world and chosen to be a phony motivational speaker in order to basically cheat people out of money. Hardened cynicism time and time again shows up in various characters within the literature of the hip-hop generation as a response to the often-subtle but still-lingering stereotypes and prejudice of and against African Americans in contemporary times.

Ellis's work provides no easy solution to the problems facing the hip-hop generation, but in his novels, he suggests that individualism and subsequent narcissism are what mainly endanger the contemporary African American community. Only Isshee and Dewayne in *Platitudes* seem able to achieve any kind of happy medium between hyper–racial consciousness and racial obliviousness, between rampant sexuality and melodramatic love, between overdone caricatures and dull realism, and finally, between the individual and the collective. Ellis suggests that, ideally, the combination of the civil rights and hip-hop generations' ethos can produce personal and community-wide advancements for African Americans. However, such an approach makes sense in theory but is much more difficult to put into practice.

2

JAKE LAMAR

Jake Lamar's memoir and four novels deal primarily with how race plays a role in the contemporary lives of middle- or upper-class, urban, African American professionals, especially those of the hip-hop generation. Lamar himself might be considered the ideal progeny of the civil rights era. Born in 1961, he was an exceptional student who attended and graduated from Harvard University and subsequently wrote for *Time Magazine*. However, as Lamar explains in his memoir, *Bourgeois Blues* (1992), he had difficulty fitting into the racially homogenous corporate environment and subsequently quit journalism to become a full-time novelist. Although on the surface Lamar's biography is a quintessential success story of integration and opportunity, his writings demonstrate the subtle but important effects of racism in contemporary America as well as the difficulties facing African Americans in the post–civil rights era. Success can no longer (or should no longer) be clearly measured by material or professional means, and achieving racial equality is not something easily measured or achieved, especially for members of the hip-hop generation.

Lamar's writings, like that of the other writers in this book, are typically labeled African American literature. This is a classification that Lamar rebels against as he seeks a nonracially exclusive audience (as do most hip-hop-generation writers): "I know from experience that plenty of white readers love my work but the ethnic label does prevent a lot of white readers from ever discovering my books" (Wells 2004). Lamar's frustration is understandable, considering that white readers as well as African Americans should be the target audience of the writers of the hip-hop generation so that their important and serious ideas gain more currency. However, Lamar's frustration with racial categorization may be driving him away from writing about race at all as evident by his latest novels, *If Six Were Nine* (2001) and *The Eighteenth Arrondissement* (2003), which veer more towards suspenseful, murder mysteries than serious novels investigating race.

In the tradition of Richard Wright, James Baldwin, and Chester Himes, Lamar currently resides in Paris, where he has lived since 1993. However, according to Lamar, he lives in Paris not so much for racial as literary reasons: "The big difference between me and someone like Wright and Baldwin is that I've never felt in exile here. I never felt that I had to escape American racism." This is not to suggest that Lamar thinks American society is racially egalitarian, for the opposite is seen in his fiction. Still, Lamar explains that he responds to Paris's "artistic freedom" and their "respect for writers," not just commercially successful authors as is more often the case in America (Patrick 2004).

After leaving *Time Magazine* in 1989, Lamar went on to work on *Bourgeois Blues,* an account of his childhood through young adulthood, his personal and family struggles, and his attempts to come to grips with the role of race in America as well as his identity as a hip-hop generation African American. To a large extent, the novel explores Lamar's relationship with his father, Jake Sr., and the generation gap between them. His father, a by-product of the segregation-era South, is a fiercely independent fighter, tormented by his own need to succeed and prove himself superior to whites, whereas the son, a more-typical representative of the hip-hop generation, is more able to move freely in the world and is less overtly concerned with whites, feeling no need to outperform them and is more relaxed and less concerned with the opinions of others. While his father tries to enforce his idea of striving for the best in everything, Lamar comes to believe that such an approach is hollow hearted in contemporary America, as it buys into white standards of success.

Unlike his father, Lamar feels no real need to be a contemporary incarnation of DuBois's talented tenth. Indeed his desire to write *Bourgeois Blues* came from a desire to counteract the often one-dimensional literary account of African Americans as economically impoverished: "I grew up hearing what the Black experience was and there was always the sense that the genuine African American is poor and in the inner city. I wanted to write about a person who didn't grow up in poverty. I wanted to say, 'This is my experience'" (Peterson 1992, 67). In that sense Lamar, from the beginning of his literary career, desires to undo stereotypes wrought mostly by the media, and he rebels against a quintessential hip-hop trope: emergence from the poverty or ghetto. *Bourgeois Blues* received high critical praise, and in 1993, Lamar received the Lyndhurst prize for it, "a three-year grant given to artists, journalists, and people in community service" (Wells 2004).

The title, *Bourgeois Blues,* is both ironic and serious. In a way it sounds elitist and condescending to those from a more-impoverished background. After all, what would someone from a middle to upper socioeconomic background know about real suffering, they might wonder? Indeed Lamar's memoirs are no gut-wrenching accounts of poverty, violence, and/or vicious racism, but that does not mean the issues he writes about are not serious and/or potentially devastating. By changing focus from the African American lower class to the middle class (which is rarely if ever done in contemporary hip-hop culture), Lamar's memoirs perform an important service by bringing to light that even the majority of economically well-adjusted African Americans have important problems, which are more often racially oriented than economically oriented.

Along similar lines, *Bourgeois Blues* is Lamar's realization of the extent to which race matters, and that despite the efforts made during and after the civil rights movement, American society is far from becoming color-blind but, rather, is riddled with subtle, institutional racism that keeps minorities from achieving on an equal basis to whites. Similar to Ralph Ellison's invisible man, Lamar first tried to "live my life by Dr. King's credo, judging people not by the color of their skin but by the content of their character" (1992, 13). However, throughout his memoir, Lamar describes himself constantly being judged and evaluated on the basis of color/race and eventually limited on the basis of that. He ultimately finds that he must address race, both in his personal and professional lives, in order to not just understand his own life but also the lives of those close to him, like his father.

Lamar devotes a good deal of his memoir to his often strained and at times nonexistent relationship with his father. A product of Southern racism and poverty, Jake Sr. views life as an unfair Darwinian struggle in which the only way for African Americans to succeed is to work twice as whites and best them at virtually everything. This is a common attitude held by members of the civil rights generation, who often scoff at the poor work habits of their seemingly lackluster progeny. Racism for Jake Sr. is a given, but for Jake Jr., "The lines between the black and white worlds had always been blurred" (1992, 12). Indeed he describes himself as reared on African American history and literature. Unlike his father, Jake Jr. was taught in integrated schools and eventually attended Harvard. Yet Jake Jr., for all his achievements, cannot fit in either the black or white world, as he tends to be excluded from the former for his "white" achievements and from the latter because he is never fully accepted by whites. One of his black friends sums up his dilemma: "You're too white for black people and too black for white people" (1992, 13). These racial expectations continually dog Lamar (as well as other members of the hip-hop generation), and try as he does, he cannot break free from them. Even if he completely isolated himself, he would still find himself judged and included or excluded on the basis of race.

Still, being the progeny of parents of the civil rights generation does not mean that Lamar grew up believing that all people are equal. Rather, through his description his parents' interracial slurs and derogatory comments about ne'er-do-well African Americans, Lamar uncovers the darker side of the civil rights movement in that in order to succeed, people like his mother and father felt the need to separate themselves from the majority of African Americans and do so by reminding themselves of their superiority over them, in an almost racially cannibalistic way. Lamar, like many Gen Xers/hip-hop-generation writers, describes himself as being more influenced as a child by popular culture (for example, the Jackson Five in the early 1970s) than by his parents. But at the same time his first real thoughts about racial exclusion occur in the late 1960s and early 1970s, when he begins "to notice the dearth of black people on television" and "wondered vaguely where people like me fit into such a world—or if we did at all" (1992, 47). This question reemerges in Lamar's memoir: Where do I fit, and with whom should I identify? Normally these identity questions might be more apropos of someone from a mixed racial background like one of Danzy Senna's characters; however, that identity questions affect a nonmixed African American indicate the large extent to which race still plays a role in the lives of hip-hop-generation writers.

What complicates the matter for people of Lamar's generation is that he and others like him, exceptionally bright African American students, are often perceived to have been given preferential treatment from programs such as affirmative action. Although this may be true in some cases, it is certainly not true in all or even most cases and not in Lamar's case. Despite this, Lamar is treated as an anomaly by "many white adults" for being "a kid who was smart, friendly *and* black." While Lamar describes such attitudes as prejudicial and somewhat sarcastically doing "no ostensible harm," he suggests between the lines that such attitudes evince a larger, subtle prejudice against African Americans that they tend to not be as intelligent or civilized as whites. This prejudice did not really bother Lamar in his adolescence; rather, it only helps him personally as he is often recognized for his intelligence, and socially because "among a lot of white kids, blackness confirmed an instant cool: they just assumed, by virtue of my being black, that I was hipper than they were" (1992, 83). This may seem like a positive stereotype and evidence that the media has actually helped hip-hop-generation African Americans, but as Lamar gets older and begins to see the bigger picture, he comes to believe such an attitude is racist and detrimental to African Americans because it places often-unrealizable expectations upon them. It also disallows whites from seeing them as varied and three-dimensional human beings.

Lamar's disillusionment and realization of how little progress has been made since the civil rights movement date from his disappointing experiences at Harvard. One would think that the nation's top university would be ethnically inclusive and welcoming, but Lamar's experiences indicate otherwise. Attending Harvard in the late 1970s and early 1980s, he finds it to be "a dull, cold, segregated place," complete with well-defined black cliques that regard Lamar with some suspicion because he has white friends, who in turn never allow him to feel included (1992, 93). For Lamar, Harvard was merely a preprofessional school in which students were joined together by one main reason, if any: "obsessive careerism" (1992, 96). That Lamar devotes only a few pages of his memoir to his Harvard experiences indicates how little those experiences meant to him, except to the extent that he has begun to seriously question the path of so-called success in America and the extent to which the country has racially integrated since the 1960s.

What the country failed to do most of all, Lamar suggests, is to adequately define racism. Instead of viewing it as a many-layered, multidimensional process, racism tends to be viewed in extreme measures as evil and vile, as manifested in pictures such as those of the animalistic hatred of white Southerners during the integration of the University of Mississippi in the early 1960s. According to this skewed schema, no ordinary white American could see him/herself as the least bit racist, for to do so would be aligning themselves with people they construe as being monstrous. However, Lamar does not see racism as the product of aberrant, vicious minds: "The civil rights movement had revealed the horror of racism so effectively that few whites could see it as something ordinary" (1992, 116). Rather, to distance themselves from the monstrosity that they believe racism to be, most whites have convinced themselves that they are most definitely not racist nor is the country as a whole. Lamar and other writers of the hip-hop generation wish to overturn this misconception.

What further awakens Lamar to an ongoing, insidious racism in America is his experiences in an interracial relationship. As interracial relationships play a role in all of Lamar's subsequent novels, the issue is clearly an important one to him (as it is to many other writers of the hip-hop generation), for it is through exposure to these relationships, Lamar finds, that implicit but powerful racism often emerges from the most seemingly innocuous of people, even self-described "open-minded liberals" (1992, 115). For instance Lamar starts dating a white woman, Deborah; her father had been "particularly fond" of Lamar before Decorah and Lamar were involved, but after learning of their relationship, her father becomes "angrier than Deborah had ever seen him" (1992, 115). Her mother is hardly better, telling Deborah, "Just don't marry him" (1992, 115). Lamar realizes something important here. If any young African American man would be accepted in upper-class white circles, it should be him. After all, he is Harvard educated, a writer for *Time,* and nonthreatening. Yet if Lamar is treated in this way, how might an unemployed, high-school dropout be treated? Lamar realizes "there was a ferocious black tax in this country, but I'd allowed myself to believe that my education, my sociability, my bourgeois credentials, made me exempt" (1992, 116). That the hip-hop generation still pays this "black tax" is something that not many Americans fully acknowledge or accept.

Instead, while working as one of only two (and eventually the only) African American writers at *Time*, Lamar finds himself facing what he believes to be subtle racism. For instance, when one of *Time*'s chief editors, whom Lamar sarcastically refers to as Whiteshirt, critiques one of Lamar's stories, Whiteshirt writes condescendingly, "You seem to have a good understanding of the English language" (1992, 126). Would Whiteshirt respond the same way to a white writer? Lamar does not believe so, and he has good reason not to, for why would there be any question as to whether a white writer at *Time* would be articulate or proficient writer? Lamar, however, does not confront Whiteshirt for fear of losing his job and because he has no hard proof of racism. Instead, Lamar continues to be pigeonholed because of his race. When *Time* decides to focus an issue upon race and poverty, they pick Lamar to write the main story, because, he comes to believe, of his race, not that he is an expert in the subject, which he is not, because he was raised in a middle-class environment. The hidden assumption is that since Lamar is African American, he will understand race and poverty better than white writers would or at least be more likely to have direct experience, knowledge, and opinions of both. Although Lamar agrees to write the story and primarily focuses upon violent African American criminals and how they were warped by poverty, the editors are concerned that their readers will be too frightened by the subjects of the story. Hence, they insist on putting Lamar's picture at the top of the story as a "nonthreatening alternative to those nasty Native Sons" (1992, 148). This attitude is typical of *Time*, according to Lamar, in that it shows no desire to understand or sympathize with casualties of racism or poverty. Therefore they portray the subjects of their story as Native Sons, not as victims themselves. This further contributes to the dehumanization and unfair categorization of African American men as violent, amoral criminals, a categorization to which hip-hop music and culture contributes.

While the response to Lamar's story on race and poverty was nearly all favorable from African Americans who were "happy that black issues were given at least some serious treatment in *Time* magazine," one of the incarcerated men Lamar wrote about does not respond as kindly to the "story's sensational aspects," as Lamar puts it. This freed, former convict, Johnnie D. Scott, describes how after leaving prison he received his G.E.D., became "a full-time Instructor aid, and a chairman in the N.A.A.C.P." Scott criticizes Lamar's article for leaving out any "hope," and he insists, "If I can still have hope, then the *Time* article should be able to show hope." This point is not lost upon Lamar, who compares his sensation upon reading the letter to be akin to a "stab of shame like a knife in the belly" (1992, 149). It becomes a turning point in Lamar's life because although he does not directly state it, he realizes and comes to believe that not only has he been acting like an Uncle Tom in acquiescing to *Time*'s demands but he has also helped perpetuate the damaging and false mythos of the African American male as a violent savage, a stereotype, as already seen in Trey Ellis's fiction, that severely damages the hip-hop generation. Hence, Lamar subsequently refuses to write any more stories on poverty and violence, and a couple years later, as he becomes increasingly disenchanted with *Time,* he quits.

Subsequently Lamar develops a better understanding of the destructive power of racism and a better understanding of his father. This allows the two to reconcile after not speaking to one another for five years. Instead of blaming his father for his emotional and behavioral lapses, Lamar comes to believe that his father has been warped by racism. This is a realization he has only been able to come to after his own experiences with institutional racism and prejudice. Similar to Dewayne in Ellis's *Platitudes,* it takes failure and disillusionment to open up a connection between the civil rights and hip-hop generations. His father, who now teaches at several community colleges, has forsaken materialism and the private industry. In his own words, "There are so many minorities here. Black and Puerto Rican kids who *want* to learn, they really do. And I have dedicated myself to making them make it" (1992, 166). His father's newfound social activism inspires Lamar, who now sees himself as "become something far worse: a self-important buppie, the corporate Tom my father had refused to be, proudly proclaiming myself a writer when all I did was hack for a newsmagazine" (1992, 171–72). The memoir concludes with Lamar making a critical decision: to write—not for a magazine like *Time* but write about important matters, matters of race, identity, politics, justice, and responsibility. He describes himself as feeling "as if a door had flung open on a dark room. I wanted to find out what was inside, hoping that I might discover definition; wondering if perhaps the searching in the dark itself was what might define me" (1992, 174). This "searching in the dark" for answers to racial, political, and individual questions is exactly what Lamar pursues in his subsequent novels.

While *Bourgeois Blues* is Lamar's attempt to define himself and his thoughts on racial issues, his next published work, the novel *The Last Integrationist* (1996), set in an alternate, possibly futuristic America, concerns race, politics, and interracial relationships. As Mary Carroll of *Booklist* writes, the novel describes where "dangerous and self-destructive American attitudes towards race . . . could take us in the not-so-distant future" (1996, 454). As the title suggests, the novel paints a rather bleak portrait of race relations in America, and while not strictly supporting a separatist or black nationalist agenda, the novel does suggest that the so-called progress in racial integration is largely artifice despite what some in the civil rights generation might suggest. This is evident in the very structure of Lamar's America in which most whites live in certain towns, and most African Americans live in separate towns that are typically economically substandard to their white counterpart towns.

The novel primarily focuses upon Melvin Hutchinson, or Hutch as he is often called, the attorney general of the United States, and the single most politically powerful African American in this futuristic America. The most popular member of the administration, Hutch is revered for his ultraconservative and militant positions on crime, drugs, and violence. He gives drug dealers the toughest punishment possible, claiming that they "must be eliminated from the body of society" (1996, 11). He gets the title Hang 'em High Hutch for his aggressive pursuit of capital punishment for criminals. A former fighter for civil rights in the 1960s, Hutch has become an Uncle Tom figure in that the majority of the criminals that he targets are African American. His popularity, Lamar suggests, which crosses ethnicities and economic classes, has much to do with an implicit racism. Hutch, by ridding society of "undesirable" criminals, most of whom are African American, makes whites feel safer. While it might seem odd, even most African Americans support Hutch, because in the novel, as in contemporary America, African Americans are often the victims of crimes committed by other African Americans. Furthermore there seems to be a fervent thirst for violence in Lamar's America. For instance, in a possible homage to Bernard Goetz, the growing group AMAP—Armed Manhattanites Against Parasites—tells "tales of heroism by ordinary New York vigilantes who had, in self-defense or on citizen's patrol, bravely murdered would-be muggers and vandals" (1996, 312). Another character, the white writer-turned-television-producer Seth, oversees the production of the new and ultimately popular show *Elimination* (sponsored by the Oprah-like Mavis), in which vicious death-row inmates are publicly executed.

Still Lamar does not place all of the blame for racial separation and prejudice upon the white characters in the novel; rather the African American civil-rights-generation characters themselves often create divisions between themselves and whites. Hutch and his wife, Dorothy, for instance, are hypersensitive to and hyperaware of their public personas as African American to the point that they worry that their wealth and privilege might make them seem less authentically African American to the eyes of others. Indeed Dorothy's main concern is "to make sure that nobody would ever be able to accuse the Hutchinsons of trying to be white" (1996, 59). In addition they are extremely concerned with their daughter, Abby being perceived as an "imitation white kid" (1996, 58). For his own part, Hutch takes part in Black Partners lunches for elite African American attorneys, and these attorneys look down upon members with white spouses, believing them to be less authentically African American. Hutch harbors his own contradictory stereotypes: "Black folks don't commit suicide;" they are instead murdered or die of drug overdoses, even though his African American mother-in-law did attempt suicide at one point. Clearly then, he has adopted or has bought into specific standards or stereotypes for African American authenticity.

Furthermore Hutch's exclusionary attitude towards whites manifests itself when Abby starts seeing a white boy, which upsets Hutch. His internalized prejudice also shows when his daughter wants to go white-water rafting with this boyfriend. Hutch wonders, "What the fuck was a nigger doing white-water rafting? Runnin' the rapids? A colored person. Now, he was, of course, all for breaking barriers. No one could doubt it. But Lord Almighty, what business did an Afro-American have runnin' the rapids?" (1996, 65–76). In many ways this is precisely the attitude that Ellis spoke out against in his essay "The New Black Aesthetic." Ellis argued that African Americans, particularly the hip-hop generation, should be allowed to choose whatever cultural activities or items that appeal to them, regardless of racial connotations. Much to his regret later, Hutch allows her to go. That Abby ends up dying in a freak accident while rafting is important because it ends up confirming Hutch's belief that African Americans are a culturally distinct group from whites. After all, had Abby never transgressed ethnic lines, she would still be alive. Any hope that Hutch might have had for integration and personal redemption as a former, liberal, civil rights fighter perishes along with his daughter. He becomes callous, violent but ironically a better politician.

Lamar hardly portrays politics in a positive light in this novel. The book begins with Hutch's fantasy of killing every member of the white audience that has come to "honor" him at a reception (more like basking in his power and popularity) with the exception of the butler, who is the sole African American there (except Hutch). At this reception Hutch feels superior and violent to the point that "if he could—instantly, bloodlessly, with a magical snap of his fingers, perhaps—he would kill them all" (1996, 3). For Lamar politics is deception and artifice, made apparent by the rise and eventual election of President Troy McCracken, a sinister doppelganger of Bill Clinton. Lamar describes Mc-Cracken as "young, rich, charismatic," but he eventually reveals himself to be utterly amoral and vicious (1996, 9). The vice president, Vin Ewell, a former anti-integrationist Southern mayor during the 1960s, meanwhile continues to be a closet racist who envies and despises Hutch. After Ewell suffers a near-fatal stroke, Hutch becomes the front-runner to replace him as vice-president when it seems unlikely that Ewell will recover. It is no accident that a man as committed to criminal responsibility and severe punishment might become the nation's first African American vice-president. Lamar suggests that it is Hutch's extremely tough stance on crime that separates him from the stereotype of African Americans in the minds of most whites, and, ironically, his ascension to vice-president would be a manifestation of hostility and fear mainly towards lower-class minorities, not a huge racial advantage as members of the civil rights generation might believe.

In *The Last Integrationist,* most characters exist in a world quite like our own in which race seems not to matter much but actually does considerably. In addition to exploring Hutch and his rise in politics, Lamar also focuses on Generation X or hip-hop generation interracial couples who try to deny that race matters but who are ultimately torn apart by racial issues. The main couple he focuses upon is Emma Person, an African American temporary office worker/ photographer, whom we later learn is Hutch's niece, and Seth Winkler, a Jewish free-lance-writer-turned-talk-show-producer, who is desperate to be famous and is rather callous, as noted by Lamar: "Nothing inspired Seth quite so much as a good friend's misfortune" (1996, 36).[1] Lamar introduces the couple about twenty pages into the novel, but he does not reveal Emma's ethnicity for another twenty pages because he wants the reader to see that there is nothing, aside from skin color, that marks Emma as African American in terms of her stereotypical behavior, actions, and speech. Similar to Trey Ellis's characters Austin McMillan and Ashton Robinson, Emma does not believe that being African American really means anything. Skeptical of labels and society, Emma wants to deconstruct images; she works on photographs of normal or less-than-attractive couples making love as a way to counteract conventional standards of beauty. She calls her photos "anti-pornography." But Lamar also implies that Emma, by denying her ethnicity, has become rather emotionally vapid in a manner similar to Ashton Robinson and according to one of her ex-boyfriends Keith, she is emotionally deadened. Furthermore Emma is drawn to the rather unattractive people whom she photographs, because she subconsciously identifies with them.

Emma's probable subverted feelings of self-loathing and/or insecurity are largely by-products of denying her racial identity. As Seth only mildly exaggerates, "Emma didn't even know she was black" (1996, 80). Of course, Emma does know, but believing that she lives in an egalitarian society, she has submerged all thoughts of race and thereby has become rather steely and cold. Granted, in a way, Emma's attitude towards race is ideal but it is also idealistic and characteristic of many members of the civil rights generation; she claims race does not matter, when in truth it should not matter, but it does. In Emma's own words: "Why should I be either proud or ashamed of being black? It's not an accomplishment—or an embarrassment. It's nothing I've ever done. It's just my race" (1996, 81). Emma does not believe in or factor in institutional racism, nor does she feel there are any cultural benefits in being aware or proud of being African American. In that, she rejects the idea that race produces culture, but, rather, she believes (in keeping with the hip-hop cultural ethos) that individuals produce culture, regardless of race. Once again, this is idealistic and, unfortunately, not accurate. Not only is it not a realistic attitude but also Emma is not able to become a successful artist if she does not address race because of societal expectations. For instance, when Emma submits her work to a gallery, the gallery owner claims, "What is very, extremely marketable is work with an ethnocentric edge to it. Work that reflects life on . . . the street. . . . What it meant to be a proud, struggling African-American woman" (1996, 42). This is the kind of stereotypical expectation that Emma keeps finding, and she responds to it in the opposite manner, by confounding racial expectations, denying that race matters at all and creating work that is basically raceless. This is another position typical of the hip-hop generation or Generation X in their elevation of the individual over society, but in this case, it is Emma's rebellion against the racial expectations she keeps encountering that ultimately backfires and prevents her from having a stable, well-rounded identity.

Racially Emma is almost a polar opposite to Seth, whom Lamar describes as growing up romanticizing black people as many young Generation X and Y non–African Americans often do. Not only did Seth only have African American heroes when he was a teenager but Lamar also describes him as having "wished back then that he had more black friends, or really any black friends" (1996, 79). His deification of African Americans is somewhat of a sham as it is based not on real experiences but on media representations of African American athletes and entertainers. For Lamar, this is a crucial distinction for a person can be committed to the racial equality in theory and can hold an ethnic group in high esteem, but in practice, or in reality, that person may actually do little or nothing to counteract racism and possibly even perpetuate it. Their seemingly good intentions may only be selfish. Seth, for instance, as a teenager, feels he holds African Americans in high esteem, generally speaking, but he only does so because he (like other predominately white hip-hop music fans) wants to possess the self-assertiveness, charisma, and agility of those African Americans he sees on television or in the movies or to whom he listens. This is one of the main reasons contemporary white adolescents (who are the largest consumer group of hip-hop music) emulate African American hip-hop artists: to co-opt their perceived power for themselves. Furthermore Seth's mother, Trudy, is also racially inclusive in theory but as it turns out, not in practice. Although an ardent supporter of civil rights in the 1960s, Trudy reacts violently to Seth and Emma's interracial relationship. She insists to Seth, "Find someone else!" and "She [Emma] will ruin your life! Don't you see you're just a symbol to her! That's how black people think!" (1996, 680). The idea that Emma could be a symbol to Seth doesn't occur to Trudy at all, even though it is closer to the truth, since African Americans have been symbols to Seth throughout his life.

Not only do whites express overt and subtle animosity towards African Americans in the novel, so do other wealthy and successful African Americans like Hutch, who denigrates lower-class, mainly hip-hop-generation African Americans. In a manner similar to Bill Cosby, Hutch purposely distances himself from urban African American youth and culture, dismissing hip-hop music as body obsession and hip-hop culture as a "tragedy" when "they think it's a party" (1996, 107). Hutch's animosity towards them is more a projection of his own conflicted feelings about being African American. Having distanced himself so much from African American culture (like Emma), he has grown emotionally isolated, his only rather insubstantial friend being Henry Beedle, whom Hutch describes as a "bald-headed ofay" with "Coke-bottle glasses and filthy little teeth" (1996, 105). Similarly the Oprah-like Mavis, an incredibly popular, wealthy, and well-received talk-show host with an audience of fifty million people, is not very supportive of other African Americans (at least in private). Her success seems contingent upon her appearing safe to her presumably white audience base. Lamar portrays Mavis as caring about only one thing: herself. In order to maintain her audience, Mavis avoids racial issues or any issue that brings attention to her ethnicity, such as interracial marriage. Furthermore, in private, she appears actively hostile towards other African Americans. This is first noticeable in that Mavis decides to hire Seth on the basis of his article, with which she is suitably impressed, "condemning the nihilism of young black rap stars" (1996, 91). In addition to that, at one point when Seth tells her that he likes Detroit because it is a city run by African Americans, Mavis replies, "No wonder it's such a shithole" (1996, 95). Still, Mavis does not completely denigrate other African Americans; aside from Seth, she hires only African Americans, and when she decides to televise a criminal execution, she insists that the criminal to be executed not be black. However, her success is not fruitful for most African Americans, given that once Mavis gets to the top of the celebrity echelon, she loses any commitment to improve the state of the larger African American community (if she ever had that desire in the first place). Once again, the individualistic tendencies of the hip-hop generation and contemporary culture do not help the greater African American community.

While Mavis may appear on the surface to be a hollow sellout who has no desire to better the lives of less-fortunate African Americans, another character, Rashid, a graduate student in Afro-American studies at Columbia University, is an outspoken hip-hop generation social activist for African Americans, or so he believes himself to be. In truth, like virtually all of the characters in the novel, he is more self-serving. Lamar first introduces Rashid as he vehemently speaks out during one of Hutch's speeches that is poorly received by an audience of primarily African American high school students. In a Bill Cosby–like manner, Hutch berates the audience for their perceived apathy, and Rashid challenges him, claiming that the "problem" may be him [Hutch] and that Hutch's message doesn't address "the black cause" (1996, 116). However, Rashid is no racial avenging deus ex machina, righting prejudice and racism whenever it appears in the novel; rather, he holds himself to unrealizable and counterproductive standards of black authenticity. In theory Rashid is an ethnocentrist, but in reality, he is infatuated with a white, English woman, Morgan, with whom he has a brief affair, which he quickly ends because of his desire to not be involved with a white woman (for to do so would violate his standards for African American authenticity). It may be Rashid's stubborn insistence on being ethnocentric that draws him into a taboo relationship with a white woman. In contrast to how Emma denies that being African American means anything, being African American for Rashid means virtually everything, but his insisting upon this leads him to become masochistic. Lamar suggests that Rashid's ethnocentrism may have originated from Rashid's rejection by a white girl when he was younger. In other words he uses ethnocentrism as armor to hide his insecurities and vulnerabilities. Even Rashid's African American girlfriend, Janet, with whom he has a rather superficial relationship, berates him for "talkin' white" (1996, 187). In response to this, Rashid cultivates an Afrocentric persona lest he be considered white.

Rashid's ethnocentrism, which might seem to be the alternative to hip-hop individualism, then is as personally damaging as Emma's ethnic ignorance because the ethnocentrism leads them both to become emotionally isolated and desolate. This is evident in how when he has sex with Morgan, Rashid finds himself experiencing "an intimacy that he found almost unbearable" (1996, 192). Because of his relentless ethnocentrism, Rashid has become incredibly hardened, unable to trust virtually anyone, especially "not a white chick" (1996, 192). For Rashid ethnocentrism is an emotional and/or personal crutch he uses to help himself feel stronger or more powerful, just as teenagers often use hip-hop. Despite his impressive rhetoric, Rashid is not fully devoted to the cause of bettering the lives of African Americans. Hence, when he rejects Morgan, in order to fulfill his standards of African American authenticity, he feels hurt because he still desires her, and he becomes further ethnocentric to help give him strength to overcome his personal pain: "He needed to go somewhere where there were no white faces in sight" (1996, 200). Rashid's solution is to abandon academics in favor of moving back to his and Hutch's hometown of Norris, New Jersey, and to start a foundation he calls the Norris Center for African-American Arts and Culture. Yet, despite what he says or even consciously believes, Rashid opens the center up for himself more than for the African American community.

That Rashid and Emma, two virtual opposites representing the social and political range of the hip-hop generation, become romantically involved, despite their initial encounter, which turns into a heated debate about the importance or lack of importance of race, indicate their hidden similarities outweigh their overt differences. Both subconsciously realize that their racial praxis is somewhat flawed or incomplete, and thereby both are attracted to the other person's positions. Through her relationship with Rashid, Emma comes to realize that being African American has some importance whereas Rashid comes to see that it isn't all-important. However, things sour between the two after Rashid invites Emma to show her photographs at his new foundation, and the audience rejects them as insulting and pornographic. In response to their breakup, both go back to their own perspectives about the importance of race or lack thereof, indicating that their stance on ethnicity is personal, not social. In fairness it isn't just Rashid or Emma who holds these extreme views on race. Toward the end of the novel, Rashid's center flourishes after a year's time with more stereotypical images of African Americans, which is what the audience wants to see. Lamar describes one of these photographic exhibits by Rashid's new, equally ethnocentric wife, Kilarti: "The show consisted of solemn portraits; dignified black women standing and singing at Norris's First Baptist Black Church; little inner-city children staring bleakly into the camera, their eyes revealing nothing but pathos; gang members, arms folded across their chests, glaring fiercely; sad-eyed old men sitting in Benny D's barbershop" (1996, 332–33). That Rashid has committed to racial separatist views becomes apparent in how he brashly dismisses Morgan, who comes to Kilarti's show. Not only does he dismiss Morgan's criticism of the exhibit as stereotypical images, Rashid claims that she cannot "understand" Kilarti's photos because she's not African American, and he ends up calling her "a silly white bitch" (1996, 335).

If anything is the undoing of the ethnic solidarity in *The Last Integrationist*, it is interracial relationships, none of which seem to produce anything beneficial. Hutch himself, it is later revealed, had a brief extramarital affair with a white ex-hippie named Willow, with whom he has an illegitimate son, Miles. Furthermore, not only is Emma treated poorly by Trudy (Seth's mother) but

Lamar also reveals that the somewhat mentally unbalanced Trudy has been defecating on the doorstep of Seth and Emma's enjoining apartment every night for weeks.[2] This act is from the same woman who took in a poor African American child after Seth starts seeing Emma, as a way to try to connect with her or understand her better but in reality as a means to convince herself that she is not prejudiced. That she believes that African Americans can be understood as a singular people indicates that she possesses rather narrow, prejudicial, even racist views, which she does her best to mask. This cuts both ways in the novel, from whites to African Americans and vice versa. Along similar lines, Emma's mother does not treat Seth much better than Trudy treats Emma: "No matter how kind Seth was to her, Alma regarded him with an attitude only slightly more gracious than contempt" (1996, 161). According to Willow, things were actually better in the 1960s, "when it was actually cool for black people and white people to talk, to hang out together" (1996, 211). In this novel, despite the common belief that members of the hip-hop generation live in a more-egalitarian society than the civil rights generation, racial relations have deteriorated since then, despite a sunny multicultural façade.

Holes show through in this multicultural façade with the progeny of interracial couples. For instance Hutch and Willow's son, Miles, who is of mixed ethnicity, is placed in a difficult situation, being not clearly white or black. While Miles is able to find a happy medium when he is a child by describing himself as "gray," when he becomes a teenager, he feels forced to choose sides: black or white. Although Miles initially chooses white because he identifies with the other excellent students who are white, he changes sides after he hears one of his white "friends" tell a racist joke. He physically attacks that student and subsequently becomes a hero to the black students. Furthermore, in order to become accepted by other black students, Miles finds a certain "code for black authenticity" (presumably at least partially derivative of hip-hop culture), which requires poor work habits, "speaking in 'black English' and keeping up with the latest slang," along with wearing specific clothing and accessories including baseball caps, sneakers, and jewelry (1996, 225). Although Lamar never states it directly, these images of authenticity have no doubt been perpetuated by the media; however, both African American and white students accept these standards for African Americans. Gradually Miles falls into drug dealing, and he does so not for the money but in order to be accepted not only by his African American peers but also by his white peers. A somewhat similar progression occurs with Gunnar Kaufman in Paul Beatty's *White Boy Shuffle* (1996).

Miles is a pivotal character in the novel because subsequent to his arrest for drug dealing, he is sent to one of Hutch's drug-rehabilitation centers. When Miles returns, he is lifelessly obedient to the point that he appears brainwashed:

"Miles did not listen to music anymore. Nor did he watch television. He went to bed at ten every night and rose at six. He made his bed every morning and kept his room relentlessly tidy" (1996, 230). When Willow confronts Hutch about Miles, Hutch becomes alarmed about the rehabilitation centers and talks to President McCracken. After doing some research, Hutch discovers that the African American inmates at the drug-rehabilitation centers have been sterilized and, in some cases, infected with AIDS. Lamar leaves no doubt that this is the beginning of a larger genocide of African Americans, because, as Hutch discovers, "Roughly seventy percent of the inmates at Fort Brandriss are black. But, of the sterile women and HIV-positive men I talked to in the last week, one hundred percent of them are black" (1996, 279). Far from being shocked, President McCracken approves of this program, which he calls "eugenics" and "practical or scientific, genetics" (1996, 282). He claims the problem is that young black men commit most crimes and that the biggest drag on the federal government is welfare, which is mostly "black single mothers" (1996, 280). Leaving no question as to his Nazi-like racism, the president suggests, "Some things are bred in the bone" (1996, 281). Reasoning that the people kept at the centers are a strain on society and will probably be executed anyhow, McCracken insists that the program is a mere extension of Hutch's own. He tells Hutch, "You don't approve of the criminal class any more than I do. In fact, you've done more to raise consciousness about the black criminal class than anyone else in the nation. If the program you're so exercised about actually existed, it would be a way of turning your very rhetoric into action" (1996, 282). In a way he is correct, and it is at this point that Hutch realizes that McCracken's program is an extension of his own, and Hutch has been a traitor to his own racial group. This change has also come about because of Hutch has learned how Miles has been affected by the program.

In the novel, Lamar's America is rather bleak and pessimistic, in which Hutch ultimately concludes that not only has the civil rights movement stalled or failed but also that any so-called racial progress (especially for the hip-hop generation) is nothing more than a façade, at best. If anything, the country has become more segregated than it was during the 1960s. Furthermore a kind of unspoken racial war exists in the novel, pitting ethnicity against ethnicity. Even Emma, as color-blind as she believes herself to be, comes to think that towards the end of the novel "that there were no people left in the United States of America, only your own people. Only races, genders, ethnicities, sexual orientations, cultures . . . blood and skin were all" (1996, 317). For his own part, after hearing the president's overtly racist agenda and realizing that the country is heading towards genocide of African Americans, Hutch shoots and kills the president and then is killed himself.

The president's death unleashes racial violence, but it is only conducted by whites upon African Americans or other whites. Lamar makes it clear that African Americans play no part in instigating the violence. A year after McCracken's death, Lamar explains, it "only widened the canyon of distrust between blacks and whites. Troy McCracken had become a God" (1996, 337–38). McCracken's death provides no end to the illicit sterilizations and AIDS infections at the drug-rehabilitation clinics as a recovered Vice-President Ewell continues in McCracken's footsteps. Feeling disillusioned by the country's backtrack towards racism, Emma leaves America for Europe, just as Lamar did, having given up on the country, believing it to be inherently racist, and she is "certain of only one thing: She would never return to the United States" (1996, 342). If there is hope in the novel, then it is symbolized by Miles, the mixed progeny of Hutch and Willow. The novel concludes with his aunt Alma suggesting that Miles, representing integration, will have a tough life ahead of him. She tells him that others will be "threatened by you and will try to crush and destroy and exterminate you," but she also calls him "the future" (1996, 344). If Miles or multicultural offspring are the future, then the only way the races will connect through common ground, possibly with interracial relationships. Although in this novel interracial relationships seem to fail, this does not mean that Lamar believes them inherently doomed to fail.

Interracial relationships play a significant role in *The Last Integrationist,* but they play an even larger role in Lamar's next novel, *Close to the Bone* (1998), as do questions of identity. *Close to the Bone* addresses the subject of defining what it means or should mean to be African American, mainly for the hip-hop generation. One of the main characters, the charlatan Dr. Emmett Mercy, a member of the civil rights generation, capitalizes on the idea that there is a distinct and genuine African American self. Mercy, who is neither a doctor (he never completed his PhD) nor the true writer of the book that bears his name (his wife, LaTonya, did virtually all of the writing, although he dubiously claims that the basic ideas were his). This book, *Blacktualization: Everyday Strategies for Reconnecting with Your Authentic African American Self,* is the basis upon which Dr. Mercy organizes workshops for African American men that are supposed to help the participants "resolve their conflicts, banish their bad habits, redeem their relationships, reclaim their unique African American identity, and gain a new sense of personal power" (1999, 4). Is there such a thing as a unique African American self? The Afrocentric portion of the civil rights generation might suggest so; however, through his use of the unreliable Mercy, Lamar suggests that such an idea is not only false but ultimately harmful because it encourages stereotypes and generalizations. Mercy's workshops also seem like failures, attracting only a few participants, who are not really interested in helping one another. In addition Dr. Mercy's questions such as "What is a black man?" are not especially penetrating, nor does he or his participants ever come up with a compelling answer or answers to that question.

Beyond his workshops, Mercy seeks to become a "designated interlocutor," or, Lamar explains, "one of the elite corps of black pundits who were paid good money—sometimes *long* money—to tell white people what to think about black people" (1998, 107). His commitment to African Americans is questionable, as he seeks to end affirmative action. Furthermore, Lamar says, his "purpose was not to provoke, to criticize, or to question" but rather to reassure whites that racism is well on its way towards being ended (1998, 107). In essence Dr. Mercy's task is to sugarcoat racial disparity through reassuring white people that there have been great strides forward in civil rights and that there is only a little ways to go before racial harmony can be truly achieved. Like Hutch in *The Last Integrationist,* Dr. Mercy is a product of the 1960s civil rights movement, and he looks with some disdain upon younger African Americans who tend to come to his workshops, believing that his generation paved the way for them, but younger African Americans haven't faced enough "adversity" (1998, 111).

The younger or hip-hop generation is the focus of the book, and they do not respond well to Dr. Mercy's message to his not-so-hidden disdain for them. After Dr. Mercy's workshop, one of the participants, Walker DuPree, tells his friend Hal Hardaway, who was also at the workshop, "Guys like Mercy are never gonna approve of guys like us. We were born in the sixties and they're never gonna forgive us for it. All they want us to do is shut up and be grateful" (1998, 181–82). During the workshop, Hal tells Dr. Mercy that he knows what it means to be a black man, but Mercy dismisses Hal's claims as the uniformed bravado of a young man.

Mercy's issues of what it means or should mean to be African American become important in a large sense because the novel takes place during the O. J. Simpson trial in 1995. In the novel (as was largely the case in real life), the Simpson trial is a fault line that divides African American and white characters in the book. It brings to the surface repressed stereotypes in whites who may subconsciously believe African American men to be inherently violent or savage. This is a belief that Hal's white girlfriend, Corky, subconsciously, if not consciously, possesses. When they both hear of the murders, "Corky took one look at O. J.'s face and said: 'He did it'" (1998, 99). Furthermore, after Hal tells Corky that his father once hit his mother, she begins to be scared of Hal even though, Lamar explains, "Hal has never really gotten angry" (1998, 98). Although she cannot admit it, Corky has come to associate violence with African American men. In all fairness Corky's suspicion of Hal might be prompted by Hal's own suspicions about Corky, for, Lamar suggests, "Hal developed an unspoken suspicion of his own: that Corky was wary of him because he was black" (1998, 97–98). Yet, we do not know if Corky has always harbored these feelings or begins to after Hal suspects she does or even if it could be a combination of both explanations, which is more likely.

To the white characters, the Simpson trial is entertainment and intellectually provocative: "To Corky and her colleagues at the courthouse, the O. J. Simpson case was like a combination of the best criminal law seminar you ever took and the sleaziest murder mystery you ever read" (1998, 288). However, to the African American characters, it is personal and reveals ingrained racial problems. Suspect of the law-enforcement system for compelling reasons (either from personal experience or from recent events such as the Rodney King incident and subsequent trial), many of the African American characters are unwilling to believe the police and/or are unwilling to take the side of the police, whom these characters do not think have ever really taken their side. Therefore the African American characters are willing to give O. J. the benefit of the doubt or believe that he is not judged fairly because his wife was white. The one exception, as described later, is Walker, but he is part white and part African American. When Hal learns of the murders, "one thought leapt to the front of his mind: 'I hope she isn't white'" (1998, 100). For the African American characters in the novel, the O. J. situation is symptomatic of a larger racial problem. They believe that whites immediately assume O. J. is guilty. If this can happen to an African American celebrity, they believe, it demonstrates how unfairly society and law enforcement treat nonfamous African Americans as compared to whites.

Heated discussion of the Simpson trial and differing views on the situation ends the Hal and Corky relationship (as well as that of two other characters, Sadie and Walker). Hal and Corky's relationship comes to a breaking point when Corky tells Hal, "Black men tend to be violent" (1998, 298). This, ironically, makes Hal almost violent himself for the first time in his life and demonstrates a self-fulfilling prophecy. By exposing people to images of violent African Americans, the media and hip-hop culture, as well as people like Corky, help perpetuate the stereotype of violent African American men, which can, like a vicious circle, lead to ever-increasing amounts of violence. Although Hal does not hit Corky after their intense argument, she repeatedly tells him, "You're just like O. J.," even though there is no real basis for her accusation (1998, 299). For Lamar the O. J. trial only increases ethnic separatism, evident by how when the verdict is announced, an entire room in a predominately African American restaurant explodes in applause.

To some extent, the solution that Lamar advances in this novel is to escape American racial inequalities by fleeing to Europe (even though he claims he left not just for racial reasons but because he felt France would be a better environment for a fiction writer). Walker, after fleeing his relationship with Sadie, goes to Amsterdam, where he feels much more accepted than in the United States. There he meets another African American man who has lived in Europe since the end of World War II. He tells Walker a riveting story about how after the end of the war, he got engaged to a white German woman, and went to her hometown. Although he thinks he will be killed, "From that moment on, I was completely accepted by the people of that town. The minister married Ilse and me a couple of weeks later and I spent the next ten years in Habichtsburg. Totally embraced by the community. Think about it, brother man: Here I was, in the heart of Nazism, in a land that represented racist evil to the entire world, and my white wife and I were more accepted there than we would have been anywhere in the United States of America" (1998, 149). Still, while Europe seems more receptive to interracial relationships, for Sadie, who has moved to Paris, it is a different story. According to her:

> The streets of Paris were packed with interracial couples. Everywhere you looked, you saw white men with black women, black men with white women. It was bizarre. Sadie was sure that white Frenchmen were just trying to live out some sick Josephine Baker fantasy, thinking every black American woman was, at heart, some nympho who wanted to jump around topless in a skirt made of bananas. And black American men, of course, were practically salivating over their white babes as they strolled arm in arm with them down the Champs Élysées. (1998, 186)

However, what really infuriates Sadie to the point that she forsakes Paris is the subtle racism she encounters there at a party. She sees a poster that it is incredibly degrading to African Americans, but no one else is bothered by it except her.

> At the top of the poster were the words LIFE'S A BALL, written in big black block letters. Just below the line was a grotesque cartoon: a dark brown face, eyes bulging, flashing crooked white teeth surrounded by ruby-red lips, crowned with a black scrawl representing nappy black hair. Below the hideous face were stubby brown fingers clutching an orange basketball, but the top portion of the basketball was missing; in its place, seemingly growing out of the ball, was the red meat of a watermelon, studded with black seeds. Below the basketball, in black block letters, were the words EAT IT UP. (1998, 230)

Contemporary racism, overt or implicit, Lamar suggests, is not strictly an American problem; rather, it is a worldwide problem. Indeed, as hip-hop music and culture have increased in popularity throughout the world, the problems that face the hip-hop generation (or its incarnations in different countries) have become more global in scope.

This is not to suggest that Lamar forsakes America in the novel, for the novel ends with the benign Tiny and his wife, Deirdre, taking a taxi with Jojo, a cabdriver who had acted extremely hostile by grabbing his crotch during Dr. Mercy's workshop and leaving in response to Dr. Mercy's question "What is a Black man?" This time Jojo is pleasant. He tells Deirdre, "You got yourself a fine husband, ma'am. It just makes me so happy to see a young black family just startin' out in the world. I can't tell you how happy that makes me!" (1999, 342). Tiny tells his son, "Someday you'll be a man. A black man. . . . But there's just one thing I want you to be. Your *own* man" (1999, 343). This is a much more hopeful ending than that of *The Last Integrationist,* indicating that Lamar is envisioning or hoping to find a way to get beyond race and racism.

With his next novel, *If Six Were Nine* (2001), Lamar moves more into the murder-mystery genre. To be sure, race still plays a significant role in the novel, which is situated at Arden University, a small liberal arts college in Ohio. The novel opens with an older African American professor, Reggie Brogus, coming to see a younger African American professor of journalism, the protagonist Clay Robinette, after the former finds a dead white student in his office, Jennifer Esther Wolfshiem, or Pirate Jenny as she is known to Clay. Pirate Jenny, unknown to Reggie at this time, was Clay's mistress. The novel covers the aftermath of the murder; at the same time, Lamar skewers the treatment of race in colleges, which are hardly portrayed as racial-inclusive bastions of intellectualism. Clay himself is a disgraced former journalist who was caught fabricating some quotes. Without so much as an interview, President Jerry Shamberg offers Clay a teaching position at Arden, despite that Clay, even by his own account, had "never even taken a journalism course let alone taught one before." Shamberg hires him in part out of loyalty, because Clay had once written an enthusiastic article about Arden and because of Clay's recent notoriety. He tells Clay, "Hey, you're controversial! Controversy's good! It sells!" (2001, 9).

Although Clay and his family take to Arden relatively well, Lamar portrays it as a rather fraudulent place, at least in terms of its attitudes towards race. Seemingly a product of civil-rights-generation ideology, on the one hand, Arden fosters diversity or, as Clay calls it, "willful diversity," but beneath the surface, there is "willful self-segregation" in which students of different ethnicities as well as faculty do not really mix and whereby faculty are judged on their personal life choices more so than professional ones (2001, 10). Consequently, Clay tells us, "For not the first time in my life, I felt lucky to have a black wife" (2001, 10). Furthermore the academic curriculum in ethnic studies is insubstantial and hollow. Instead of an African American–studies program, they have an Afrikamerica-studies program; the spelling errors are just a superficial way to grab attention and to illustrate a connection between Africa and America, in that they are sharing the *a*. The head of the program is Kwanzi Authentica Parker, whose middle name is a sarcastic jibe at her Afrocentrism, which Lamar mocks by describing her as "righteous, kente-clothed sister," who is married to a foppish, white Englishman, another professor, Roger Pym-Smithers (2001, 52). In Lamar's description, not much of any significance occurs in the Afrikamerica-studies program. Kwanzi, for instance, teaches courses in "Black Consciousness, elusive, catchall classes with ever-changing reading lists comprised of social theory, history texts, polemical tracts, self-help books, poetry, and novels. What the courses actually amounted to were bull sessions where black students could vent all their racial frustrations, anxieties, and self-justifications under the sympathetic guidance of a gregarious professor" (2001, 101). Once again, Lamar shows how the quest for ethnic solidarity has changed from being socially committed to more of an individual search for happiness and confidence, an emblem of the hip-hop generation.

Along similar lines, Lamar also illustrates how fragmented the civil rights movement became after the 1960s. When discussing his parents, Clay describes them as "especially earnest, idealistic people," members of a "generation of Negroes that were running the civil rights movement, smashing barriers, changing America" (2001, 20). However, Clay describes his parents as becoming disillusioned after the Martin Luther King Jr. assassination in 1968: "Their optimism about the future had changed to a bitter fatalism. Their faith in integration was replaced by a sense that white and black Americans could never peacefully coexist. Their belief in non violence had been irrevocably refuted by the violent death of their leader" (2001, 22). Similarly Reggie Brogus is also portrayed as a disillusioned product of the 1960s. Reggie used to be a militant revolutionary in the 1960s and wrote an extremely radical book called *Live Black or Die!* which promoted "executions of white males" and "rape of white women by Black men" (2001, 24). However, over time, Reggie becomes a conservative Republican, writing a right-wing book called *An American Salvation: How I Overcame the Sixties and Learned to Love the USA*. While throughout most of the book, Reggie seems characterized as a sellout, it is later revealed that his radical behavior in the 1960s was a sham and that he was actually an undercover government agent whose purpose was to scare whites into demonizing the leaders of the Black Power movement and to divide African Americans through his radical ideology.

Still, in times of crisis, racial solidarity is most apparent. Clay does drive Reggie most of the way to the airport even after he sees Jenny's dead body in

Reggie's office, because they are both African American, and Clay still has some respect for Reggie. In addition, after Reggie is noted as the prime suspect, Kwanzi, who previously seemed to be Reggie's nemesis, comes to his defense, again presumably because they are both African American. Despite the mounting evidence suggesting otherwise, Kwanzi wants Reggie to be presumed innocent. Clay himself wonders, "Perhaps in a situation like this, racial loyalty mattered more to Kwanzi than Brogus's racial betrayals. Had I been governed by a similar impulse when I drove Brogus almost all the way to Arden Airfield?" (2001, 62). Racially these characters are on shaky ground. They help each other but also savagely compete with one another. For Lamar, just as with Trey Ellis, this is endemic in the African American community, and it is what ultimately threatens them the most.

In all of Lamar's novels, significant racial and economic divisions are not only between whites and African Americans but also between other African Americans. According to Lamar, there really is no safe space in America for minorities, In this novel, Lamar critiques the one institution, if any, thought to be above the practice of stereotyping and prejudice: the university. However, as Lamar describes, not much changes for the better even after the events of the murder, which turns out to be committed by Kwanzi's husband, Roger Pym-Smithers, who was also having an affair with Jenny. Roger, who has planned to kill Clay, confesses to him first; Clay is saved at the last moment by Reggie, who kills Roger. Arden University's Afrikamerika-studies department, which Lamar not so subtly criticizes, ends up flourishing, even though Lamar makes it clear that it does little or nothing to improve race relations. What can then? Lamar does not provide a clear answer, because there are no clear answers; rather, identifying the current racial problems, which is what he does in his fiction, is the first step towards coming up with a kind of solution.

3

Of all of the writers of the hip-hop generation, none has received as much critical acclaim as Colson Whitehead, which is perhaps best demonstrated in that he is the youngest writer to be included in the second edition of the Norton Anthology of African American literature. Born in 1969, Whitehead, like Jake Lamar, is a Harvard graduate, as well as a former journalist, who, before turning to fiction, wrote television reviews for *The Village Voice* and advertisements for an Internet company (Whitehead 2006). Whitehead's first novel, *The Intuitionist* (1999), won the Quality Paperback Book Club's New Voices Award and was an Ernest Hemingway–PEN Award for first-fiction finalist in 1999. His next novel, *John Henry Days* (2001), was a finalist for the National Book Critics Award. To add to his laurels, in 2002, Whitehead was awarded a MacArthur "genius grant" (New York State Writers Institute 2006). Subsequently he published a nonfiction account of New York City, *The Colossus of New York* (2004), and another novel, *Apex Hides the Hurt* (2006). Whitehead sees himself as part of group of African American writers who approach race in a different way in that they are not as "polemicized" as the previous generation of African Americans can be (especially 1960s black-arts writers), but they still are "dealing with serious race issues" (Miller 1999). Although he never uses the label, it can be surmised that the group he refers to is the hip-hop generation.

One case in point would be Whitehead's first novel, *The Intuitionist,* which on the surface, is an unusual suspense story concerning elevator inspectors and a suspicious elevator mishap, but the novel has much larger aspirations than merely building up suspense. Reminiscent of Thomas Pynchon and Don De-Lillo, Whitehead gradually uncovers a shadowy underworld of mobsters, criminals, would-be power mongers, and racists beneath the surface of everyday life. The novel is also an allegory about the struggle for racial equality and the divisions that the struggle creates both between whites and African Americans and also between African Americans as well. On the simplest level, the elevator serves as a symbol for racial mobility, but it also comes to represent race itself later in the novel. The main protagonist of the novel is Lila Mae Watson, the first-ever female African American elevator inspector, who symbolically oversees the extent to which there is racial mobility.

In this novel, elevators and elevator inspection are a serious business, to the point that there have developed powerful, competing, political, and philosophical groups that have differing approaches on how to manage elevators. The two main groups are the Empiricists and the Intuitionists. Empiricists, as the name suggests, rely on experiences for knowledge; they can only comment upon what is visible or tangible. Empiricists believe that everything is scientifically knowable, and they follow the same procedures and "search for a national standard" (1999, 45). In addition they are homogenous, as evident by how all of the Empiricist elevator inspectors look similar, having identical haircuts. Intuitionists, on the other hand, rely more upon their feelings and believe there is an unseen, almost spiritual world existing underneath or parallel to the visible one. Lila Mae, an Intuitionist herself, seems able to discern the quality of an elevator by just feeling its vibrations while in it. That "she is never wrong" about the quality of elevators indicates that Intuitionists are more accurate and reliable than the Empiricists (1999, 6). Racially, Empiricists are like individuals (often civil-rights-generation members) who believe racism has been eradicated because they cannot perceive it; they do have the insight to see subtle racism nor the ability to conceive of institutional racism. Furthermore they do not have the ability to fully understand or empathize with anyone because they can only see the surface of things. This is a societal criticism that writers of the hip-hop generation often make.

Intuitionism and Empiricism are not just basic philosophies; they are also akin to political parties, complete with candidates for higher offices in the elevator-inspection bureaucracy. While the two groups are not necessarily separated by race, Intuitionists are clearly associated with stereotypes about African Americans, as evident by the nicknames Empiricists use for Intuitionists: "swamis, voodoo men, juju heads, witch doctors, Harry Houdinis. All the terms belonging to the nomenclature of dark exotica, the sinister foreign" (1999, 58). Given these stereotypes of savages, it might be surprising that the Intuitionists are apparently more accurate in determining the efficacy of elevators, as compared to the Empiricists (1999, 58). What Empiricists, then, misconstrue as backwards and savage is actually more reliable and accurate than their own purportedly scientific and objective approach. Still, it is the Empiricists who hold the vast majority of the power, evident how at the Institute for Vertical Transport, the Intuitionist classes Lila Mae attends are marginalized, kept to "the dingy recesses of the course catalog" (1999, 59).

The association between race and Intuitionism becomes clear when we later discover that the founder of Intuitionism, James Fulton, author of the book *Theoretical Elevators,* is himself, at least partially African American, and his ideas about elevators have much to do with breaking down the stereotypes of African Americans. According to Lila Mae, Intuitionism focuses on communicating with the elevator on a nonmaterial basis: "Separate the elevator from elevator-ness" (1999, 62). This is akin to the suggestion that one should separate the person from the race. Furthermore, if an elevator is a symbol for racial mobility, Fulton suggests that it is the kind of elevator that matters, in terms of how fast it takes them and where it takes them in the metaphorical building. Theoretically an ideal elevator would help them rise from the economic bottom.

This is what Fulton worked on towards the end of his life: the construction of a perfect elevator. In school Lila Mae remembers studying Fulton's design problem: "What does the perfect elevator look like, the one that will deliver us from the cities we suffer now, these stunted shacks?" (1999, 61). According to Fulton, we cannot envision this perfect elevator because "it's something we cannot imagine, like the shapes of angels' teeth. It's a black box" (1999, 61). What could he be suggesting about a black box? First of all, it is significant that Fulton choose the color black because he is himself part African American and in the era of the "one-drop rule," would have been considered to be black. Fulton's elevator can take passengers wherever they want to go. The problem is that people do not often know where they want to go. In other words, they don't have clear ambitions. Fulton's ideal elevator possesses the ability to somehow get beyond language and understand the true desires of its occupants. Furthermore Whitehead describes how in this theoretical black box, verbal language is transformed into something more pure but abstract, "understood by the soul's receptors and translated into true speech" (1999, 87). Language, of course, is an imperfect medium, and it can manipulate a person's emotions or intentions. Somehow, Fulton's ideal elevator would be able to get beyond that.

Fulton's beliefs about his ideal elevator are also somewhat religious in tone, as we discover when Lila Mae reads his *Theoretical Elevators.* Fulton writes that he believes "the second elevation is coming," insisting that all the entire perceived environment and reality "will come down. All of it" (1999, 182). As irrational as Fulton's ideas sound (and to some degree they are quite incomprehensible, and he appears to have lost some touch with reality, possibly a result of his passing as a white man for so long), his ideas gain currency among both Intuitionists and Empiricists. The latter seek to destroy any plans for constructing the black box as it would lead to the end of structured cities and to their unchecked power, whereas Intuitionists such as Lila Mae come to think of the black box as their salvation. Indeed Lila Mae comes to believe that "whoever owns the elevator owns the new cities" (1999, 208).

Given the dismal manner in which Whitehead describes the urban setting of the novel, one can see why there could be a desire for a new kind of city. This never-named large city is reminiscent of New York City in the 1940s and 1950s, and Whitehead portrays it with Edward Hopper–like imagery. Lila Mae believes the city is defined by "metropolitan disaffection" that is "situated in the heart of the city" (1999, 4). The city is also located near a contaminated river and appears like a labyrinth or trap with an "internecine system of one-way streets and prohibited U-Turns making retreat a difficult enterprise" (1999, 17). It is important to remember that the ordered city is a product of the Empiricists; they are responsible for its rather abysmal condition. Despite its overtures of racial inclusion, the city is quite racially separated and volatile, just as is the case with contemporary major American cities. There have been a few transparent attempts to satiate the African American population, for instance, by naming a building after a former slave who taught herself to read: the Fanny Briggs Memorial Building. However, this was done for purely political reasons and is merely a symbolic act that does nothing to ameliorate the conditions of African Americans.

The superficial, calculating, and rather racist manner in which the Empiricists operate can be seen when the president of the elevator inspectors, an Empiricist named Chancre, gives Lila Mae the Briggs Building purportedly to help him get more of the minority vote. In truth Chancre doesn't care a bit about racial equality, which can be seen in how, at the Department of Elevator Inspectors, most African Americans are only able to get jobs as mechanics, and the vast majority are banished to the garage, where "there are no windows permitting sky, and the sick light is all the more enervating for it" (1999, 18). These African American employees are Intuitionists, who live in a kind of unseen underworld that is more genuine and realistic than the aboveground "white world." They deface pictures of Chancre: "No one notices them but they're there, near-invisible, and count for something" (1999, 18).

As one of the only African American elevator inspectors (and the only female African American inspector), Lila Mae believes that her job security is virtually nonexistent, having learned from her father "that white folks can turn on you at any moment" (1999, 23). The few other token African American elevator inspectors are presumably hired only because it makes the department seem racially inclusive. In reality they are treated abysmally by their white superiors: one African American was promoted only after he let his white boss literally kick him in the behind (1999, 25). Lila Mae herself lives in a predominately African American area, and the extent to which the city is segregated is evident in how the real-estate agents try to "reassure their clients that they are not moving into the colored neighborhood, but into the farthest reaches of the adjacent white neighborhood" (1999, 30). Tellingly there is no elevator in Lila Mae's building, which signifies how the residents are denied the opportunity for upward mobility and further shows Lila Mae's alienation to her own job as she works on objects (elevators) that she cannot even use at her apartment building.

Whitehead also describes Lila Mae's struggle to become an elevator inspector, which was extremely difficult for an African American, let alone a woman, in that time period. While a student, Lila Mae is forced to live in "a converted janitor's closet" because the segregation-era Institute lacked dormitories for African American students (1999, 43). African American students are so uncommon at the school that Lila Mae is sometimes mistakenly called the name of the last attending African American student by her professors. Indeed Lila Mae ends up becoming the first African American elevator inspector. However, Lila Mae's ethnicity is an asset when she seeks answers about Fulton and finds a willing talker in Marie Rogers, an African American maid who served Fulton, and Rogers is willing to talk to Lila Mae because of their shared ethnicity. At this point, Lila Mae doesn't know for certain that Fulton is at least part African American, nor does anyone else. Through her searches, Lila Mae finds Fulton's nephew, Natchez, who explains to her, "They always take away from our people. I don't know if they know he was colored, but if they do you know they ain't going to tell the truth" (1999, 139). Furthermore Natchez insists that those in power in the Intuitionist camp would never admit that their primary founder and designer, whom they tend to worship, was African American because that would "make them puke all over their expensive carpets they got. They'd die before they say that" (1999, 139). After discovering Fulton is black, Lila Mae comes to see his ideas and Intuitionism differently. She sees racism even within the Intuitionist camp, believing that had everyone known he was African American, not only would he not have been so almost divinely celebrated but also his books probably would not have been published at all (or he would have to use a pseudonym (1999, 151). This is the case even though all of the Intuitionists in the novel are African American (and it may be that all Intuitionists are African American). The African American Intuitionists do not exhibit much solidarity or allegiance to one another.

Furthermore, throughout the novel, Lila Mae is sabotaged by the other African American elevator inspector, Pompey, who is much more subservient than Lila Mae. Pompey was the first African American elevator inspector (irrespective of gender), and he acts against Lila Mae under orders from his white superiors, who, he obeys because he feels he has no other option (1999, 195). When Lila Mae tells him that he serves his white superiors like a "slave," he responds, "What I done, I done because I had no other choice. This is a white man's world. They make the rules" (1999, 195). Because of this, Lila Mae believes that Pompey or the Empiricists have sabotaged her when one of the elevators she had inspected comes crashing to the bottom of the elevator well. However, by the end of the novel, she comes to believe it was "a catastrophic accident" (1999, 227).

Lila Mae comes to personify the elevator as a light-skinned African American who passes for white to the extent that he/she truly comes to believe that he/she really is white. She speculates, "The elevator pretended to be what it was not. Number Eleven passed for longevious. Passed for healthy so well that Arbo Elevator Co's quality control could not see its duplicity" (1999, 229). Rather than destroying her Intuitionist ideals, the catastrophic elevator accident actually strengthens them. She comes to believe that it shows "the dull and plodding citizens of modernity that there is a power beyond rationality" (1999, 231). In addition she comes to believe that it reveals some limitations of Intuitionism that she does not account for such as that light-skinned African Americans, such as Fulton, who pass as white and elevators "must rely on luck, the convenience of empty streets and strangers who know nothing" (1999, 231). However, they also "dread the chance encounter who know who they are. The one who knows their weakness" (1999, 231). In other words, there is no way to truly know for sure if your intentions are correct, and there is power beyond that of Intuitionist theory.

In her quest to discover more about Intuitionism and its founder James Fulton, Lila Mae uncovers his journals and comes to see that Fulton initially intended Intuitionism to be a "big joke" (1999, 232). That is to say, he did not really believe that there was really a way to understand an elevator, let alone a person, through intuition. However, as time progresses and more people start believing in Intuitionism, so does Fulton. He begins to believe that Intuitionism is a good model in teaching people how to escape from their own established and rote mentalities and how to break from mental limitations and prejudice. Lila Mae learns that Fulton believed that the Empiricists "were all slaves to what they could see" (1999, 239). In other words, Empiricism, which is based on perceiving appearances as truths, fails to account for how perceptions can be misleading, such as the belief that Fulton was white when, in fact, he was African American. Lila Mae comes to believe that Fulton's theory of Intuitionism comes from a desire not just to outdo or deceive the Empiricists, which he had already been doing virtually all his life by passing as a white man, but it also comes from a deep-seated hatred of himself as an African American in a society that devalued African Americans. Recognizing himself as African American and hating himself for that, Fulton wanted to be treated equally just as members of the civil rights generation did, but he knew he never would be fully respected as an African American, so he had to pretend to be a well-adjusted white man. Lila Mae comes to believe that Fulton could never fully believe that he or any other African American could fully transcend race. Rather, he ends up thinking that "his race kept him earthbound, like the stranded citizens before Otis invented his safety elevator. There was no hope for him as a colored man because the white world will not let a colored man rise" (1999, 240).

Yet, just as Fulton grew to believe in the idealism of his perfect elevator or completely egalitarian society, so does Lila Mae. At his death, Fulton had written two volumes of books called *Theoretical Elevators,* and Lila Mae begins work on a third part, which envisions a different kind of elevator and society. The one that Fulton designed, the so-called black box, was purely utilitarian, but the ones Lila Mae designs are more traditional in appearance and design: "She particularly likes the cab design, which takes care of engineering necessity without sacrificing passenger comfort. Just like they did in the old days. This third volume of Fulton's truly understands human need, she's found. The elevator she delivered to Coombs, and then to Chancre and Ben Urich, should hold them for a while. Then one day they will realize it is not perfect" (1999, 255).

Metaphorically the elevator, a symbol for racial mobility, should be designed for comfort, as the ascension towards something better might take a long time. Lila Mae truly believes that this new elevator will bring forth a new city and society: "They are not ready now but they will be" (1999, 254). Yet Whitehead leaves it uncertain whether Lila Mae has fallen into similar delusions as Fulton and ends the novel: "She returns to the work. She will make the necessary adjustments. It will come. She is never wrong. It's her intuition" (1999, 255). However, Lila Mae had been wrong once before about believing the Fanny Briggs Memorial Building's elevator had been sabotaged when it had actually accidentally malfunctioned. In any case, the novel ends on an optimistic note, whereby Whitehead suggests that racial progress, even racial equality may one day be approachable, if not for the hip-hop generation, then for the next.

Whitehead switched gears for his next novel, *John Henry Days.* In his article, "I Worked at an Ill-Conceived Internet Start-Up and All I Got was This Lousy Idea for a Novel," Whitehead discusses how he got started on the book. He already had the idea to write about Henry, but during his plentiful free time at his rather insubstantial job at an Internet company, Whitehead started doing some research about Henry and found that the U.S. Postal Service had recently made a stamp of him as part of a folk-heroes series. For Whitehead, "This was a nice modern hook—a real live contemporary event I could pin a story to. What kind of monument was a postage stamp? It was so banal that it addressed something about our debased age. And the fact that there was an actual press release for it resonated with me." Whitehead also learned that not only was there a historical basis for the Henry story but also that the town of Talcott, West Virginia, was holding its first "annual John Henry Days festival," and that "coincided with the release of the Folk Heroes stamp" (Whitehead 2006). These real-life events gave Whitehead the impetus to write about the loss of history, myth, and heroism in the pre–9/11 contemporary age, in which trivial matters often dominated the news and in which the differences between the news and entertainment had been mostly effaced. Furthermore Whitehead uses the John Henry story/myth to demonstrate how the African American culture and folklore dissipated over time and matters much less to the hip-hop generation than to previous generations of African Americans. As John Henry scholar Brett Williams explains, Henry "has undeniably been a hero to black Americans, who sang of him in the nineteenth century and knew of his prowess at least through the 1920s. . . . John Henry is less a hero to black Americans today" (117). Indeed this is the case in Whitehead's novel.

The main protagonist of John Henry Days is J. Sutter, a disaffected hip-hop generation African American free-lance writer of small, relatively inconsequential news stories, or, as Whitehead calls him, a junketeer. He is a corollary to John Henry in the sense that both are competing against something nonhuman, and both face tremendous odds. For Henry, of course, his competition is a drilling machine, but for Sutter, it is an inconsequential junketeer record of attending consecutive newsworthy events every day or night, which he seeks to break. Revealed later, the previous record holder, Bobby Figgis, went insane during and after setting the record and was never heard from again, which hints at the difficulty of J.'s task. Whitehead explains that Figgis subsequently disappears because "he had been devoured by pop" (2001, 111). In the contemporary age and to members of the hip-hop generation, Whitehead suggests, popular culture has become extremely powerful, an entity onto itself, devaluing human life and determining what we consider to be reality. However, whereas Henry's nineteenth-century act was an important statement about the power of human drive and determination, celebrating man over the machine, Sutter's is meaningless. Thereby, Whitehead suggests that the late twentieth century is an era of fluff, of the elevation of the trivial over the significant, and J. is a good representation of the self-investment and the social disengagement that Whitehead perceives in contemporary America and/or in the hip-hop generation.

John Henry has become a national legend as well as a figure of some debate. Was he an actual living person? If so, who was he? Did he really compete against a drilling machine and die immediately after winning? Whitehead does not seek to answer these rather unanswerable questions. Rather, he begins the novel by discussing the various theories people have about the identity of Henry. For instance one researcher-writer claims that Henry was white, another that he was Jamaican, and yet another that he was hung for murder (2001, 4). Whitehead states that there is a lack of consensus on John Henry's appearance because "he was everyman. Every freed slave, travelling under the most common freed slave name. He was a six-foot-tall bruiser, big as a barn, dark as chocolate, darker. He was a wiry trickster figure who lived by his wits, quite obviously had some white blood, gentle, mean" (2001, 262).

In the novel, Whitehead writes from the perspective of many characters, including John Henry himself, whom the author portrays as a tough but kindly man who lived in an incredibly racist era in which African American workers were considered to be literally disposable. In his passages from Henry's perspective, Whitehead displays how such African American workers were exploited for their labor. In Whitehead's treatment, the Henry story becomes somewhat of a tragedy in that Henry is forced to work when he is sick, and "he knew the mountain was going to kill him the first time he saw it" (2001, 240). He is a casualty of the cruel working environment as shown by how when one of Henry's coworkers shatters his hand, only Henry cares enough to help him. The bosses do not care because from their skewed perspective, "There was no shortage of niggers" (2001, 86). In Whitehead's depiction, Henry is valued only because he is a highly productive worker. Unlike the usually docile images of Henry, Whitehead's Henry derives his energy from his internalized anger and frustration at the racist behavior he witnesses against African Americans. He dreams of "crushing the face of the white man" (2001, 147). Not being able to do that, he takes out his aggression in his work. In contrast to that, J. remembers watching a cartoon about John Henry when he was in grade school. This cartoon portrays Henry as larger than life and makes no mention of slavery. Instead, Henry is welcomed by the railroad companies and idolized by the other white railroad workers, which is most certainly not accurate. It is an overly sentimental and false portrait of race relations at that time.

While John Henry means little or nothing to the disaffected J., who can be seen as an example of how much of the hip-hop generation has forsaken or ignored African American history and culture, he or his legend comes to signify a great deal both to other African Americans and to whites. The mostly white town of Talcott, West Virginia, seeks to capitalize upon the Henry legend through their festival; their purpose is purely economical. However, it is unclear whether Henry, if he existed at all, was from Talcott. If so, he would not have been allowed in the white town but rather would have lived in the African

American shantytown nearby. The U.S. Postal Service also seeks to capitalize on Henry through their commemorative stamp.

For postslavery generations of African Americans, Henry becomes a symbol of strength and racial pride, a kind of precursor to the proud and unapologetic African American future boxing-champion Jack Johnson. According to one researcher whom Whitehead describes, African Americans of the late nineteenth and early twentieth century regarded John Henry as "a hero of their race" (2001, 5), and the researcher claims that within communities of African American blue-collar workers, "John Henry had become a byword, a synonym for superstrength and superendurance" (2001, 162). In the novel, Whitehead also describes the obstacles an African American scholar and professor, Guy Johnson, faces while researching John Henry. Although Johnson finds there is a large amount of interest in Henry from African Americans, when he goes to Hinton, West Virginia, to conduct research, he is not only dismissed by the white residents but he is also refused a room there and only is able to stay in the area by convincing an African American woman to put him up at her house. When he returns to his college, Johnson struggles to convince his rather prejudicial department that Henry is worthy of scholarship. For older, African American characters, such as Mr. Street, Henry becomes an idol, a symbol of an ideal African American man. Mr. Street becomes an obsessive collector of Henry memorabilia and eventually opens up a small John Henry museum in his apartment, which virtually nobody visits, signifying how African American legends and folktales are decreasing in importance for the hip-hop generation. After his death, his daughter, Pamela Street, goes to John Henry Days to sell off or donate Mr. Street's collection.

In Whitehead's historical description of Henry, white people keep trying to subvert the Henry story/myth for their own ends. In another part of the novel, Whitehead describes the stage production of a play in 1940 about John Henry starring the celebrated actor Paul Robeson. However, the show is a critical and commercial failure because, as it is suggested, of the abysmal stereotypes of the playwright Roark Bradford, who claims he is qualified to write about African Americans because "he had a Negro for a nurse and Negro playmates when he was growing up" (2001, 226). In his script, Bradford uses an overdone African American idiom and makes his characters simpletons or noble savages at best. In that sense, it becomes little more than a minstrel show, and what was once a symbol of African American independence, pride, and strength becomes a mockery.

This debasement of African American folklore continues in the present. When Talcott actually puts on the fair commemorating Henry, it is hollow and signifies the commercialization of modern American society, in which virtually everything has become disposable entertainment. The fair seems like a sham; no one really cares about or even knows much of anything about Henry. Even when they stage a false reenactment of Henry's steel-driving, a white man acts out the part of Henry, symbolizing how the town leaders, who, in all probability, are mostly white, are even excluding African Americans from their own cultural history: "Nothing life or death here, just a chance to show off for the crowd" (2001, 319). J. concludes, after watching the reenactment of Henry's penultimate act, that it has devolved into entertainment, "a fun time, pay per view" (2001, 319). Further contributing to the debasement of African American folklore and culture is the large amount of commercial Henry merchandise for sale during the Days, best displayed in how the John Henry statue has been sponsored by Jim Beam whiskey.

As for J., a member of the hip-hop generation, he is likewise unconcerned with African American history and folklore, wanting only to cover John Henry Days because he wonders, "Who in the world would possibly care about this event?" (2001, 19). While J.'s question is somewhat understandable, he misses out on the importance of the John Henry story in African American folklore. This is not to suggest that he is any different from others of the hip-hop generation, for when J. goes to the John Henry Days in Talcott, he sees many African Americans there "dressed in the hip-hop gear he'd see on any Brooklyn ave; there are even one or two hardrocks around, fronting. . . . Cable allows every teenager, no matter how country, to catwalk into the latest styles. And maybe looking at these woods frees them to reach for what they see on TV as ghetto realness, and they cling to it. A life raft in this cracker wilderness" (2001, 313).

J. is not much better than that himself, if at all, as he can be seen as an emblem of a disposable, anonymous society, as evident in how his first name is never revealed. J., like all of Whitehead's protagonists, is a rather alienated hip-hop generation urbanite, for whom, while race is not his main concern, it does help create his feelings of alienation and anomie. For instance J. is still sufficiently race conscious that he, an urban Northeastern African American, is rather apprehensive about traveling to West Virginia, where he goes to a write a story about the "unveiling" of the John Henry Stamp and the subsequent John Henry Days festival. He describes West Virginia as a part of the South, even though it is more like a Border State: "Forget the South. The South will kill you" (2001, 14). Possibly influenced by media images of prejudice and discrimination against African Americans, J. is hyperconscious of racism, believing, "It's always Mississippi in the fifties" (2001, 127). While J. encounters no indication of racism while in West Virginia, he comes to believe "these people are liable to eat me" (2001, 15). Furthermore, when J. chokes on a piece of prime rib during a buffet for the junketeers, he thinks to himself, "All these crackers looking up at me, looking up at the tree. Nobody doing nothing, just staring. They know how to watch a nigger die" (2001, 79). Yet, it is a white man, Alphonse Miggs, who eventually saves him. He is also drawn to Pamela Street because she is also African American, and Whitehead describes how seeing her makes him feel comforted and reassured because of their shared race in an all white environment (2001, 50).

Whitehead describes J. as "always up in the air," because he travels so frequently to cover trivial news stories (2001, 12). Metaphorically J. is up in the air because he lacks a distinct identity, and he is seemingly unable to make significant connections with anyone. His immersion in the flotsam and jetsam of pop culture has affected him to the point that he is becoming dehumanized and emotionally deadened or numbed. He also lacks moral integrity because his only real concern is capitalizing on his assignments by getting as much as he can free, free food and travel, for instance. J. even picks up discarded receipts so he can claim them as expenses even though he did not buy what was purchased. In short J. only has allegiance to himself, and in that sense he represents the dark side of the hip-hop ethos: extreme egotism. Whitehead, himself a former journalist, satirizes the "work" that J. and the other junketeers do. Even J. realizes that much, if not all, of what he covers is trivial and meaningless, but he continues in his profession because he finds that it is easy work and it is easy for him to cheat his employers by tacking on dubious charges to his expense account and writing superficial, nonsubstantial stories.

Beyond his apparent lack of morality, J. seems unable to have a serious or steady relationship, only a purely physical intermittent relationship with Monica the Publicist (2001, 221). Their relationship is just a sexual one, lacking emotional commitment or connection, but is rather just mechanical and routine. Whitehead explains that Monica and J. compulsively see one another precisely every two weeks over a period of "years" (2001, 224), and, furthermore, "they despised each other," keep an open relationship, and barely ever converse. They continue their relationship as a matter of habit and because, as both Monica and J. are rather lazy, it is easier to continue than end it (2001, 223). Yet, Whitehead does not condemn their relationship, nor does he want the reader to do so: "Circumstances had thrown them together, life under pop had forced them to find solace wherever they could" (2001, 225). Still, Whitehead describes their relationship as a war, with J. as a soldier and Monica as his nurse. The regimental, hollow, and mechanical affair J. has with Monica mirrors his own job as a free-lance writer/junketeer.

This is not to suggest that Whitehead portrays J. as any less moral or sympathetic than the other characters. The other junketeers are portrayed as equally, if not more, callous and hollow as J., yet they have an amazing power in setting trends and making people and events seem newsworthy even if they are not. For instance Whitehead compares junketeer Dave Brown's writings to a cockroach in their seeming indestructibility and for the way they spread to virtually all newsstands. The extent to which the junketeers write regimented, insubstantial material can be seen through their categorization of subject material into five categories: Bob's Debut, Bob Returns, Bob's Comeback, Bob Is Hip, and Bob's Alive, or Simply Bob. That they use the same name for these events indicates how meaningless and interchangeable these supposedly newsworthy events have become. Furthermore they have become experts at making the mundane and trivial seem important, and that there is a market for this indicates the increased audience's appetite for fluff such as celebrity profiles and up- and supposed-up-and-coming artistic and commercial successes (2001, 73).

Whitehead describes the junketeers as fighting a phony battle to champion free speech, when their writings serve to more accurately obfuscate their readers from real and serious issues. Their real "ideals," Whitehead suggests, are "the holy inviolability of the receipt, two dollars a word, travel expenses" (2001, 47). Freedom of speech, of course, is not at stake, nor are the junketeers contributing to American society in any way. Although there are no overt racial overtures to the above quote, it can be construed that the trivial stories the junketeers work on help distract the larger populace from more-important issues such as institutional racism and poverty and thereby lull their readers into a false sense of security as well as a false sense that we live in a racially egalitarian society.

For Whitehead, the technology and information age threatens to subsume the individual, just as in John Henry's time, the machine was threatening to subsume the worker. The junketeers ominously signed up (or were signed up) to an e-mail listserv that posts events of tabloid-like interest. The junketeers personify the List, as they call it, claiming that it "knew if writers moved, switched from this newspaper to that magazine, if they died or retired, and updated itself accordingly" (2001, 55). The List is more like a compendium of so-called important pop stories, which are in actuality irrelevant, like "the next big thing" and "behind the scenes at the award ceremony" (2001, 55).

It is not the junketeers, however, who determine what becomes popular or newsworthy; rather, it is whoever controls the List itself. The junketeers are mere pawns, and they have no idea who controls their choice of assignments. Some believe the List controllers to be a "consortium of publicity firms or solitary and mean-spirited visionaries," while J. "thinks it's a game" (2001, 125). People like Lucien, a wealthy corporate executive, who is also in West Virginia, might control it. It may be both. The amoral, cynical J. does not care who controls the list or how it works; rather, as long as it functions, it's fine with him. According to J., the List seeks out apathetic, morally shady individuals "who don't give a fuck, who want things for free" (2001, 137). Rather than portraying such individuals as aberrant, Whitehead describes the junketeers as "quintessential" or "key Americans" because of their greedy and selfish behavior, evident how "they want and want now and someone else is picking up the check" (2001, 137). If indeed the junketeers represent quintessential Americans, this hardly paints an uplifting portrait of turn-of-the-millennium America and, along with it, the hip-hop generation.

However, whose fault is it for the cultural and intellectual ennui Whitehead perceives in late twentieth-century America? The consumers or the producers or both? Either way, J. sees a kind of cultural boredom setting in, affecting virtually everybody and everything, including himself. This is especially evident in how J. is a member of the hip-hop generation and at one point wrote about hip-hop, but he has come to believe that even hip-hop has become rather superficial and meaningless. Therefore he rejects an offer from a book agent for him to write a book about it, even though J. "admitted that he wanted to write a social history of hip-hop at one point, when he was younger" (2001, 136). However, he comes to believe that he and hip-hop itself have become too old and "jaded." Furthermore he suggests that they "grew up together and are too old to pretend that there is anything but publicity" (2001, 136).

J. and the other junketeers are not the only itinerant workers who feel little or no allegiance to their jobs. Similarly Pamela Street, daughter of an obsessive John Henry collector, is a temporary office worker who moves from job to job with no real connection to her work and/or fellow employees. Similarly her story and the stories of other low-level computer/Internet workers also mirror the John Henry story, just as J.'s does. That is, technology, in this case computer technology, threatens to render the human worker almost obsolete and if not obsolete, then devalued. When Pamela works an upstart Internet company, she rightly fears that her job may not last very long because the company has plans to develop a fully autonomous computer accessory, which they call the Tool, that would replace many of their workers (2001, 228). Furthermore the environment in which Pamela works in also seems to be contributing to the process of dehumanization. Her company determines the success of their Web sites on the basis of the number of "the hits, the eyeballs, the clicks," not on the basis of the number of people who visit their site(s). They also call the main workroom "the Box" (2001, 288). Unlike John Henry, Pamela does not challenge machines or technology. Rather, she quietly leaves after the company develops the Tool that replaces the need for her. In that, Whitehead suggests that either the technology has become too powerful to challenge and/or we (or at least the hip-hop generation) have lost the desire that John Henry had to prove human superiority. Rather, we have let technology dehumanize us and grown apathetic in process.

This is not to suggest that dehumanization in the workplace and society is anything new. Another character in the novel, Alphonse Miggs, works in an industry notorious for contributing to violent, mental breakdowns: the U.S. Postal Service. Alphonse is as alienated as J., except that Alphonse, unlike J., is in a rather loveless marriage with his wife, Eleanor. Whitehead shows Alphonse's emotional deadening when he tries to save J. while J. chokes on prime rib, not because he is a good Samaritan who truly cares about his fellow human beings but more out of shame "when he realized his indifference to whether the man lived or died" (2001, 135). Just as J. and the junketeers try to come up with fluff to fill the minds of their often-disconnected readers, Alphonse grows obsessed with stamp collection as a way to give his life meaning. Specifically he grows enamored of stamps with pictures of trains. Alphonse is drawn to trains because he seeks to escape from his rather empty, insubstantial life. What appeals to Alphonse the most in the pictures of trains on stamps is how "anything could be in those cars, anything he wanted" (2001, 284). In all probability, he longs to be on one of the trains he sees in order to get away from his unsatisfying life. However, it is Alphonse, not J., who ultimately becomes a contemporary incarnation and/or twisted doppelganger of John Henry, as Alphonse brings a gun to John Henry Days, for reasons that are never fully explained in the novel. It may be that Alphonse was sickened by the debasement of the John Henry myth/story, or he irrationally attempts to defeat the technological world, or he may have just cracked up. His last words were "I wasn't going to shoot you," which was presumably directed towards the policeman who shot him (along with two other bystanders), but that does mean that Alphonse didn't intend to shoot anyone (2001, 368). However, Alphonse's death and the injuries of the two bystanders hardly affect the public. The two postal employees who discuss the events in the novel do so nonchalantly and conclude their discussion by having a beer and discussing a seminar one had recently attended.

A friendship and/or the beginnings of a romance start between J. and Pamela. He helps her to try to find John Henry's grave or the actual mountain he worked on or in where she can scatter her father's ashes, because her father was so completely devoted to John Henry memorabilia. Pamela begins to think that the festival is somehow contingent upon her father's death. She wonders, "Would this have still happened, the fair, the museum, if he was still alive. Or did he have to give up himself for this to happen. The price of progress. The way John Henry had to give himself up to bring something new into the world"

(2001, 378). In a way, Pamela's father, a member of the civil rights generation, sacrificed his own life in order to make sure that John Henry's story and myth live on. Hearing about this from Pamela touches J. (as much as he is able to be emotionally touched), and he thinks about writing a story: "It is not the thing he usually writes. It is not puff. . . . He does not even know if it is story. He only knows it is worth telling" (2001, 387).

J., experiencing intellectual curiosity, morality, and possibly even affection for the first time in years, is then faced with a dilemma. Pamela asks him to take an earlier flight with her, or he could stay and continue in his quest to beat Bobby Figgis's record for consecutive days of junketeering. In other words, he has to choose between Pamela and the contest. Whitehead ends the novel with the arrival of Pamela's taxi and J. standing, "deciding, as if choices are possible" (2001, 389). Although Whitehead does not give away whether J. goes with her or not, I believe he does because Whitehead also says at the end of the novel that Pamela asks J. for his complete first name, and "He told her" (2001, 389). Telling Pamela his name is an important symbolic event in that it represents the rehumanization of J. As J. can be seen as a representative member of the hip-hop generation, Whitehead suggests that learning the importance of the John Henry myth and along with it African American folklore and history help give his life more purpose and meaning and, along with it, the lives of other hip-hop-generation members. J. realizes how much of his life was devoted to the trivial and seeks to change that.

As with *John Henry Days,* in his next novel, *Apex Hides the Hurt* (2006), Whitehead's main protagonist is a hip-hop-generation social isolate who visits a small town on a job-related mission. Whereas J. had at least the beginning of a name, the protagonist of *Apex* is never named, ironically so because he is a so-called nomenclature consultant, one who invents and markets consumer names. He goes to the town of Winthrop to help rename the town. Both J. and the protagonist of *Apex* work in jobs whose primary purpose is to manipulate their audience into reading and/or buying. For Whitehead, it seems, much of contemporary life, as well as the main tropes of hip-hop culture, revolves around consumerism, consumption, and illusion.

Realizing this, probably through his job, the protagonist develops a post-modern perspective; he sees what we consider to be real as a fictional construct, based upon language. This has made him increasingly skeptical and suspicious of other people. Rejecting contemporary culture and the hip-hop ethos helps make him into a hermit; his brief discussion with a bartender shortly after his arrival in Winthrop is "more human contact than he'd had in months" (2006, 25). Furthermore, at an awards dinner, the narrator's animosity towards his coworkers appears. The narrator envisions his co-workers wearing their "true names" instead of their real names on their nametags, such as "LIAR, BED WET-TER," and he concludes, "That would be something. That would be honest" (2006, 170). Instead, the protagonist comes to believe along the lines of what William Burroughs once said, "To speak is to lie." As Whitehead explains, "Of course, it [dissimulation] began at birth—by giving their children names, parents did their offspring the favor of teaching them to lie with their very first breath. Because what we go by is rarely what makes us go" (2006, 170). Believing that there is no true reality frees the protagonist to do anything he so chooses, regardless of moral concerns, but also makes him into somewhat of a misanthropist and social isolate.

At the same time, he becomes drawn to the power of naming. Naming is an important device in hip-hop culture. Instead of using their actual names, many of the most popular hip-hop artists use and create invented, almost inhuman names such as Diddy and 50 Cent, which makes them appear more powerful. The protagonist in this novel accidentally stumbles into his position as a nomenclature associate, but he finds that not only does he have a talent for inventing lucrative names but he also becomes drawn to their power, concluding that "to have a name imprinted along the bottom of a Styrofoam container: this was immortality" (2006, 5). To a large extent, the protagonist, hungry for power, is already delusional, for how many people look at the bottom of a Styrofoam cup, let alone know or care about the brands of any of them? Yet he accurately sees a way through which he can shape the world: through naming. Consequently he starts calling his names his "most excellent dispatches" (2006, 35). However, what the protagonist does not consider is that he is himself a tool of major corporations, and the names he comes up with ultimately serve them and them only in selling merchandise and making them rich in the process. This mirrors the revelations that often come to hip-hop performers who believe themselves to be fully independent, only to realize that they actually serve the record companies with whom they have signed.

In the novel, Whitehead suggests that contemporary society has become more superficial, relying on façades or names instead of substance. For instance the protagonist himself gets his job as a nomenclature consultant not because he has extensive experience in the field but because he is a "Quincy man," in other words, a graduate from a prestigious Ivy League institution. Quincy, we learn, is the third-oldest university in the country.[1] Furthermore most founders of the protagonist's firm went to Quincy. This fact alone allows the protagonist to "fit right in" and demonstrates the power of the name (2006, 29). Along similar lines, Albie, the descendent of the wealthy Winthrop, for whom the town was named, tells the protagonist that he trusts him because he's a Quincy Man (2006, 68). Clearly the Quincy name carries great weight, and Whitehead compares graduating from Quincy to being "anointed new" with a royal title (2006, 69).

Names can not only influence others and create beneficial or negative prejudice; they can also create expectations and become a self-perpetuating industry onto themselves. For example, when the protagonist was younger, he associated the name *Winthrop* with wealth, class, and privilege. While at Quincy, he lived next to the Winthrop Library and so associated it with intellectualism, but he later realizes it is also a product name used to sell luxurious items; hence, he associates it with wealth as well. Similarly we see how certain names become associated with certain chain stories that have spread across the country like a consumer/corporate virus. This kind of cultural homogeneity creates expectations for what defines a good town and encourages consumers to reject anything different.

Even the protagonist, who, one would think, would be the least susceptible to the power of consumer names, is easily manipulated. When he first sees the town of Winthrop, he is immediately comforted by the familiarity of its chain stores: "They had the new computer chain, the sneaker chain, the convenience-store chain, Admiral Java of course. Affirmations of a recognizable kind of prosperity and growth" (2006, 39).[2] The protagonist has not only named one of these chain stores, Outfit Outlet, but he has also designed its logo, the infinity sign or two interlocking zeros. The brilliance of this logo is that infinity or total, endless domination is the ultimate goal of any consumer name or the name of any shrewd performer. Although Outfit Outlet or any store never achieves this goal, Outfit Outlet becomes increasing popular with an almost cult-like following: "Some people drive miles to watch foliage; he had heard of people who made regular pilgrimages to the windows of Outfit Outlet to watch the color change" (2006, 41). A similar attempt is made to capture an audience by any means possible through hip-hop music itself. For instance the protagonist describes a hip-hop song, "Peep This," which "had attached itself to his nervous system. He was more or less powerless against it, a blinking automaton" (2006, 176).

With the superficial rise in the importance of names and appearances, it becomes easier to manipulate people. Financial and occupational successes become the primary measurement of attractiveness. Consequently, as the protagonist becomes adept at naming, he becomes more desirable to others. As Whitehead describes, the protagonist "had a kind of vibe he projected. Wage earning. Self-actualizing. Nice catch. A local magazine picked him as one of the City's 50 Most Eligible Bachelors" (2006, 58). The key word here is *vibe*, as Whitehead suggests that reputation and desirability are or, rather, have become largely artifice. Furthermore one of the ways to most influence people and to build up their interest is to build up their expectations of the future. This is why the protagonist comes to think that New Prospera would be a good name for the town: "The lilting a at the end like a rung up to wealth and affluence. . . . New, new, new money, new media, new economy. New order. New Prospera. He reckoned it would look good on maps. Nestled among all those Middle-towns and Shadyvilles" (2006, 52). Whitehead suggests that naming for influ-ence and appearance is more of a contemporary approach and thereby more specific to the hip-hop generation, whereas naming used to be more individual and meaningful during the civil rights era or earlier. As the protagonist ex-plains, the former name of the town, Winthrop, is "a traditional place-name, insisting on the specific history of the area and locating it in one man. The man embodies the idea, and the name becomes the idea" (2006, 105). To most mem-bers of the hip-hop generation as well as Generation X, who are often rather cynical, it has become difficult to look up to one individual as a key example of success, wealth, and class. Rather, they want the attributes for themselves rather than merely being associated with individuals who possess those attributes.

The protagonist suggests that this rampant consumerism creates a kind of mental torpor in people, especially in the hip-hop generation. Furthermore cultural homogeneity produces individual homogeneity, whereby everybody wants to be the same. This is where eventually race factors in or, rather, does not factor in, as the society in which the protagonist lives desires the total effacement of race. When meeting people in the bar, he says to himself that they live according to a "script": chasing success, motherhood, wearing the trappings of success, like an "expensive watch" (2006, 45–46). At this bar, the bartender bemoans the loss of the old days in which people would come to him for advice, and there was some kind of camaraderie between them, but now he describes people as more frequently disappointed because of having higher expectations for what consists of a good life and jealous of those who do achieve a seemingly appropriate level of personal and professional success (2006, 47–48). With those expectations of life, most people choose to ignore racial issues or cover them up rather than confront them. As seen in the writ-ings of Trey Ellis and Jake Lamar, this makes things even worse for the hip-hop generation, as they not only have to deal with institutional racism but they also have to deal with a majority of people who do not even believe it exists.

There is certainly a shady side to the business of naming and homogeneity and one important aftereffect is the way it affects minorities, especially African Americans. Whitehead does not reveal that the protagonist is African American until about one-third of the way through the novel. This indicates that race does not matter a great deal to the narrator, no doubt a result of his experiences in the naming business, which leads him to believe that "reality" can be whatever one constructs it to be. While that may be true to some extent, there is a "reality" in which he is devalued, excluded, and isolated because of his race. We learn how, underneath the surface, being African American has certainly made the protagonist feel more disconnected and alienated. For instance, when Albie tells the protagonist about a black friend he had at Quincy, Whitehead describes the protagonist as feeling extremely uncomfortable, even wanting to "flee when white people felt compelled to inform you about their black friend, or black acquaintance, or black person they saw on the street that morning" (2006, 81). One of the reasons Quincy University becomes interested in him is their supposed commitment to fostering "diversity" (2006, 70). However, the protagonist feels that this is only a façade Quincy projects in order to foster a better public image. That the protagonist never feels comfortable at Quincy becomes apparent with Whitehead's description of the protagonist, who "never bought into the Quincy mystique" and "did not learn the words of the drinking songs" (2006, 70). Rather, the protagonist becomes coldly rational, embracing Quincy merely because it "was a name that was a key, and it opened doors" (2006, 71).

Furthermore white people control most of the power behind naming, we discover, through the protagonist's library research into the history of the town of Winthrop. He concludes, "With names there is no coincidence. Only design, design above all. There were a lot of rich white people named Winthrop and they were all related, if not by blood then by philosophy" (2006, 68). Not only are whites behind naming, their names cover other names that were significant to African Americans and that carry with them aspects of their culture. The protagonist discovers, for instance, that before Winthrop came with his factory, the town was settled by ex-slaves who named the town Freedom. Unlike New Prospera or Winthrop, this name, Freedom, actually has meaning and purpose; it does not aim to bring glory to one person as Winthrop does or to manipulate people into settling and investing there as New Prospera does but, rather, Freedom aims to express the collective emotional state and desires of its inhabitants. Yet the protagonist calls them "the laziest namers he'd ever come across" (2006, 95). He describes them this way because, as a more typical representative member of the hip-hop generation, he cannot fathom any reason to name a town other than for self-aggrandizing reasons.

In contrast to the protagonist, the mayor of Winthrop, Regina, a descendant of the original ex-slave settlers, wants to rename the town Freedom in honor of her ancestors. Indeed there is some rationale to this, for the name Winthrop comes to metaphorically whitewash the importance of the town to its African American residents. In a flashback, Whitehead describes the original settlers of

the town, their decision to name the town Freedom, and their eventual acquiescence to change it to Winthrop. At first, they decide to name the town Freedom because it expressed what they held most dear (2006, 144). However, they
realize that such a name is idealistic and exclusionary in a time when African
Americans could hardly afford to be exclusionary if they wanted to obtain
decent employment through a white-dominated industry (which was the case
for all industries). Consequently they agree to change the name to Winthrop
after Winthrop himself bribes one of the African American leaders of Freedom.
Far from criticizing their decision, Regina tells the protagonist that it's possible
he might have done it out of financial necessity (2006, 206). Yet she sees renam-
ing the town Freedom as a way to reclaim African American history and to help
the struggling African American community of Winthrop. Still, her desire to
rename the town Freedom meets great resistance among all residents, white and
African American, who prefer an illustrious town name that can help bolster
their own self-image.

They also resist the name Freedom because, in the novel, race is something
that most characters do not want to address but instead want to ignore completely. This is seen in the most commonplace of items: the adhesive bandage.
In this case, a marketer comes up with an extremely popular idea: multicultural
bandages that adapt to a person's skin color. This kind of bandage is marketed
by the newly named Apex bandages (named by the protagonist). Whitehead
relates that the protagonist "had been saving Apex for a while," but he decides
to use it for these adhesive bandages because he sees their broader significance
and how they metaphorically represent contemporary life as he sees it (2006,
89). Most people seek homogeneity and sameness, not difference. Hence, they
respond well to these multicultural bandages because they keep racial divisions
and homogeneity. Not only does Whitehead describe the bandages as "raceless"
but also as something that could literally and metaphorically conceal "the deep
psychic wounds of history and the more recent gashes ripped by the present
(2006, 90). Apex represents the ideals and ideology of multiculturalism as well
as the dominant ideology of the civil rights generation in that it envisions a
world in which all cultures are equally respected. This is apparent in their advertising campaign, which includes television commercials with families of different ethnicities in which "multicultural children skinned knees, revealing the
blood beneath, the commonality of wound" (2006, 109). The commercials lead
the viewers to believe that "they were all brothers now . . . united in polychro-
matic harmony, in injury, with our individual differences respected" (2006,
109). The final chimera is that Apex would heal them all, when in actuality, it
serves to exacerbate deeper-seated injuries and wounds.

This utopian vision of multiculturalism often characteristic of the civil rights generation turns out to be a chimera because Apex actually can exacerbate wounds by concealing them so effectively, which encourages people to neglect them. In the protagonist's case, this leads to a severe situation. After he suffers an injury to his toe, the protagonist covers it up with an Apex bandage, which encourages him to ignore his wound because the bandage blends into his skin color. Consequently his toe gets increasingly worse, and by the time that he actually has it examined by a doctor, it is so diseased that it must be amputated. With this example, Whitehead suggests that multiculturalism, at least in its Disney-like "It's a Small World" belief that all cultures can be equally respected is naïve, for by neglecting the deeper, subtle prejudice and inequalities among the different ethnicities, it actually backfires, creating an increasing amount of subverted animosity among and towards people. In the larger society of the novel, the phrase "Hides the Hurt" becomes a national tag line, indicating how people are not able or willing to deal with uncomfortable and/or painful issues.

Throughout the novel, the protagonist grapples with the different names strongly endorsed by the different characters (New Prospera by Lucky the computer mogul, Freedom by Regina, and Winthrop by Albie). It is not until the protagonist goes to Times Square in New York City and comes up with a new name that he feels that he really gets beyond race and ethnicity and captures something universal: struggle. When he goes to Times Square, the protagonist realizes an inherent level of competition is involved in generating successful names (2006, 181). However, he also comes to believe, "We spent our lives trying to keep our true names inside and hidden, because if they were let out we would be known and ruined" (2006, 181). Rather he seeks "a name that got to the heart of the thing" and believes that such a name "would be miraculous" (2006, 183). He rejects the town names of New Prospera and Winthrop because they appear to him aimed to profit a single individual or family, but he also rejects the name of Freedom because he believes it to be overly idealistic; it was what the ex-slaves "sought," while "struggle" was what they truly experienced (2006, 210). Furthermore he comes to believe that the name *struggle* was more honest and reflective of what ultimately binds people together. While struggle is not "the highest point of human achievement," the protagonist comes to believe that "it was the point past which we could not progress, and a summit in that way" (2006, 210). Essentially then, the protagonist realizes that struggle is part and parcel of human existence, if not the core of existence itself. He decides to name the town Struggle, believing that people will say, "I was born in Struggle. I live in Struggle and come from Struggle. I work in Struggle. We crossed the border into Struggle. Before I came to Struggle. We found ourselves in Struggle. I will never leave Struggle. I will die in Struggle" (2006, 211).

After coming to this decision, the protagonist feels that his honest admission of the universal vulnerability of human beings has helped cure his isolation, as well as the limp he has developed in response to his amputated toe.[3] Admitting vulnerabilities and showcasing them go in direct opposition to the ethos of hip-hop culture. However, Whitehead does not merely suggest that the hip-hop generation has it wrong. Rather, the situation is much more complex. The novel ends with Whitehead describing how as weeks pass and the protagonist adapts to a different lifestyle, he confesses "that actually, his foot hurt more than ever" (2006, 212). In that, Whitehead suggests that acknowledging pain can actually increase it, because awareness makes one focus on it. In a way, then, the honest admission of pain and vulnerabilities is counterproductive, and to some extent it can be; however, the protagonist would never have been in this situation in the first place had he not tried to cover up his literal wound with an Apex bandage. While on the surface it might seem that this is a nonracial conundrum, when analyzed further, it expresses one of Whitehead's main ideas about race in his novels: that there's a middle ground between multiculturalism and cultural nationalism, whereby we can honor racial differences but also acknowledge and confront the lingering racial problems that still exist in America. This harkens to the main ideas expressed by Ellis and Lamar: that the different racial approaches and attitudes of the civil rights generation and the hip-hop generation can be blended into a more productive symbiosis.

4

Born in early 1960s Los Angeles, Paul Beatty, while older than Colson White-head, owes a great deal to the burgeoning hip-hop/rap movement in the 1980s, which inspired his spoken-word poetry in the late 1980s and early 1990s. Beatty received a master's degree from Brooklyn College, where he was taught by Beat guru Allen Ginsberg, who compared Beatty's work to Miles Davis's "short, melodic bursts" (quoted in Lewis 1991–92, 6). According to Kevin Powell, "Paul Beatty's highly publicized triumph at the Nuyorican Poets Café's inaugural grand slam contest, in the spring of 1990, was a watershed moment for the Word Movement. It was, in a sense, the bridge from the 80s into this new thing" (2000, 5). The linguistic wordplay and musicality of quintessential Beat writing can be seen throughout Beatty's writing, especially in his first two books of poetry, *Big Bank Take Little Bank* (1991) and *Joker, Joker, Deuce* (1994).

In an interview, Beatty describes why he rarely ever reads his poetry after publishing his subsequent two novels and rarely even writes poetry anymore: "For me, if I could convey all the energy on a page, that's what I wanted to do. Reading a poem aloud is complementary, but I don't think it's essential. It's part of the reason why I kind of stopped writing poetry. I realized, this is not my bag. It becomes performance, and I'm just not a performer. I felt very out of place sometimes" (Weich 2005). In large part Beatty consciously chose to move away from poetry to focus on his fiction, which better reflects his more recent views on race, society, and culture. Beatty's follow-up to his two poetry collections was the critically acclaimed novel *The White Boy Shuffle* (1996). It is full of oppositions and polarities, at once wildly sarcastic but emotionally affecting, sincere, and outlandish, bleak but hopeful about race relations with a protagonist who is part hero and part antihero. Its ambition and scope are remarkable. In it Beatty seeks to address the present and future state of African Americans, the extent to which race does or should matter, and the extent to which there will ever be anything approaching racial harmony and/or equality in America.

From the very beginning of the novel, one of Beatty's goals is to demolish the overwhelming demands of racial authenticity, especially for hip-hop generation members, that in order to be an "authentic" African American, one must act or behave in certain ways, and that by not doing so, one can be labeled a traitor, white, or phony. Beatty does this by presenting an unusual narrator who comes from a long line of Uncle Toms. This narrator, Gunnar Kaufman, rises to become the most prominent African American in the nation (a kind of anti–Martin Luther King Jr.), eventually encouraging other African Americans to commit suicide because they will never be fully respected and treated equally in America (by whites). Although it might seem that such a character would undoubtedly be a villain, Beatty not only makes Gunnar, in his role as schlemiel, a loveable loser, he also places a significant portion of the blame upon society and upon African Americans and whites alike, whites for helping to foster the institutional inequality and African Americans for eventually thrusting Gunnar unnaturally into the position of leader/prophet.

In the prologue to the novel, Gunnar speaks from his present role as a prominent African American leader/messiah. He suggest that the climate is such in the African American community that extreme pessimism makes a leader popular, as it gives the audience, many of whom are presumably poor, not only someone to blame but also comfort in their own economical and personal plight. Gunnar writes, "I spoon-feed them grueled futility, unveil the oblivion that is black America's existence and the hopelessness of the struggle. In return I receive fanatical avian obedience" (1996, 1). Gunnar appeals to people who are tired of struggling for equality and respect, for indeed it is much easier to give up and claim the struggle is futile than to continue in a difficult fight. Therefore Gunnar's words resonate with his African American audience and sadly, have a certain logic, although Beatty is more lampooning those who give up the struggle as metaphorically destroying themselves: "In the quest for equality, black folks have tried everything. We've begged, revolted, entertained, intermarried, and are still treated like shit. Nothing works, so why suffer the slow deaths of toxic addiction and the American work ethic when the immediate gratification of suicide awaits?" (1996, 2). However, Gunnar hardly appears to think very highly of himself, as he compares himself to Jim Jones, David Koresh, and Charles Manson and describes himself as a "frightened deserter in the eternal war for civility" (1996, 2).

Beatty creates Gunnar as an antithesis to the literary African American ubermench, who, he suggests, is no real role model but rather creates unrealizable and unrealistic standards. In addition, Beatty aims to break down so called positive stereotypes. Gunnar says, "There are no comely Kaufman superwomen. No poetic heroines caped in Kinte cloth stretching welfare checks from here to the

moon. No nubile black women who could set a wayward Negro straight with a snap of the head and a stinging 'Nigger, puh-leeze'" (1996, 23). In contrast to "the typical bluesy earthy folksy denim-overalls noble-in-the-face-of-cracker-racism aw shucks Pulitzer-Prize–winning protagonist mojo magic black man," Gunnar describes himself as "preordained by a set of weak-kneed DNA to shuffle in the footsteps of a long cowardly queue of coons, Uncle Toms, and faithful boogedy-boogedy retainers. I am the number-one son of a spineless colorstruck son of a bitch who was the third son of an ass-kissing sellout house Negro who was indeed a seventh son but only by default" (1996, 5). Beatty is being sarcastic here, but there is a serious undertone in the sense that one rarely, if ever, hears of these disempowered or even cowardly individuals in African American literature or history. Yet, in a sense, the Kaufmans are not only adaptful and cunning but are also admirable in a way. Beatty largely absolves them of blame, and furthermore he illustrates how it is the racial environment in which they live that forces them to step on as well as over other African Americans in order to survive.

This pattern is discovered as Gunnar describes his ancestors, going back to Euripides Kaufman, who in 1770 Boston egged on the British militia and subsequently "dodged a redcoat's musket shot with his name on it and Crispus Attucks woke up in nigger heaven a martyr" (1996, 9). Another ancestor, Swen Kaufman, a would-be dancer and choreographer, became "the only person ever to run away into slavery. Being persona non anglo-saxon, Swen was unable to fulfill his uppity dreams of becoming a serious dancer. . . . So on a windy night he packed his ballet slippers and stowed away on a merchant ship bound for the Cotton Belt" (1996, 12). When Swen gets to a plantation in North Carolina, "the rise-and-fall rhythm of the hoes and pickaxes and the austere urgency of the work songs gave him an idea for a 'groundbreaking' dance opera" (1996, 13). Swen happily stays at the plantation: "He considered himself dancer-in-residence at the Tannenberry plantation, free room and board and plenty of rehearsal space" (1996, 13). Despite being mercilessly whipped by his master, Swen continues dancing and, in a way, achieves a kind of mental freedom in his dogged determination to live out his desires, however trivial they might seem, in the face of slavery.

Gunnar continues to tell the stories of his submissive ancestors with ridiculous-sounding European names such as Franz von Kaufman and Wolfgang Kaufman, the chief of the Department of Visual Segregation in the 1920s who "spent muggy afternoons under a splotchy painter's cap, painting and hanging the FOR WHITES ONLY and FOR COLORED ONLY signs that hung over quasi-public places throughout Nashville" (1996, 18). Wolfgang continues in his Uncle Tom–like behavior when he later moves to Chicago, and he helps inspire the

creators of Amos 'n' Andy: "Soulless white American radio was destined for droll hours of Fibber McGee and Molly till Wolfgang Kaufman shucked 'n' jived to its rescue. America got a pair of stumbling jitterbugging icons; Wolfgang Kaufman got a ten-cent raise" (1996, 20). Yet is it really Wolfgang's fault? He is merely trying to survive in a racist environment, rather like a Nazi–enlisted Jewish guard" in a concentration camp, and it is he who ends up getting gypped with only a ten-cent raise. As with Wolfgang, his son Ludwig becomes "a manager of white acts that ripped off the Motown rhythm-and-blues hysteria" and later is trained by the FBI to sell out Malcolm X (1996, 20).

Gunnar goes all the way up to his father, who works as a sketch artist for the Los Angeles Police Department. Thereby, his father continues in the Uncle Tom tradition of his Kaufman ancestors by helping the department catch criminals, many of whom are presumably African American. In *The White Boy Shuffle*, Beatty makes no effort to hide his scorn for the post–Rodney King LAPD, as well as how meek and subservient his father is, willing to be submissive and acquiesce in order to be accepted by whites. Gunnar describes how when he would visit his father at work, his father's "fellow officers would stand around cluttered desks breaking themselves up by telling how-many-niggers-does-it-take jokes, pounding each other on the back and looking over their broad shoulders to see if me and Daddy were laughing. Dad always was" (1996, 9). Gunnar's father laughs because he must, in order to fit in and keep his job. However, Gunnar does not describe himself as laughing, which indicates that, at this point in his young life, he wishes to break away from the cycle of Uncle Tom–like subservient and acquiescent behavior of his forebears.

When the novel begins, Gunnar lives in the predominately white community of Santa Monica, just outside Los Angeles. Living as he does, surrounded by whites, Gunnar adopts their persona to some extent, at least to the extent to which he can. He is certainly never allowed to completely forget that he is African American, as he is often "escorted by the police" (1996, 25). Furthermore, in this age in which being African American is often held in great esteem by hip-hop–loving white teens who long to have the power and self-assured attitude they perceive in their favorite performers, it is hard for a student at a predominately white school such as Gunnar to merge into the crowd. Instead, he is labeled "the funny, cool black guy" (1996, 27): "In Santa Monica, like most predominately white sanctuaries from urban blight, 'cool black guy' is a versatile identifier used to distinguish the harmless black male from the Caucasian juvenile while maintaining politically correct semiotics" (1996, 27). This process alienates Gunnar from himself and disconnects him from the other white students. His internalized disdain for them shows in his description: "I learned early that white kids will believe anything anybody a shade darker than chocolate milk says. So I'd tell the gullible Paddys that I was part Gypsy and had the innate ability to tell fortunes" (1996, 28).

Like certain white hip-hop fans who believe they hold African Americans in esteem while they are really exoticizing them, Gunnar's school in Santa Monica hypocritically espouses multiculturalism. This "all-white multicultural school," in which Gunnar is the only African American student, is in reality just succumbing to the pressures of being politically correct and multicultural (1996, 26). Beatty shows how it has become easy to subscribe to these positions yet still be contributing to racial separatism and inequality. By espousing multiculturalism but still attracting almost entirely white students, white parents and administrators who might be subconsciously, if not consciously, racist are allowed to metaphorically have their cake and eat it, too. Gunnar points out that for all their attempts to force-feed multiculturalism, the school fails and even backfires in their mission, for outside the classroom, "the kids who knew the most Polack, queer, and farmer's jokes ruled" (1996, 28). For Beatty multiculturalism can, and in this case has, become an excuse to ignore race, to pretend it does not matter and to believe that everyone is treated the same. Beatty subtly criticizes this dogma. When the school preaches that "the sun doesn't care what color you are," the students learn the complete opposite in their biology class: that dark colors absorb sunlight, and white colors reflect it (1996, 29). So, in point of fact, the sun does care what color a person is. Along similar lines, their teachers stress the importance of being color-blind, but the students are also checked by a doctor to make sure that they are not color-blind.

With these examples, Beatty uncovers a duplicity and hypocrisy behind the seemingly good intentions of the multiculturalist movement. In this case, though, their attempt to ignore the existence of race, ethnicity, and color does more damage than good, leaving its teachers and students to essentially lie to themselves, rather than confront the painful realities of overt and subtle racism as well as of ethnic difference. In vignettes on different colors, Beatty uncovers the importance and beauty of color and difference, exactly what his teachers at the multicultural school are trying to teach him to ignore. Color goes beyond race as Gunnar relates under the "Blue" section: "We splashed in the postcard blue of the ocean and stuck out our Slurpee blue tongues at the girls two towels over. Eileen's light-saber blue eyes cut through me like lighthouse beacons lancing the midnight" (1996, 34). Likewise, under the section for "Psychedelic," Gunnar recounts, "When you're young, psychedelic is a primary color and a most mesmerizing high. Santa Monica was full of free multihued trips. The color-burst free-love murals on Main Street seemed to come to vibrant cartoon life when I passed them. The whales and dolphins frolicked in the clouds and merry-go-round horsies turned cartwheels in the street" (1996, 34). Outside his school, which preaches being color-blind, Gunnar and the other students ironically become more sensitive to color and, thereby, what they are taught at their multicultural school ultimately backfires.

Gunnar has more-conflicted feelings about the colors of black and white, which represents his own conflicted feelings about race and what it means or should mean to be African American. He correlates white with a façade, a hollow insubstantiality he perceives in his friends and even himself: "White Gunnar was a broken-stringed kite leaning into the sea breeze, expertly maneuvering in the gusty gales." White, for Gunnar, is nothingness and holds no possibilities, because his life, at this point, has been a masquerade: "White was the expulsion of colors encumbered by self-awareness and pigment" (1996, 35). For Gunnar, alienated as he is from virtually all of African American culture, the color *black* has even more negative connections.

> Black was an unwanted dog abandoned in the forest who finds its way home by fording flooded rivers and hitchhiking in the beds of pickup trucks and arrives at its destination only to be taken for a car ride to the desert. Black was hating fried chicken even before I knew I was supposed to like it. Black was being a nigger who didn't know any other niggers. The only black folks whose names I knew were musicians and athletes: Jimi Hendrix, Slash from Guns 'n' Roses, Jackie Joyner-Kersee, the Beastie Boys, and Melody the drummer from Josie and the Pussycats. (1996, 35)

Of course, the Beastie Boys are white, which points out Gunnar's naïveté. Furthermore, he describes, "Black was a suffocating bully that tied my mind behind my back and shoved me into a walk-in closet. Black was my father on a weekend custody drunken binge, pushing me around as if I were a twelve-year-old, seventy-five-pound bell clapped clanging hard against the door, the wall, the shoe tree" (1996, 36). A vicious circle of violence runs in the Kaufman family. Gunnar's father, belittled at work, takes out his anger on Gunnar, who becomes personally and socially self-loathing.

This leaves Gunnar in a precarious position of not being able to identify with either blacks or whites. Therefore he seeks a kind of postethnic identity beyond racial categories. Like Birdie in Danzy Senna's *Caucasia* (1998), Gunnar affiliates with Judaism. In his subsequent novel, *Tuff* (1999), Beatty also explores African American and Jewish American relations through use of an African American rabbi in Harlem. In an essay entitled "Revisiting Literary Blacks and Jews," Andrew Furman explores the Afro-Jewish connections in the novel, suggesting that it highlights "locations of ongoing affinity between African- and Jewish-Americans," as well as highlighting "locations of crisis between these two groups that ought to be strenuously addressed both inside and outside the pages of fiction" (2003, 133). He also suggests that Beatty "even more subtly implicates Jewish-Americans in the long history of American racism through Gunnar's arguably Jewish last name, Kaufman. Beatty never broaches the origins of the Kaufman name directly, but the implication is clear enough. A Jewish slave-owner and rapist most likely sits atop the Kaufman family tree" (2003, 143). However, historically, there were not many Jewish slave owners.[1] Still, while Furman may be accurate, Kaufman, as translated from German, also means a merchant or trader. Beatty may also have chosen the name as a play on words, as Gunnar describes himself as a traitor to other African Americans. He is also unscrupulous and trades new identities for old ones, depending on his surroundings and what's expected of him.

As Furman suggests, *The White Boy Shuffle* does seem to exhibit conflicted feelings towards Jews. It is with a Jew that Gunnar makes his first connection or friendship while in Santa Monica: "Of all my laidback Santa Monican friends, I miss David Joshua Shoenfeld the most. He was off-white and closest to me in hue and temperament" (1996, 38). David, however, is no moral beacon for Gunnar; rather, he could be considered a rather negative influence. They discuss and play imaginary World War II games, but rather than aiming to defeat the Nazis, "We concerned ourselves with whether it would be more fun to fantasize about world domination attired in crushed Gestapo black velvet with red trim or in crumpled green Third Army gum-chewing schleppiness" (1996, 38). Yet they form a connection through their shared minority status as noted by how they also debated "who Hitler would kill first, David the diabolical Jew or me the subhuman Negroid" (1996, 40). Gunnar also copies David's actions. Still, in a letter to David, Gunnar's conflicted feelings towards him and possibly towards Jews as well come out. This makes sense in that Gunnar, like his father, feeling disempowered, may seek out anther equally vulnerable minority to whom he can transfer his subverted anger: "David, somehow through being with you I learned I was black and being black meant something, though I've never learned exactly what. *Barukh atah Adonai*"; the letter's closing, however, translates, "Shalom, motherfucker" (1996, 40). This indicates that Gunnar does not completely respect David, and indeed his association with David ends when he subsequently moves to Hillside, an impoverished, predominately African American section of West Los Angeles. Thereby, Beatty suggests that the ghetto culture within which Gunnar is soon immersed (and which so often represents hip-hop culture), stymies interethnic and interracial connections.

Through his description of Hillside, Beatty criticizes Los Angeles as an ethnically segregated city. According to Gunnar, Hillside is built at the bottom of the surrounded, walled-in, upper-class, white community of Cheviot Hills: "At the bottom of this great wall live hordes of impoverished American Mongols.

Hardrock niggers, Latinos, and Asians, who because of the wall's immenseness get only fifteen minutes of precious sunshine in summer and a burst of solstice sunlight in the winter" (1996, 45). The Hillside residents are deprived of sunlight, or, metaphorically, of hope and sustenance. They are treated as potential criminals by the LAPD, who come to "welcome" the Kaufmans in the first week. The police officers try to justify their racism by claiming that they practice "preventative police enforcement" (1996, 47). Their treatment of the Kaufmans and, specifically, of Gunnar, which is presumably the same way they treat all African American men, creates a self-fulfilling prophecy. They ask Gunnar his gang affiliation, assuming that all young African American males in the area belong to one and, by doing so, ironically encourage Gunnar and/or any other young African American male to join one.

Certainly gang life is a key element and theme in harder edged hip-hop music and culture, and it plays an important role in this novel. Beatty uncovers the darker side of gang life while he also debunks the mythos that surrounds it. However, Gunnar quickly learns that it is not so simple to just go out and join a gang. Rather, there is a code for authenticity and a social hierarchy in Hillside that Gunnar must learn in order to survive and thrive. His exposure to white culture in Santa Monica does him no good in Hillside, because there (just as in hip-hop culture) an emphasis is placed upon being tough and never showing weakness. Any show of fear—by crying. for instance—Gunnar learns, could lead to a verbal or even physical attack: "I've seen kids get hit by cars, ice cream trucks, bullets, billyclubs, and not even whimper. The only time it's permissible to cry is when you miss the lottery by one number or someone close to you passes away. Then you can cry once, but only once. There is no brooding; niggers got to get up and go to work tomorrow" (1996, 51). In Hillside everything is determined by attitude and posture; it is "where body and spoken language were currency" (1996, 52). There is also no real sense of community or connection in Hillside as seen in how the residents treat simple eye contact as aggression. Because Hillside appears to represent much of the tropes of the hip-hop generation, it might seem that Beatty is blaming hip-hop for helping to create the environment of a place such as Hillside. While there may be a measure of truth to this is, Beatty does not implicate the residents for their behavior. Rather, he suggests their actions are a product of their environment: "The people of Hillside treat society the way that society treats them. Strangers and friends are suspect and guilty until proven innocent. Instant camaraderie beyond familial ties doesn't exist" (1996, 53).

For Gunnar, an intelligent, studious young man, it is incredibly difficult to do what he desires, and he is forced to hide his interests; therefore he secretly reads Kant, Hegel, and Greek tragedies lest he be ridiculed, considered "white," and/or uncool. In the new, decrepit school he attends, Manischewitz Junior High school,[2] which is more like a jail than a school, Gunnar comes to believe he is phony, that growing up in a predominately white environment has subverted his true identity: "I realized I was a cultural alloy, tin-hearted whiteness wrapped in blackened copper plating" (1996, 63). This is only partly accurate. What he does not fully realize is that the tough-appearing and tough-acting African American students at the schools are also performing their idea of authentic black identity (presumably at least in part because of the caricatures of African Americans in the media, especially through hip-hop), which he eventually emulates. Although their conception of what it means to be African American is performative and not necessarily any more authentic than is Gunnar's identity in Santa Monica, Gunnar finds it necessary to adapt to the identity they deem acceptable. A performance becomes not only real if it is commonly accepted as real by the majority of Gunnar's fellow students but also in a hostile, dangerous environment, it is the only way for Gunnar or any other resident to be accepted.

Just as Gunnar ridiculed the all-white multicultural school he attended in Santa Monica, he also ridicules the hollow-hearted attempts of his new school to rehabilitate its minority students. Gunnar describes the school as essentially buying into civil-rights-generation ideology, aiming "to liberate us from a cult of self-destructiveness and brainwash us into joining the sect of benevolent middle-class American normalcy" (1996, 112). However, the school's guest speakers at an assembly seem phony, such as those who "tried to sway our self-destructive sensibilities with the flashy, super-bad, black businessman-pimp approach to empowerment. . . . No matter who the delivery boy, the message was always the same. Stay in school. Don't do drugs. Treat our black queens with respect" (1996, 113–14). This message has no real effect on the students as they have come to disregard authority and believe that the speakers have no knowledge of how difficult it is to live in Hillside, just as hip-hop-generation members often criticize the members of the civil rights generation for their lack of insight into their own lives and culture. Dealing drugs, for instance, to those of the hip-hop generation, might be the only way they feel they can escape the dismal Hillside environment.

Gunnar, like his Kaufman ancestors, is, above all else, adaptful and resilient. While at first he is isolated at school and in Hillside, he soon makes a friend, Nick Scoby, whom he first describes as looking like "an autistic hoodlum," but whom we discover is actually a jazz-listening, straight-A student, neither of which would be appreciated in a hip-hop dominated environment (1996, 66). Gunnar makes friends with Nick, no doubt largely because of their shared intelligence. However, it is notable that Gunnar becomes incredibly moved when, in a penultimate exchange, Nick calls him a "nigger"; Gunnar relates, "My euphoria was as palpable as the loud clap of our hands colliding in my first soul shake" (1996, 67). Gunnar, at least subconsciously, if not somewhat consciously wants to belong in Hillside, and to belong, he realizes he must appear unkempt, dangerous, and somewhat ignorant. Hence, his happiness goes beyond merely finding a friend; from Nick's greeting, he also starts believing he is beginning to become more authentically African American, at least according to Hillside codes and hip-hop-generation tropes.

Gradually, Gunnar does learn how to act and behave in manners that his fellow hip-hop-generation students find more appropriate and even admirable. For instance, during a Shakespeare competition in which members of the Manischewitz Drama Club compete (including Gunnar and Nick), Gunnar attempts to rewrite a scene in *King Lear* by combining Shakespearean dialogue with hip-hop tropes: "Gazing directly at the judges, I grabbed my dick and ripped into my makeshift monologue. 'What dost thou know me for? A knave, a rascal, an eater of broken meats; a base, proud, shallow, three-suited, hundred-pound, filthy, worsted-stocking whoreson . . . one-truck-inheriting slave . . . beggar, Nigger . . . I will beat you into clamorous whining if thou deny'st the least syllable of thy addition'" (1996, 71). While his performance does not win the club the competition, it does win him the admiration of other African Americans as well as from Nick, who praises him by calling him "a crazy nigger" (1996, 71). Indeed Gunnar's behavior seems to mirror that of the hip-hop stars, the Stoic Undertakers, who are filming a video nearby. Beatty describes them as "reciting their lyrics and leaning into the camera with gnarled intimidating scowls" (1996, 77).

Gunnar's popularity in his community rises as he imitates the accepted tough façade of a gangster in the mold of a hip-hop performer. In a comic scene, he is pursued and eventually loses his virginity to two adolescent would-be gangster girls, Betty and Veronica. He is also invited to join the Gun Totin' Hooligans, a gang headed by the appropriately named Psycho Loco. This gang, in their questionable wisdom, actually does not carry guns but, rather, uses antiquated weapons such as bows and arrows. They adopted their gang name, supposedly, as a way to deceive rival gangs. Gunnar becomes the gang's poet, and he composes poetry that combines Greek myth and street slang. For instance, from his poem, "Negro Misappropriation of Greek Mythology or, I Know Niggers That'll Kick Hercules's Ass":

> I lift the smoggy Los Angeles
> death shroud
> searching for ghetto muses
> anyone seen Calliope?

heard she emigrated to the San Fernando Valley
fulfills her ranch-styled dreams
with epic afternoon soap opera
and bong water bubble baths

. . .

ham radio signals
s.o.s. a.p.b. 911 electronic prayers
to the goddess Urania's voicemail
go unanswered
(1996, 86)

That Calliope, who was the Greek muse of epic poetry, has deteriorated into a blasé suburban housewife indicates that Gunnar believes that there has been a loss of meaning and purpose in contemporary society or at least for the hip-hop generation and that Urania, the Greek muse of astronomy, ignores prayers indicates that Gunnar believes that no one really cares about the plight of the downtrodden in Hillside or in any inner-city community. Unfortunately these poems, like the Gun Totin' Hooligans's weapons, are ultimately insignificant. They do not change anyone's mind or behavior and pale in comparison to the power of contemporary hip-hop lyrics and music, which, in this case, only seem to exacerbate the problems in the African American community.

But, more than anything, what makes Gunnar and to a lesser extent Nick popular is their newly discovered talent and skill in basketball. That basketball has become important in the African American community, especially to the hip-hop generation, is common knowledge, but in *The White Boy Shuffle*, Beatty uncovers how it has become a huge industry and culture. This is because basketball is not just a sport but also a culture, a fashion, and an attitude. Hence, just buying basketball shoes becomes a highly important activity for Gunnar, and Beatty describes his purchase in great detail as more like a corporate rip-off, whereby the shoe manufacturers, capitalizing on the desire of so many to become basketball stars, market shoes that are increasingly expensive but dubious in their supposed performance-enhancing attributes. Gunnar eventually opts for the "high-tech Adidas Forum II's, an outrageously expensive pair of white basketball shoes, computer-designed for maximum support" (1996, 89). In all likelihood, though, these shoes are barely different, if at all, from any generic-brand basketball shoe, presumably not worth the $175 Gunnar pays for them, but Gunnar does buy them because they are the same ones Nick wears.

Gunnar wants to impress Nick and others and believes he can through shoe choice as well as with a specific haircut that Nick insists "was more important than having a basketball" (1996, 90). That the haircut is identical to every other male's, "a concentration-camp baldy with a hint of stubble," shows the homogeneity of Hillside's male African American community (1996, 90). One reason for their shaved heads is because, adhering to the hip-hop generation's code of conduct, they do not want to seem human and vulnerable. Having a shaved head equals being perceived as strong. Now, possessing the appropriate image and look, Gunnar begins to blend in with his peer group: other inner-city African Americans and Latino/as: "By high school I was no longer the seaside bumpkin, clueless to the Byzantine ways of the inner city. But I hadn't completely assimilated into Hillside's culture. I still said 'ant' instead of 'awwwnt' and 'you guys,' rather than 'y'all,' and wore my pants a bit too tight, but these shortcomings were forgiven because I had managed to attain a look. My sinewy physique drew scads of attention" (1996, 95).

In *The White Boy Shuffle*, other codes for authenticity in gang life are seen, specifically that of the Gun Totin' Hooligans. The members tend to model themselves after media images of gangsters, such as Joe Shenanigans, who acts like someone in an Italian mobster movie and claims that "he was a Sicilian from a long line of mafiosi" (1996, 98). Gunnar explains, "Holding a conversation with Joe was like talking to someone who was simultaneously channeling Martin Scorcese, Al Pacino, and Mama Celeste" (1996, 98). As the gang gradually comes to accept Gunnar, he becomes tougher and learns how to use a gun. Tellingly, when Gunnar goes home that night, he tells his mother, "I'm becoming so black it's a shame" (1996, 102). He has reached a point at which he readily associates being African American with being violent. Associating with the gang changes Gunnar, making him more hostile and violent, as signified by the dream he has of killing a white boy who used to be his friend (1996, 103).

Yet, as Gunnar gets older, basketball, not gang life, becomes the focus of his and Nick's life, signifying how he has become a commodity. At first they are not all that noticeable players, in large part because Nick is not a flashy player: "His team always won, but it wasn't like he was out there performing superhuman feats. He didn't sprout wings and fly, he didn't seem to have eyes in the back of his head. There was always someone who jumped higher than he could, handled the ball better. Nick would make five or six baskets and that was it" (1996, 93). As basketball is or has become at least as much spectacle or entertainment as athletic contest, Nick is initially ignored because he is not flamboyant. However, Nick's fame and respect gradually build up because he never misses a basket. Yet he does not immediately become a star because he does not display the necessary flash and arrogance, like a Dennis Rodman might. What the public wants, Beatty suggests, is entertainment (for example, backwards dunk shots), not necessarily a simple, quiet, but impeccable player such as Nick. Similarly one could explain the evolution of hip-hop music from socially and politically charged to individual- and physical-based as being a response to the public's desire to be entertained and not challenged.

One thing seems certain, though, basketball at school and in the African American community holds an almost sacred space: "Unlike at the playground, here a collective self-esteem was at stake. People who didn't give a fuck about anything other than keeping their new shoes unscuffed all of a sudden had meaning to their lives" (1996, 116). This is also evident at school in how Gunnar and Nick become celebrities, which Gunnar describes, "Everywhere we went we were Wheatley High's main attraction. Teachers and students treated us with unwanted reverence. The murmur of everyone clamoring for our attention rang in my ears like a worshipful tinnitus" (1996, 117). That basketball and not social or academic issues has become preeminent indicate that priorities are placed upon the individual and entertainment, not upon the collective good. When Nick tells Gunnar that he cannot miss a shot, Gunner concludes, "Watching his hands shake, I realized that sometimes the worst thing a nigger can do is perform well. Because then there is no turning back. We have no place to hide, no Superman Fortress of Solitude, no reclusive New England hermitages for xenophobic geniuses such as Bobby Fisher and J. D. Salinger. Successful niggers can't go back home and blithely disappear into the local populace. American society reels you back to the fold" (1996, 118–19).

Nick has other talents than basketball—academic and musical talents—but no one really cares about those. Rather, he is only treated as an athlete/performer and is not allowed to be anything else. The pressure would probably have overwhelmed him had he not been playing along with the increasingly popular Gunnar. Gradually Nick takes second stage to Gunnar, who becomes the star, not because Gunnar is the better player, but because he is showier than Nick. Meanwhile Nick suffers scorn for his shooting perfection because he is African American: "In the past two years Scoby had scored over a thousand straight baskets, and a local media usually clamoring for perfection from its athletes could not accept the perfect athlete. Instead of appreciating Nicholas's gift, they treated Scoby as an evil spirit, an idiot savant with a bone through his nose who made the basketball sail through the hoop by invoking African gods" (1996, 163). This would not happen, Beatty suggests, if Nick were white. Rather, the American public can accept African American athletes but not if they seem absolutely infallible, for to do so would be akin to admitting the superiority of African Americans over whites.

Despite his athletic success, Gunnar spends an increasing amount time with the Gun Totin' Hooligans (an activity that is reinforced by his community), and he becomes more militant and callous, so that when the Los Angeles Riots come in 1992, he comes to some important realizations. First of all, he no longer thinks about his father and Kaufman ancestors with complete disdain: "Suddenly [I] understood why my father wore his badge so proudly. The badge protected him; in uniform he was safe" (1996, 130–31). In other words, he comes to believe that in an unequal, racist society, African Americans do not always or very often do not have at all the luxury to live according to idealistic morals. Furthermore he comes to question the worth of his poetry, or any poetry for that matter, in comparison to direct social action, like that of his friend and gang member, Psycho Loco, and the Gun Totin' Hooligans. At this point, Gunnar describes his poetry as "little more than an opiate devoted to pacifying his cynicism" (1996, 131). He questions whether poetry can really do anything, especially in comparison to Psycho Loco's direct actions: "The day of the L.A. riots I learned that it meant nothing to be a poet. One had to be a poet and a farmer, a poet and a roustabout, a poet and soon-to-be revolutionary" (1996, 132). Consequently Gunnar begins to act in morally questionable ways, participating in the looting during the riots and having no remorse for doing so whatsoever and experiencing little repercussions either. Even though he is caught by his father, the police officer, Gunnar's only punishment is being transferred to a predominately white school in the San Fernando Valley.

As Gunnar's basketball stardom rises, so does his confidence, to the point of arrogance. At his new mostly white school in the San Fernando Valley, unlike his experiences in Santa Monica, Gunnar no longer feels so insubstantial. Unlike the other African American students whom Gunnar describes as performing for the whites "with vaudevillian panache, like adolescent interlocutors entertaining the troops back from the Rhine," Gunnar has learned "that I wasn't in arrears to the white race. No matter how much I felt indebted to the white folks, I owed them nothing" (1996, 154–55). Whereas the old Gunnar hid his intellectual interests, this new Gunnar no longer cares if other people think he is overly studious. In short he no longer cares so much about fitting in and spends much of his time (outside of basketball practice) reading in the library. It is doubtful Gunnar would have found this level of confidence had it not been for his basketball celebrity, which explains why athletics has become so important in the African American community: it is one of the only ways to reach a point at which one can do what one wants without having one's supposed authenticity as an African American constantly put to the test. Unfortunately only a tiny fraction of African Americans are in Gunnar's enviable position.

Gunnar's studies also pay off in that he does extremely well on his college-entrance exams and thereby garners attention from major universities such as Harvard. However, it is doubtful that the schools actively recruit him mainly for his intellectual abilities and accomplishments. Rather, while Gunnar and Beatty do not directly state so anywhere in the novel, it is probable that Gunnar garners such attention from prominent universities because he is African American in addition to being a basketball star. As the college recruiters[3] visit Gunnar to try to get him to enroll in their school, Beatty critiques the upper echelon of African American intellectual society.

The Harvard recruiter, a member of the civil rights generation, for instance, appears amoral, lacking fortitude, and seemingly tries to forsake his identity as an African American. This is immediately evident in that he "moved west to Los Angeles to set up a think tank of mulatto social scientists called High Yellow Fever" (1996, 157). Revealing his predilection for Asian over African culture, he also takes Gunnar to a Hawaiian restaurant, thus showing the ease to which he denies or subverts his racial identity. He is an unabashed elitist, having written a book called *Antebellum Cerebellum: A History of Negro Super-Genius*. He likes soulless white music performed by black musicians. Gunnar fears that he would turn out the same way were he to attend to Harvard: "After one listen to 'Surrey with the Fringe on Top,' I'd pretty much decided I wasn't going to Harvard" (1996, 157). Furthermore the recruiter admits that he would get a sizeable finder's fee if he convinces Gunner to attend Harvard. He also tries to get Gunnar to become coldly materialistic and to forsake less-privileged African Americans as well as the larger African American community: "Those poor people are beyond help, you must know that. The only reason I and others of my illustrious ilk pretend to help those folks is to reinforce the difference between them and us" (1996, 159). Clearly Beatty is critical of Harvard, which may have some real-life basis, because Beatty attended Boston University as does Gunnar.

Boston University appeals more to Gunnar because the university seems rebellious in its attempt to buckle the academic and corporate system. The BU recruiter says, "A couple of months back, the Massachusetts lottery was up to five hundred million dollars. The trustees of BU decided to buy thirteen million dollars' worth of lottery tickets, figuring if they covered every possible number combination they would at least win their money back, if not more. As luck would have it, BU was the sole winner. A little hush money in the right pockets, a few well-publicized millions to each member school, and Boston University is in the Ivy League" (1996, 161).

At BU, Gunnar attends only a creative-writing class when he is there, probably a result of his basketball stardom. Gunnar has become relatively famous because of his poetry, and he is known as a street poet, even though a good deal of his poetry has classical allusions and Gunnar grew up mostly in affluent Santa Monica. This suggests that a hip-hop-generation writer, especially a poet, has become almost synonymous with "street poet," even if that may not be an accurate description. Thereby, even in academics, an area supposedly above pre-judgments, there continue to be stereotypes of African Americans and the hip-hop generation. Indeed the ultraliberal, politically correct, creative-writing-class students embrace Gunnar because they assume he is an authentic street poet, which he is not. One such class member who embraces him is a white woman who is named Negritude, a product of extremely liberal but patronizing parents who named her that so she "would be a reminder of the hagiocratic innocence possessed by black people around the world" (1996, 179). With Negritude, Beatty mocks extreme liberalism as ultimately counterproductive for African Americans. This is evident when even though Gunnar's class encourages him to publish a book of his poetry, they also begin to treat him as a poetic demigod. Both of these help lead to Gunnar's catastrophic ascension to collectively destructive African American leader.

Gradually Gunnar and Nick become disillusioned with basketball, realizing that they are merely entertainers for a white audience. Inspired by his wife, a mail-order bride named Yoshiko, who, Psycho Loco "ordered" for Gunnar, given Gunnar's failures and fears of women, Gunnar begins reading Japanese literature. One writer particularly affects him: Yukio Mishima. According to Gunnar, "Mishima said that to reach a level of consciousness that permits one to peek at the divine, one must sacrifice individual idealism" (1996, 191). From this Gunnar begins to develop a political philosophy beyond himself, a big step for a member of the hip-hop generation but in this case a misguided step as well. Meanwhile, Nick becomes hounded by people who are trying to figure out why he cannot miss, having "thrown every theory, every formula, every philosophical dogma out of whack" (1996, 192). Philosophers hope he will miss, but he does not, and Gunnar thinks, "They would be a lot better off if they simply called Scoby a god and left it at that, but no way they'll proclaim a skinny black man God" (1996, 192). Rather, most of the time the crowd is against them because they cannot stand Nick's perfection.

Still, despite its drawbacks and imperfections, Beatty demonstrates that basketball is a way to create solidarity among African Americans. As Gunnar describes, "When we played Columbia, I swear, all of Harlem was in the gym. They were quiet except when one of us scored; they could give less than a care who won. Remember at the Harvard game, black folk from as far away as Peabody and Scituate were in the house. I bet the Harvard kids didn't even know so many niggers existed" (1996, 193). The problem is that the community that basketball engenders is short lived and does not extend outside the basketball court. It also does not have any broader social goals or purpose and can create animosity or rivalry against competing teams and fans of competing teams. Gunnar also begins to realize that all of the energy directed towards basketball could be redirected into something more socially important and/or uplifting for the African American community.

Certainly there are members of the hip-hop generation who are politically and socially active, but in *The White Boy Shuffle*, Beatty satirically portrays them as superficial. Gunnar soon discovers that the standard political outlets for African Americans in the Boston area, like a citywide black student union called Ambrosia, are largely ineffectual. "I purposely arrived late at the gathering," Gunnar says. "Harvard, BU, MIT Negroes were wearing loud African garb over their Oxford shirts and red suspenders, drinking ginger beer, and using their advertising skills to plan how best to package the white man's burden" (1996, 183). At the meeting, they boast that they are courageously fighting a race war, but they actually do little or nothing. For instance one member, Dexter, ridiculously insists that the way to racial improvement is through fashion, with little educational lessons printed on clothes. Another equally ineffectual group is Concoction, "an organization of mixed-race kids who felt ostracized by both white and colored students" and who want to "celebrate . . . ethnic hybridization" (1996, 186). In truth Concoction is a self-serving group; they have no political agenda but only seek to make themselves feel better. On the other hand, Beatty satirizes white campus liberalism in the guise of SWAPO, "Spoiled Whities Against Political Obsequiousness" (1996, 187). That they are ineffectual can be seen in that they have only one black member—Gunnar—who claims to come only for the marijuana they provide: "No one could possibly care enough to be treated like a baby seal. Colored people are not mascots for your political attitudes" (1996, 187). Indeed their sit-ins and rhetoric achieve nothing, except maybe to allow the white students to feel less guilty about their wealth and privilege.

All of these political groups, be they run by African Americans, whites, or those of mixed ethnicity, are politically ineffectual, leading Gunnar to want to try his hand at socially charged politics. This begins when Gunnar speaks at a rally to extremely enthusiastic fans of his poetry. Gunnar denigrates the audience, even other African Americans, claiming that they are ignorant. He asks them if they have ever before looked at what was on the Martin Luther King Jr. statue. He yells out, "You motherfuckers pass by that ugly-ass sculpture every day. You hang your coats on it, open beer bottles on it, meet your hot Friday night dates there, now here you are talking about freedom this and whitey putting-shit-in-the-game that and you don't even know what the plaque says? Shit could read 'Sieg Heil! Kill All Niggers! Auslander Raus!' for all you know, stupid motherfuckers, African-Americans, my ass. Middle minorities caught between racial polarities, please. Caring, class-conscious progressive crackers, shit. Selfish apathetic humans like everyone else" (1996, 199). Even though he berates them, the crowd still embraces Gunnar, possibly because they have low opinions of themselves, or they only respond to the fervor of his passion without paying attention to what he's really saying. As it turns out, the plaque contains a real quote from King: "If a man hasn't discovered something he's willing to die for, he isn't fit to live," and Gunnar asks, rather rhetorically, if any of them are willing to die for South Africa or anything else, and no one rises up (1996, 199–200). He claims the problem with current African American political leaders and along with them the entire hip-hop generation is that nowadays no one has anything they are willing to die for, but they did during the civil rights movement. Gunnar declares, "What we need is some new leaders. Leaders who won't apostatize like cowards. Some niggers who are ready to die!" (1996, 200).

Gunnar's speech goes over well in an alarming way, because people begin taking his message seriously and interpret it as a call to start committing suicide, which to some extent, it is. Twisting Gandhi and King's philosophy of nonviolent resistance into violent self-destruction, Gunnar claims that suicide is not giving in but defeating the enemy. However, in claiming this, he has now become a veritable Uncle Tom in the tradition of his Kaufman ancestors; Gunnar is misguided in that instead of fighting or sacrificing for a cause or fighting against the established white power structure, they surrender through suicide. Gunnar's uncertain mental state is seen when Nick asks Gunnar if he's really serious about suicide, and he expresses some hesitancy, "I guess so. I meant everything I said, but that don't mean shit, you know. Don't mean I'm right, wrong. The poems, the magazine interviews are just words, man. I'm just saying, Look, I'm outta here, all you motherfuckers who act like you give a shit— stop me, you care so much" (1996, 204). In actuality Gunnar wants to be accepted and loved by the African American community. That no one cares enough to stop him or anyone else shows serious problems and/or failings in the African American community. The power of Gunnar's rhetoric is such that it convinces Nick to commit suicide but not Gunnar himself—he and Yoshiko move back to Los Angeles while the mass suicides continue. Inspired by Gunnar, they write poems just before they die in response to small prejudicial or racist acts like a checkout clerk who refuses to place change in a black woman's hands or when a white principle asks an author if she would sing an old Negro song (1996, 213). The reasons for the suicides, Beatty suggests, are repressed anger and self-loathing in the African American community, exacerbated by living in a country that tends to think of itself as egalitarian (as opposed to the pre–civil rights era). Rather than act on these emotions by speaking out or confronting whites, which they feel they cannot do—whether this is a result of perceived powerlessness or the commonly held belief that American society is largely unprejudiced—they internalize these corrosive feelings, which eventually leads to literal self-destruction.

These latent, corrosive feelings are shown in what Gunnar helps inaugurate through a Friday night ritual in which "we held outdoor open mikes, called the Black Bacchanalian MiseryFests" (1996, 219). In addition to singing, dancing, poetry, and car shows at the MiseryFests, the African American audience complains about being stigmatized in some way. While no doubt some if not most of the complaints are legitimate, it becomes counterproductive in that they only focus on the problems of racial oppression, not the solutions. The MiseryFests begin to be broadcast on television, and they become popular not so much for their content but for their potential spectacle. That is, viewers think that Gunnar might commit suicide on live TV, especially on the two-year anniversary of Nick's death. Although Gunnar does not do that, he does cut off his pinky in homage to one of his Japanese mafia, or Yakuza. He describes the reaction his act gets from the public: "That night cemented my status as savior of the blacks. The distraught minions interpreted my masochistic act as sincerity, the media as lunacy. The more I tried to deny my ascendancy, the more beloved I became. Spiteful black folks and likeminded others from across the nation continue to immigrate to Hillside, seeking mass martyrdom" (1996, 223). It does not take much, Beatty suggests, for African Americans to collectively destroy themselves, as they live in a society that is already slowly destroying them. In response to the collective suicides, "Congress passed a motion to quell our insurrection by issuing an ultimatum: rejoin the rest of America or celebrate Kwanzaa in hell. The response was to paint white concentric circles on the roots of the neighborhood, so that from the air Hillside looks like one big target, with La Cienega Motor Lodge and Laundromat [where Gunnar and Yoshiko are staying] as the fifty-point bull's-eye" (1996, 224). We never find out for certain whether the targeting of Gunnar is successful.

The epilogue begins just after this description. Gunnar proclaims, "It's time to go. . . . Black America has relinquished its needs in a world where expectations are illusion, has refused to develop ideals and mores in a society that applies principles without principles" (1996, 225). He suggests that the past African American movements have withered away and had no staying power. While there may be some truth to that, we cannot confuse Gunnar's rhetoric with Beatty's as Gunnar is essentially a hypocrite because has no real desire to commit suicide himself. Rather, he mostly stays in the motel with his wife, infant daughter, and mother. When Psycho Loco asks Gunnar why he does not fight back, Gunnar suggests it's useless. He believes he cannot beat the white-dominated system and does not want to give it the satisfaction of killing him:

"The trippy part is that when you think of it, me and America aren't even enemies. I'm the horse pulling the stagecoach, the donkey in the levee who's stumbled in the mud and come up lame. You may love me, but I'm tired of thrashing
around in the muck and not getting anywhere, so put a nigger out of his mis-
ery" (1996, 226). Beatty suggests that this self-defeatist philosophy ultimately
can be the death knell for African American progress.

The novel ends with Gunnar passing the Kaufman torch by telling his
infant daughter their family history, including about his father's recent suicide
and the poem he left.

> Like the good Reverend King
> I too "have a dream,"
> but when I wake up
> I forget it and
> remember I'm running late for work
> (1996, 226)

The poem leaves a sense, common to writers of the hip-hop generation, that
despite the progress since the civil rights movement, the idea that there is racial
equality in contemporary America is a dangerous chimera. In reality people are
not fully judged by the content of their character but still, at least in part, by
the color of their skin. *The White Boy Shuffle* provides no clear hope that this
will change but leaves the frightening thought that in contemporary America,
the greatest threat to the African American community may be from certain
segments of their own population who have become so twisted by frustration,
anger, and prejudice that, like Gunnar, they can become the catalysts for collective self-destruction. The hope Beatty provides in the novel is through awareness of the problems. Most of all, *The White Boy Shuffle* can be seen as a wake-up
call to contemporary American society, the African American community, and
the hip-hop generation, emphasizing the need to change focus from the personal and immediate to the social and lasting as well as emphasizing the importance of recognizing that prejudice and racism directed towards African
Americans still exist implicitly and explicitly in this country.

In contrast to the rather bleak ending of *The White Boy Shuffle,* Beatty's next
novel, *Tuff* (2000), is more of a playful, uplifting account of the life of a quintessential member of the hip-hop generation, one Winston "Tuffy" Foshay, a
twenty-two-year-old, 320-pound Harlem gangster. Tuffy, as he is commonly
called, is almost a polar opposite to Gunnar. Whereas Gunnar is book smart but
rather cowardly, Tuffy is street smart and fearless, possibly based on deceased
hip-hop icon, Biggie Smalls, whom Beatty paraphrases in the epigraph to the

novel. Beatty describes Tuffy's face as being "so impenetrable, so full of East Harlem inscrutable cool is his expression that usually even he doesn't know what
he's thinking" (2000, 3). The novel begins after a drug deal gone bad in which
the rather cynical and amoral Tuffy, who works as a menacing bodyguard and
money collector, barely escapes being shot and killed. Beatty describes Tuffy's
job as merely to "answer the door, look mean and yell: 'Pay this motherfucker,
now!' to the balky customers" (2000, 7).

Despite his inscrutable exterior, Tuffy, toward the beginning of the novel, is
not more than a façade of toughness, an emblem of the hip-hop generation.
Although he is married to Yolanda and has an infant son, Bryce Extraordinaire,
whom they call Jordy, he rarely pays much attention to either, not because he
does not care about them but because he has trouble showing his emotions or
is reluctant to show them, which is a typical attitude of the hip-hop generation.
In an environment in which romance is a sign of vulnerability that is to be
avoided at all costs, Tuff cannot or does not express his emotions. Tuffy met
Yolanda when she worked as a cashier at Burger King, and the only "date" they
ever had was a boat tour around Manhattan one Christmas Eve (2000, 33). Still,
this is not to suggest that Tuffy is without his charms and positive attributes.
Yolanda likes Tuffy because she believes him to be inherently honest and
thereby trustworthy (2000, 36). In addition he also possesses some strong natural intelligence. He enjoys watching foreign art-house films and claims with
some insight that mainstream films are predictable in the sense that they tend
to be suspense movies focused on determining who the killer is and/or are
merely sexually titillating. He tells his friend Fariq that if the lead actor is a
man, particularly if the actor is white, "then the film has to be about right and
wrong"; Tuffy insists, "Whiteys is [sic] the last motherfuckers on earth to be
teaching me about right and wrong. Much less charging me for the lesson"
(2000, 98). This is not to suggest that Tuffy's ideas about his own possible films
are much more substantial, for his main idea for a Hollywood blockbuster is
Cap'n Crunch—the Movie in which the Cap'n, played by Danny DeVito, would
be "sailing on an ocean of milk, having adventures and shit" (2000, 63). However, it is conceivable that such a movie could be commercially successful, and
Tuffy, like many mainstream hip-hop performers, is more interested in immediate monetary success and entertainment rather than intellectual depth
(which usually does not sell very well).

To a large degree, Beatty implicates American society for excluding Tuffy and
along with him a sizable portion of the hip-hop generation and thereby helping
to steer him into a life of crime. From an early age, Tuffy did not take well to
school because for him, "Language was an extension of his soul. And if his
speech, filled with double negatives, improper conjugations of the verb to be,

and pluralized plurals (e.g., womens) was wrong, then his thoughts were wrong" (2000, 104). Beatty also charges the civil rights generation with contributing to Tuffy's delinquency. He grew up under the less-than-illustrious shadow of his former Black Panther father, Clifford, who in later years becomes a poet. Even Clifford admits there has been some deterioration in the African American community over recent years. When an intervention is scheduled to help steer Tuffy onto the right path, Clifford is extremely skeptical, claiming that an intervention would not have been necessary during the civil rights era because "Things was [*sic*] together. The community raised the children" (2000, 107).

A black nationalist, Afrocentrist, and quintessential civil-rights-generation member, Clifford wants Tuffy to develop into a "strong black man . . . a descendant of African aristocracy" (2000, 108). However, to Tuffy, his father's Afrocentrism and civil-rights-era dogma are nothing more than empty rhetoric that does nothing to ameliorate the conditions he must face in the inner city. For his own part, Tuffy is very skeptical of his father's Black Panther–like friends, who he thinks are just freeloaders. Beatty lightly ridicules Clifford as a foppish performer who gives poetry readings "resplendent in a Bengal tiger-patterned djellaba, topped off with an intricately woven macrame kufi, accessorized with wooden beads and yellowed lion's teeth" (2000, 128). Despite his self-righteous, politically charged demeanor, Clifford's poetry is actually self-serving, mainly autobiographical, glorifying his own rather-feeble political activism and personal life. In that, Beatty critiques the Black Nationalist and Afrocentrist movements as often devolving into insubstantial self-serving and hollow exercises. Although it might seem that Clifford is more admirable than Tuffy, for at least Clifford is somewhat idealistic, it is Tuffy, not Clifford, who wants to change his life for the better, and it is Tuffy who ultimately grows somewhat of a moral conscience. In that, Beatty displays that the two generations are similar in purpose but that the potential for change lies mostly in the hands of the hip-hop generation, in part because they are younger and also because they have more to gain.

After nearly losing his life in a drug deal gone bad, Tuffy decides that he wants to turn his life around by getting a Big Brother (2000, 44). Unlike his father, who believes he knows most everything about life and people, Tuffy comes to the conclusion that he is looking for a mentor with answers, because "I don't understand nothing about life, me—nothing" (2000, 99). This, Beatty suggests, is the first positive step towards change: admitting one's limitations and lack of knowledge rather than arrogantly and mistakenly claiming that one knows most everything. Despite his age (twenty-two), Tuffy actually does get a Big Brother, albeit one he did not expect: an African American rabbi whose name is Spencer Thockmorton.

As with *The White Boy Shuffle, Tuff* is a conflicted portrayal of Judaism. While on the one hand, Beatty portrays Spencer as rather naïve and weak in his attempt to deny his ethnic or racial roots, it is Spencer (along with Tuffy's friend/mentor Inez) who ultimately helps Tuffy begin to turn his life around for the better. Unlike Tuffy, Spencer is a product of an upper-middle-class African American household, and it is because of his privileged upbringing, Beatty suggests, that he comes to abandon or forsake his African American cultural roots and thereby dissociates from the larger African American community. Beatty tells us that Spencer finds it a "mystery" why the media devotes a significant amount of time looking at "the crisis of the black family" (2000, 80). It is a mystery to Spencer because he does not conceive of or fully realize the additional problems of discrimination, poverty, and racism that affect African American families. At college, Spencer dates a Jewish woman and claims that he only feels African American when he looks at his hands. Spencer converts to Judaism when he plans to marry the woman. When their relationship ends, and he has little other career possibilities, he enrolls in a rabbinical school. Once he becomes a rabbi, Spencer is readily accepted by the larger New York community, because they now view him as harmless (in contrast to their preconceived notions of the hip-hop generation as thugs). Because Spencer is often "the only black friend of many of the city's political organizations," whom often are completely disassociated from the larger African American community, organizational leaders typically approach Spencer to see if he knows any "like-minded and like-tempered black folks for those high-paying display-window positions for which qualified black candidates were invariably hard to find" (2000, 85). Despite his initial skepticism, Tuffy decides to keep Spencer around because with Spencer, "He'd have a person in his life to whom he wasn't emotionally attached." (2000, 101). Tuffy comes to think that Spencer might be able to function as "an impartial voiceover that would cut through the white noise of Yolanda's bickering, Fariq's proselytizing, and Ms. Nomura's good intentions" (2000, 101).

In contrast to Spencer is Tuffy's friend, the paralyzed wheelchair-bound Fariq, an active member of the Nation of Islam. While Spencer seems hollow and rather insubstantial, Fariq is a rather unsympathetic anti-Semite who engages in verbal battles with Spencer: "The jew is the black man's unnatural enemy. . . . Wherever he goes, the Jew be [*sic*] stirring up trouble" (2000, 93–94). The third wheel in Tuffy's sphere of influence is Inez, the Japanese head of a Harlem school. She became mesmerized by Harlem in the 1960s and moved there in order to work for Malcolm X. After he dies, Inez decides to found a community center in Harlem and seeks out "the next Malcolm" (2000, 68). She comes to believe, quite idealistically, that Tuffy might be the one. All of these characters hold unrealizable expectations for Tuffy. Inez wants him to become a political leader in the manner of Malcolm X, just as a civil-rights-generation member might. Spencer wants him to covert to Judaism and lead a normal life. Fariq wants Tuffy to hate but emulate Jews by becoming coldly materialistic. Neither approach ends up being the right one for Tuffy, but he does decide to follow Inez's lead, to some extent, by running for city council.

It has been suggested that one of the failings of the hip-hop generation and of contemporary hip-hop music as well is its lack of political agency. Tuffy's rise to become a political candidate is improbable yet signifies how the hip-hop generation could conceivably change its society should the members become more politically active. At first, Tuffy, considering other employment, thinks of running for city council as a kind of joke, but gradually he becomes more serious about it, at first because he desires the power, but as time progresses, he begins to see outside himself, probably for the first time in his life. Instead of merely gagging when going into buildings with nonfunctioning sewer systems, he begins to ponder what or who might be responsible for these abysmal conditions. He is "stupefied" when realizing that along his neighborhood block, "abandoned dwellings outnumbered occupied ones by two to one" (2000, 133).

Tuffy is quite politically naïve, and in part, Beatty's aim is to show, through Tuffy, the political naïveté of the hip-hop generation. Tuffy admits that the only things he knows about politics he learned from television, specifically *School-house Rock*. Furthermore his ideas are somewhat simplistic. A kind of libertarian, Tuffy wants his neighborhood to become a "paradise ex nihilo, an idyllic shtetl of midnight swimming holes and hassle-free zones where denizens would be free to 'drug, fuck, suck, and thug' to their heart's delight" (2000, 138). However, such a community would quickly descend into chaos and extreme violence. Still, Tuffy has noble ambitions as well. He also wants a community in which "children would never have to know what it is to eat sugar sandwiches for breakfast, frozen broccoli for lunch, and sit down to dinners of Spam, canned corn, and moldy pieces of bread" (2000, 138).

Even Tuffy realizes the rather flippant and cynical manner in which most of his African American peer group regard politics and/or any authority figures. He therefore decides that he wants to start a new political faction, which he calls "A Party" because he believes, with good reason, that his apolitical and rather hedonistic hip-hop-generation peers would like that name and thereby vote for him. Tuffy's promotional posters are clearly aimed at a more anarchical audience as one says that he is "ambivalent on drugs, guns, and alcohol in the community" and frequently repeats that he is "anti-cop"; they include a menacing picture of Tuffy underneath a caption, "a scary motherfucker" (2000, 172). Being a candidate makes Tuffy somewhat more politically engaged. Ironically, in order to garner support, he gets himself thrown in a jail for a misdemeanor. There he gives a speech to the inmates, presumably the first political speech of his life. He describes the disparity in the judicial system between African Americans and whites, concluding that African Americans are "treated like animals" (2000, 181). Tuffy's animosity is directed not towards just whites and authority figures but also towards affluent African Americans such as the black golfers he sees when he goes to New Jersey.

Beatty portrays politics in a rather cynical manner in the novel. After publicity from Spencer, who writes a three-part article about Tuffy and his campaign, Tuffy gets an increasing amount of attention from American third parties. Despite what they say, these parties seem to have little commitment to the African American community and/or in improving existing racial inequalities. Their overtures of multiculturalism are hollow, as they are ultimately fatalistic—"Race was a dead-end issue," and "No matter what you do, racism will still be, if not prevalent, at least present" (2000, 211). Tuffy comes up against the rampant apathy of his peer group. For instance, at one point, in a half-hearted effort to get some votes, Tuffy tells some young, voting-age African Americans, "I ain't saying waste your vote on me, because I ain't the somebody that give [sic] a fuck, but you need to vote for somebody" (2000, 230). However, they are resistant, not wanting to be part of the system that they distrust or despise and not wanting to show emotion or concern because to do either would be interpreted as weakness by those around them.

As the novel progresses, Beatty's sympathies lie more with Tuffy, who begins to appear like a refreshing, honest alternative to the other rather phony-seeming characters, such as the incumbent, civil-rights-generation member German Jordan, who is a professor, astronaut, and writer, among other things, but whose approach seems hackneyed and uninspired, always delivering the same speech regardless of circumstance or audience. He is unrealistic in his desire to have people get beyond race in his insistence that Christianity is virtually a universal panacea (2000, 234–35). To Beatty, Jordan is a sellout, representing all that the hip-hop generation has come to despise about the civil rights generation. In contrast Tuffy does not try to inflate himself. He begins his speech by calling himself a motherfucker and then quickly calling his audience the same name. Astutely though, Tuffy tells the audience that if they truly want to support disadvantaged youth as they claim, then they should vote for him because he is not only in that group but is trying to make his life better (and presumably the lives of others). He asks them, "Now that you have a brother like me by the scruff of the neck, what you going to do with him?" (2000, 236). He tells them that unlike the other candidates, he is part of the community, knows people there, and is more committed to those people: "Imagine Jordan, Ms. Tellos,

Mr. Cienfuegos, Ms. Cox goin' to the hospital with you to watch your uncle die of AIDS, posting your bail, writing you letters while you upstate, sending commissary money, defending you on the street. Shit I've done for and with many of the sons, daughters, and grandchildren of many folks that's up in here tonight" (2000, 237). Tuffy's tactics seem to work, as at the conclusion of the debate, it becomes clear "from the number of strangers wishing him good luck come Tuesday, that Winston had won over a few of the electorate's more cynical voters" (2000, 238).

That is not enough to win Tuffy the election, but he comes close. In that, he has succeeded in turning his life around to some degree. This is seen earlier: when voting, Tuffy does vote for candidates with Jewish surnames, which indicates that Spencer has had some influence upon him (2000, 252). "For a grassroots campaign in a community with no grass, Team Tuffy had done well," mentor Inez says. "Now all that had to be done was to make sure Tuffy would live to see his twenty-third summer" (2000, 259). Tuffy, as Inez realizes, has a difficult road ahead of him. With no immediate job prospects and few marketable skills (if any), he will be tempted to go back to his criminal activities. Because he does fail in his political endeavor, he might give up being concerned about anyone else except for himself and his family. This, Beatty suggests, is one of the main dilemmas facing the hip-hop generation: how to create a community out of a group of people who, believing that they live in a dog-eat-dog world, feel they can only have allegiance to themselves and possibly their family or gang. While Beatty provides no exact solutions, Tuffy's story is a somewhat optimistic one in that he does end up changing for the better, with a little help from his friends.

5

Danzy Senna, author of the novels *Caucasia* (1998) and *Symptomatic* (2004), was born in 1970 in Boston. Senna received a bachelor's degree from Stanford University and an MFA from the University of California at Irvine (Arias 2002, 447). The daughter of a Bostonian white woman of WASP heritage and a Louisiana man of mixed African and Mexican heritage, Senna says, "Unlike people who are automatically classified as black or white, my race has always been up for debate. I am forever having to explain to people why it is that I look so white for a black girl, why it is my features don't reveal my heritage." Senna adds that she chose to self-identify as African American because in her home-town of Boston in the 1970s, "there were only two choices for me: black and white." Her decision was all but made for her by her parents whom she describes as "smitten with the black-power politics of the time" (1998, "Passing," 76). Senna's novels largely concern the difficulties that multiethnic hip-hop-generation members face, and she concurrently deconstructs the categories and notions of race. Caught between two ethnic groups, along with their respective expectations, but unable to fit in with either and not satisfied with the multiethnic or multicultural movement, Senna's characters often try to find places beyond race, a kind of postracial or postethnic condition.

Senna's first novel, *Caucasia*, focuses on ethnic hybridity in post–civil rights America. It was highly praised by critics such as Donna Seaman, who describes the novel as "thematically and dramatically rich as fiction be, infused, as it is with emotional truth" (1998, 985). No doubt, Senna has much in common with the narrator/protagonist of *Caucasia*, Birdie Lee, who is likewise ethnically mixed and reared in Boston. However, *Caucasia* is a work of fiction whose importance lies in Senna's descriptive and theoretical categorization of racial construction and identity. At a time in which an increasing number of Americans (especially members of the hip-hop generation) hail from ethnically mixed backgrounds and/or are exposed to different cultures through popular culture, one of the most pressing questions has become: How much, if at all, does or should racial or ethnic identity mean in America? Furthermore one of the important questions facing postsegregation society is to what extent should ethnicity or race play a role in determining a person's identity? To explore these questions, it is helpful to consider the plight of the ethnically or racially mixed persons because they are situated on the borders between ethnicities. Thereby, they are at once able to see and experience both or a number of perspectives. Furthermore, with a growth in the number of interracial couples and their progeny in America (and globally), the increased presence of the ethnically mixed threatens the legitimacy of racial and ethnic categories.

Although not a utopian text, *Caucasia* envisions alternatives to racial categorization by championing post–ethnic identity divorced from race. At the same time, Senna argues that race is more performative than biological, impeding identity more than elucidating it. By centering on a racially mixed young woman and her family, *Caucasia* complicates and deconstructs the black/white binary and challenges multicultural theory. In exploring the boundaries of race, Senna also participates in the contemporary backlash against race as determining identity and community. This is especially evident in Alvin Schmidt's *Menace of Multiculturalism* (1997) and David Hollinger's *Postethnic America* (1995), but it is also evident in the work of Cornel West who, in *Prophetic Reflections* (1993), calls "into question the prevailing myths perpetrated by both the so-called Eurocentric crowd and the so-called multiculturalist crowd" (125). In the tradition of James W. Johnson's *Autobiography of a Colored Man* (1912), Nella Larsen's *Passing* (1929), and Langston Hughes's "Passing" (1934), *Caucasia* is a hip-hop-generation, post-passing novel, arguing that race itself is performative and considers the possibilities for its gradual effacement.

According to Lacanian theory, a child first develops a sense of individual identity during the "mirror stage," at which time the child begins to perceive of him- or herself as possessing a separate identity from other people (usually his/her parents). In *Caucasia*, Birdie Lee (as well as her entire family to some extent) passes back and forth between a series of mirror stages, never cementing her identity. At the beginning of the novel, Birdie announces, "Before I ever saw myself, I saw my sister. When I was still too small for mirrors, I saw her as the reflection that proved my own existence" (1998, 5). A person who defines herself in contrast with others, Birdie forms a self-enclosed binary opposition with her darker sister, Cole. Birdie does not perceive herself as being a distinct person until she realizes that her sister looks significantly different than her. As Birdie ages, she only becomes conscious of her racial identity when she sees other ethnically mixed people. When she is amid ethnically homogenous groups, she becomes a chameleon, taking on the attributes of the majority in order to protect herself from being ostracized or from social scorn. To a large extent, Birdie never feels entirely comfortable anywhere except when she is alone. She is damned and blessed by her outsider status, which allows her to peer beyond race and ethnicity.

Caucasia begins in liminal, 1970s, post–civil rights Boston, which "still came in black and white, yellowing around the edges" (1998, 1). Senna portrays Birdie and Cole's parents, Deck and Sandy Lee, as well-intentioned but ultimately naïve baby boomers, products of the civil rights movement, who believe that they can raise their children free of racism, possibly even divorced of an ethnic and racial identity as well. In a sense, the intellectual Deck and Sandy become involved and have children to disprove accepted theories of ethnicity and to prove their own rather than out of genuine love for one another. Birdie notes that Deck "liked to joke to his friends that Cole and I were going to be proof that race mixing produced superior minds, the way a mutt is always more intelligent than a purebred dog" (1998, 26). Later in the novel, Gideon, an old friend of Deck, calls Sandy and Deck "mad scientists" and their children "experiments" (1998, 349). Deck and Sandy's "experiments" include educating Cole and Birdie at home and exposing them at an extremely young age to different religions and sophisticated texts such as Frantz Fanon's *Black Skin, White Masks*.

Senna goes to great lengths in describing Sandy and Deck when they meet, and rightly so, for she shows how both are involved in the process of passing and are, to a large extent, changelings such as Birdie. Thereby, she argues that passing is more of a general phenomenon; it is not necessarily race specific. In a flashback, Senna describes Sandy as an awkward, isolated, overweight teenager who feels alienated. Sandy meets Deck the year after she graduates from high school, a year she spends at home trying to determine her identity and future career. Senna notes, "Her interests were literature, existentialism, and the Holocaust" (1998, 32). Meanwhile, Deck, a student in a course taught by Sandy's father at Harvard, and Sandy meet at a cafe when she is with her father. According to Senna, "She had no particular interest in Negroes at this time—not in them or in their cause" (1998, 34). However, Sandy soon becomes involved with Deck and, more important, becomes passionately involved with the civil rights movement. Deck helps give her a sense of identity as a white revolutionary, which, in turn, gives substance to her less-justifiable feelings of alienation as a privileged white woman. It is an identity that Sandy can never relinquish because it gives her a perceived sense of social significance and importance. Although the extent to which Sandy is truly a revolutionary, renegade, and/or criminal is never completely verified or denied, it is doubtful that Sandy is as much of a hunted woman as she believes herself to be.

As the utopian 1960s deteriorate into the race-conscious 1970s, Deck and Sandy grow distant, and, like many members of the civil rights generation, their utopian ideology is deteriorated by the rampant racially sparked violence in Boston. Like Birdie, Deck is also caught between the white and African American worlds. He becomes more conscious of race and concerned with his own perceived authenticity as an African American male, especially when around others of his ethnicity. Deck's divided loyalty is representative of two primary schools of thought at that time. As Kimberly DaCosta and Rebecca King argue, "Although the biracial baby boom emerged in the context of an integrationist cultural attitude, at the same time a counter-ideology of black cultural nationalism put forth new standards of what it meant to be black and new criteria for authenticity" (1996, 238). Although Deck is not ethnically mixed, he, too, is a changeling. As time goes by, Deck becomes concerned that he is trying to pass as a white intellectual and begins to act differently, especially when he is around other African Americans, like his friend Ronnie. Birdie notices, "My father always spoke differently around Ronnie. He would switch into slang, peppering his sentences with words like 'cat' and 'man' and 'cool.' Whenever my mother heard him talking that way she would laugh and say it was his 'jive turkey act'" (1998, 10). Eventually Deck and Sandy separate, which puts an end to Cole and Birdie's home schooling. Seemingly changing from race effacement to ultra race-consciousness, Deck insists that they attend an all-black school.

The Afrocentric Nkrumah school that Birdie and Cole subsequently attend, a by-product of the civil rights generation, forces them to reconsider their identities. It ends up not being a source of nourishing African culture but a contribution to their feelings that they must perform in order to be accepted. Unlike a traditional passing narrative in which the main character would attempt to pass as white, at the Nkrumah school, Birdie and Cole try to pass as African American and have a difficult time doing so. Though they are technically African American, Birdie and Cole do not behave, dress, or talk in the same ways as their African American classmates, who accuse them of acting and/or wanting to be white. Birdie quickly learns how her lighter skin separates her from Cole, who has a much easier time being accepted. During her first weeks of school, Birdie is taunted and ostracized because of her light skin. Cole escapes for the most part but is also scorned because of her white knees and elbows.[1]

Senna uses Birdie's and Cole's experiences at Nkrumah to criticize the growing rigidity of socially or culturally legislated ethnic identity that has been further perverted by media images in post-1970s America. While the Nkrumah school provides a seemingly empowering atmosphere for its African American student body, that same student body, governed by codes for "black" authentic-ity, does not tolerate ethnic difference. Birdie emphasizes that she "learned the art of changing at Nkrumah," but at the same time, she describes it as "more of a game" (1998, 62). Indeed she and Cole set out to find the rules of the "game." They attempt to decipher the rules of "black authenticity" by reading maga-zines such as *Ebony,* which explains how to speak like an "authentic" African American. Skimming through the magazine, Cole tells Birdie, "They have examples in here. Like, don't say, 'I'm going to the store.' Say, 'I'm goin' to de sto.' Get it? And don't say, 'Tell the truth.' Instead say, 'Tell de troof.' Okay." (1998, 53). Desperate to be accepted, Birdie also buys clothes to match those of the other students and practices her speaking technique in order to make it sound more like that of her classmates: "I stood many nights in front of the bathroom mirror, practicing how to say 'nigger' the way the kids in school did it, dropping the 'er' so that it became not a slur, but a term of endearment: *nigga*" (1998, 62). Birdie's efforts are rewarded as her classmates gradually accept her, once she dresses and talks more like them. However, the lessons she learns "how to become someone else, how to erase the person I was before" make her feel void of a stable core or identity (1998, 62).

While both Cole and Birdie become consumed with passing, their father, Deck, similarly becomes obsessed with achieving a sense of authenticity as an African American male. With Deck, Senna shows how racial pride or solidarity can, in some ways, do more harm than good, for one of the negative aftereffects of Deck's newfound race consciousness is that he gradually ignores Birdie in favor as Cole: "Cole was my father's special one. I understood that even then. She was his prodigy—his young, gifted, and black. . . . Her existence comforted him. She was the proof that his blackness hadn't completely blanched. By his four years at Harvard. By so many years of standing stiffly in corners, listening to those sweatered tow-haired preppies talk about the Negro Problem, nursing their vermouth, glancing at him with so much pleased incredulity in their eyes. . . . He usually treated me with a cheerful disinterest—never hostility or ill will, but with a kind of impatient amusement" (1998, 56). To some extent, Deck's contrasting attitudes toward his daughters on the basis of their skin color are responses to others who have trouble accepting Deck's kinship to Birdie. For instance, when Deck goes to the park with only Birdie and not Cole, he attracts the suspicion of others because of their contrast in skin color. One couple reports them to a police officer, who believes Deck has abducted Birdie and has trouble accepting that she's his daughter, even after Deck shows them his iden-tification and a picture of his entire family in his wallet. This experience further distances him from Birdie and makes him conscious of color and appearance. When Deck drops her off at Sandy's, after the incident, Birdie remembers,

"Usually he kissed me on the top of my head before he said good-bye, but this time he just touched my forehead with the back of his hand, as if he were checking for a fever" (1998, 61).

Deck's response to the frequently mistrusting, glaring eyes of whites is to embrace the African American community and to emphasize and exaggerate his ethnicity, nearly to the point of pantomime. Separated from Sandy, he becomes involved with Carmen, an African American woman. Still, Deck's efforts do seem to give him the interracial acceptance he so desires. Unlike the cold disregard from other African Americans that he would normally get when he was with Sandy, Deck receives and revels in the warm friendliness with which they now regard him and his woman. Playing along, Deck calls Carmen his "brown sugar" when they are in "all-black establishments," and he basks in compliments such as, "That's a fine sister for you, Lee" (1998, 90). Deck's racial performance is an understandable defense mechanism from the perceived threats of the white world, but it is also a selfish act, notable by his complete disregard of how Carmen demeans and ignores Birdie in favor Cole on the basis of skin color. Carmen's treatment has a profound effect upon Birdie: "Others before had made me see the differences between my sisters and myself—the textures of our hair, the tints of our skin, the shapes of our features. But Carmen was the one to make me feel that those things somehow mattered. To make me feel that the differences were deeper than skin" (1998, 91).

Like Carmen, Sandy sometimes treats her daughters differently on the basis of skin color. Sandy "sometimes spoke of Cole as if she had been her only black child," Birdie relates. "It was as if my mother believed that Cole and I were so different. As if she believed I was white" (1998, 275). As much as Sandy prides herself on being color-blind, she also makes scornful, stereotypical comments about WASPs. While they are in New Hampshire, Sandy tells Birdie "how to spot a real WASP from a fake one" and makes a list called "How to Spot a Real WASP," composed of derogatory comments such as "A Real WASP is generally a failure in life," and "A Real WASP speaks with a drunken slur, even when he has had nothing to drink" (1998, 152; 154). At the same time, Senna does not place Birdie upon a moral pedestal. Despite being a casualty of stereotypical attitudes and incomplete categorization, Birdie also harbors stereotypical notions of ethnicity. When in New Hampshire, Birdie writes a short novel, which she calls *El Paso*, about a Mexican American family. Birdie gives television the credit for inspiring her short novel: "I had seen such a family on a news show about alien abductions, and had decided, watching the rowdy, exotic lot, that I wanted to be Mexican. . . . It featured a religious, perpetually pregnant mother; a banjo-playing, sombrero-donning papa; and their teenage son, the main character, Richie Rodriguez, who is a bad seed looking for a way out. Throughout the course of the novel, Richie gets in knife fights, beats and impregnates his girl-friend, and fails out of high school" (1998, 171–72). Sandy praises Birdie's work because Sandy is not able to see how Birdie has interiorized stereotypes about Mexican Americans. Rather, Sandy is so blinded by her purported commitment to fighting racial oppression of African Americans that she can only see racial prejudice towards that one ethnicity.

To a large extent, Sandy's and Deck's performative identities pull them and their family apart more than their perception of societal disdain of their inter-racial relationship. When they decide that Deck will take Cole and Sandy takes Birdie, Senna makes it clear that their tacit agreement is based on color. Deck's purported love for Birdie is not stronger than his newfound racial identity. With his newfound racial nationalism, Deck forsakes America in favor of Brazil, tak-ing Cole and Carmen with him, and he proclaims, "Black people need to start thinking internationally" (1998, 121).

Sandy, whose identity was largely formed after meeting Deck, reverts to see-ing herself as a countercultural revolutionary. Sandy must maintain this iden-tity, for without it, she would feel empty, devoid of purpose or meaning. At first her rebellious behavior manifests itself in childish, performative acts such as shoplifting small items such as candy bars from supermarkets. These acts, how-ever insignificant, are important to Sandy because they allow her to confirm her self-perception as a criminal. Through these acts, she believes she combats the oppressive racist and capitalistic powers that she believes dominate America and that she has come to despise. After Deck and Cole leave for Brazil, Sandy's rebellious behavior transforms into fear that she is in imminent danger of being captured by the federal authorities, a belief that may have some truth to it but is never resolved. Sandy decides that she and Birdie must go on the run and change their identities. To maintain her preferred outsider status, Sandy decides that she and Birdie will take on Jewish identities: Sandy becomes Sheila Gold-man, and Birdie becomes Jesse Goldman.

For the first few months, Sandy/Sheila and Birdie/Jesse go from women's communes to boardinghouses, and Birdie reverts into a Lacanian pre–mirror stage. In hindsight Birdie describes her flight with her mother, "In those years, I felt myself to be incomplete—a gray blur, a body in motion, forever galloping towards completion—half a girl, half-caste, half-mast, and half-baked, not quite ready for consumption. And for me, there was comfort in that state of incom-pletion, a sense that as long as we kept moving, we could go back to what we left behind" (1998, 137).

Birdie later discovers the sense of "completion" is not only an illusion, but it can be destructive in its own way. With time, Birdie feels more vibrant but also devoid of an identity and ethnicity: "At some point during our wanderings, the gypsy life had grown on me. Staying still for too long felt unnatural. I had begun to savor even that moment upon waking up when I had no idea which city we were in, which day of the week it was, even where we had just been the day before. I felt somehow more lucid in that half-waking state, as if that place of timelessness and placelessness and forgetfulness was the only space one could possibly inhabit" (1998, 155). This is Birdie's first movement towards postethnicity, her first recognition that racial constructions are made through comparison with others and are determined by place. Furthermore she becomes aware of how race can be performative, describing their new identities as "like a performance we put on together for the public" (1998, 140).

This realization allows Birdie to see beyond race. In *Neither Black nor White Yet Both,* Werner Sollors argues, "Passing may even lead an individual who succeeds in it to a feeling of elation and exultation, an experience of living as a spy who crosses a significant boundary and sees the world anew from a changed vantage point, heightened by the double consciousness of his subterfuge" (1997, 253). Amidst white people while in New Hampshire (where Birdie and Sandy eventually settle), Birdie, pretending to be Jesse Goldman, sometimes thinks of herself as a spy in the white world, playing a game, fantasizing about giving a report about her experiences but never feeling connected. In her first few months on the road with her mother, Birdie tries to maintain a connection to African American culture by looking at a box of "Negrobilia" that Deck gave her before he left for Brazil. This box contains items such as a "black barbie doll," a James Brown cassette, and the "Black Nativity program from the Nkrumah School" (1998, 127). These consumer items and publicity publications possess little or no real historical or cultural relevance. It is not surprising, then, that by the time they settle in New Hampshire, after about a year on the road, Birdie barely looks at her box of Negrobilia and begins to forget her previous life in Boston as a product of two different cultures and ethnicities.

However, just as at the Nkrumah school, Birdie/Jesse becomes fully aware of her staged identity when her peers surround her at public school in New Hampshire.

> Wandering through them, I felt a yearning that surprised me. Something I hadn't felt at Aurora. A yearning to belong to something ordinary, the same way I had felt at Nkrumah. I looked at these girls with their clownish makeup, their brassy bubble-gum faces, and felt an urge to be one of them. I saw myself from above that first day, saw with a rush of embarrassment what a strange creature I really was: a pitiful creature called Jesse for lack of a better name; a girl who dressed in oversized tomboy clothes, her hair in twin braids, who tapped her fingers against her lips in a rhythmic pattern, a nervous habit that looked like some religious tick. (1998, 220)

At the beginning of their flight, Birdie understandably feels her "real self" remains "frozen solid" within her; now she starts feeling more like Jesse Goldman. Birdie later wonders, "Maybe I had actually become Jesse, and it was this girl, this Birdie Lee who haunted these streets, searching for ghosts, who was the lie. . . . I wondered if whiteness was contagious. If it were, then surely I had caught it. I imagined this 'condition' affected the way I walked, talked, dressed, danced, and at its most advanced stage, the way I looked at the world and at other people" (1998, 329). While it has been argued, "Passing may lead to the higher insight of rising above and looking through the 'veil' of the color line, to an experience of revelation, to seeing while not being seen," if one passes long enough, one's staged identity becomes more real than one's previous identity (Sollors 1997, 253).

Ultimately what jogs Birdie/Jesse into action is encountering an ethnically mixed student, Samantha, who attends the homogeneous New Hampshire school. Birdie sees herself in Samantha, which reminds her that she is passing and of her staged identity. She rummages through her mother's things, finds a postcard to Sandy from Deck's sister, her Aunt Dot, and takes a bus to Boston to try to track down her father and sister. Three to four years of passing make Birdie feel understandably mistrustful and lead to her belief that identity is itself an illusion. Even after Sandy tracks Birdie down at Dot's house, Birdie refuses to go back with her mother: "She was the person in the world who was closest to me, the person who had been my other half all these years. But it hit me now how little I knew about her. In some deep way, she had remained a mystery even to me" (1998, 337). Birdie wonders whether their whole purported flight from the authorities might have been the result of fabrications from her mother's paranoid mind.

The last section of *Caucasia* concerns Birdie's attempt to find her father and sister. In the process, she gravitates towards an identity without ethnicity or racial affiliation. Some critics have called this state "postethnicity," which David Hollinger describes: "Postethnicity prefers voluntary to prescribed affiliations, appreciates multiple identities, pushes for communities of wide scope, recognizes the constructed character of ethno-racial groups, and accepts the formation of new groups as a part of the normal life of a democratic society" (1995, 116). As children, Birdie and Cole make their first strides toward postethnicity by creating their own private, asocial, and aracial language, which they call "Elemeno." Birdie remembers what Cole told her about it, "It wasn't just a language, but a place and a people as well. . . . The Elemenos, she said, could turn not just from black to white, but from brown to yellow to purple to green, and back again. She said they were a shifting people, constantly changing their form, color, pattern, in a quest for invisibility" (1998, 7). Later in the novel, when Deck and Sandy get together in what becomes a strained meeting, Birdie and Cole revert to their old ways, speaking in Elemeno, with Cole "telling me a story about how a girl named Aphrodite who would come and take us away to that land called Elemeno" (1998, 118).

Along similar lines, in Boston, Dot tells Birdie of her own attempts to shed race and ethnicity by fleeing America to India. Birdie recounts Dot's reasoning: "She wanted to go deeper than skin color, deeper than politics, to something more important. Something spiritual. Something she thought she could only find in India" (1998, 313). Dot tells Birdie that she decides to come back to America after hearing black music on the radio, which reminds her of her heritage. However, when Dot returns, she refuses to submit to ethnic categorization. She tells Birdie that she still has "a yearning for some place that doesn't exist. . . . I'm never completely at home anywhere. But it's a good place to be, I think. It's like floating. From up above, you can see everything at once. It's the only way how" (1998, 315). Dot's rejection of race is a brave one, for as DaCosta and King comment, "Most people realize that race is socially constructed, which means that although they know that race is not 'real' in a biological sense, they cannot just refuse to use race as an analytical category, cannot simply individually change what they want race to mean, nor can they ignore that race has very real consequences" (1996, 229).

After a rigorous search, Birdie tracks down her father, who resides in San Francisco, completing his book, "The Petrified Monkey: Race, Blood, and the Origin of Hypocrisy" (1998, 390).[2] Jaded by his experiences in Brazil and realizing his foray into African American nationalism was largely self-serving, Deck scoffs at Birdie when she tells him that she passed as white: "There's no such thing as passing. We're all just pretending. Race is a complete illusion, make-believe. It's a costume. We all wear one. You just switched yours at some point. That's just the absurdity of the whole race game" (1998, 391). Although Birdie believes Deck to be right, she begins to think him "mad" as well when he tells her his theory that "the mulatto in America functions as a canary in the coal mine" and that "likewise, mulattos had historically been the gauge of how poisonous American race relations were" (1998, 393). Deck's overdramatic, overintellectualized theories of race do not resonate with Birdie, whose life has been in one way or another, mediated by race. She angrily asks Deck, "If race is so make-believe, why did I go with Mum? You gave me to Mum 'cause I looked white" (1998, 393). Caught up in his own intellectual pursuits, Deck ignores Birdie's accusation but subtly acknowledges his mistake in favoring Cole when he tells Birdie, "Cole turned out to be as different from me as any child could be" (1998, 394).

Birdie's reunion with her father is bittersweet and pales in comparison with her desire to reunite with her sister, whom she sees as the only person who can

truly understand her plight. Deck takes Birdie to Cole, who lives nearby in Ber-
keley. After an emotional reunion with Cole, Birdie talks to her about her
father's theories about race. They agree that race is a construct, but they both
feel it "exists" (1998, 408). To deny race or the importance of race, as their
father does, just exaggerates the problem, while to obsessively focus on race, as
their mother does, also serves to exacerbate the problem. For Birdie racial identity is merely one form of identity. She realizes that while racial identity is not
necessary, some form of identity is crucial for emotional stability if not survival:
"Everybody had their own way of surviving. My mother had her way, my father
had his, Cole had hers. And then I thought of me, the silent me that was Jesse
Goldman, the one who had not uttered a word, the one who had removed even
her Star of David. It had come so easily to me. I had become somebody I didn't
like. Somebody who had no voice or color or conviction. I wasn't sure that was
survival at all" (1998, 408). The lingering question is whether Birdie can achieve
a satisfying identity divorced from race or ethnicity. Rejecting race, Birdie
learns, can lead to feelings of extreme isolation, paranoia, or possibly madness
in the case of Deck and Sandy, but accepting and amplifying race as the primary
determinant of an individual's identity can nullify a person's identity, which
Birdie comes to believe is by definition fragmented and multiple and in flux.

At the end of *Caucasia*, Senna identifies a middle ground that Birdie has
been gravitating towards, a paradoxically stable condition of postethnicity and
identity in flux. This vision appears at the very end of the novel, at which point
Birdie has just reconciled with Cole and arranged a meeting between the two of
them and her mother for the following summer. Leaving Cole's house, Birdie
sees a bus filled with students of different and mixed ethnicities and experiences a small epiphany.

> They were black and Mexican and Asian and white, on the verge of puberty,
> but not quite in it. They were utterly ordinary, throwing obscenities and
> spitballs at one another the way kids do. One face toward the back of the
> bus caught my eye, and I halted in my tracks, catching my breath. It was a
> cinnamon-skin girl with her hair in braids. She was black like me, a mixed
> girl, and she was watching me from behind the dirty glass. For a second I
> thought I was somewhere familiar and she was a girl I already knew. I began
> to lift my hand, but stopped, remembering where I was and what I had
> already found. Then the bus lurched forward, and the face was gone with it,
> just a blur of yellow and black in motion. (1998, 413)

In this final vision, Birdie learns to look beyond color. She prevents herself from
identifying with the mixed girl who looks like her, and in the process Birdie

rejects racial categorization. The last image of the blurring of colors is a fair representation of Birdie's mindset. Instead of seeing a set color or ethnicity, Birdie sees ethnicity as permeable categories. Blurring of ethnicity is a hallmark of postethnic theory, which "promotes solidarities of wide scope that incorporate people with different racial and ethnic backgrounds" (Hollinger 1995, 3). Birdie is beginning to pass into postethnicity.

Senna leaves it an open question as to whether or to what extent Birdie and Cole will be able to progress in their quest towards postethnicity, but she makes it clear that Birdie has learned how destructive the arbitrary boundaries of race or ethnicity can be. This is a realization that runs contrary to contemporary multicultural theory, which champions the equality of cultures but seeks to keep their boundaries intact. Alvin Schmidt argues, "Multiculturalists are convinced that their philosophy will usher in a new millennium, enabling people to overcome cultural prejudice and discrimination. When prejudiced Americans, for example, finally learn something about cultures, they will drop their prejudices regarding other cultures, races, and ethnic groups" (1997, 17).

Caucasia suggests that ideals of multicultural thought are chimeras, and with the increasing amount of the mixing of races and cultures, it has become progressively difficult if not impossible to determine which cultural phenomenon, if any, "belongs" to an ethnicity. "With our generation, what Black and white Americans want and desire has become more generally American than either Black or white," Bakari Kitwana states. "This is a phenomenon that sociologists long attributed to membership in the middle class, but it is a phenomenon that seems to defy class with our generation" (2002, 113). Indeed *Caucasia* deconstructs the black/white binary, paving the way towards postethnic hybridity and postethnic fiction.

Senna's next novel, *Symptomatic* (2004), continues in the tradition of *Caucasia* by focusing on a hip-hop-generation, multiethnic female protagonist who, similar to Birdie, feels caught between the often-conflicting white and African American worlds. *Symptomatic* is more of a suspense novel than *Caucasia*. In an interview, Senna describes the novel's origin: "I definitely wanted to write something that was hard-edged and kind of minimalist. It was a style that I was drawn to and that fit the atmosphere of the book. I was really influenced and inspired by thrillers" (Weber 2004). The never-named narrator, like Colson Whitehead's never-named protagonist in *Apex Hides the Hurt,* has trouble establishing a stable identity. This is evident from the very beginning of the novel in which we find the narrator, a recent college graduate in New York City on a journalism fellowship, living in an apartment with her white boyfriend, Andrew. She longs for invisibility and power and is aware at some level that

Andrew's and her different ethnic backgrounds are getting between them. The narrator says that every night she spies on Andrew while he fixes them dinner: "This was the moment I savored every night, when I could see him but he could not see me" (2004, 1). She does this because she longs to stop feeling like the exoticized Other and to experience a sense of power as the perceiver rather than the perceived.

To a large extent, the narrator exists in a rather-discombobulated state, divorced from her family and friends and unwilling to disclose much of any of her personal information or background. She reveals very little about her college experiences and her familial background, and her avoidance of both indicates that she has been living in a state of impermanence for some time. It may be that the narrator has been so overwhelmed by the self-consciousness of being multiethnic that she seeks to be blissfully unaware and therefore does not tell anyone of her ethnicity but rather just passes for white: "Every day in this new city I was trying to live in the purity of the present, free from context" (2004, 5). The narrator likes her work because it allows her to disappear "into someone else's story. Of watching and not being seen. Then and only then do the secrets reveal themselves" (2004, 6). Denied or denying herself a stable identity, the narrator feels that she can only really exist through others. Her relationship with the white Andrew at the beginning of the novel suggests that she seeks the comfortable racial ignorance of being white. Not only is Andrew white, but he is quintessentially Aryan looking with "Sleepy blue eyes. Full pink lips. Tousled blond hair. Skin pale and milky" (2004, 1). Presumably she is drawn to Andrew because he is the physical embodiment of Nordic whiteness. However, the narrator can only stay in this state of relative blissful racial ignorance for so long, and once it is broken, her relationship with Andrew also disintegrates because her relationship with him was based on lies and illusions. When meeting Andrew's rich and insensitive friends from Andover, Massachusetts, for the first time, the narrator becomes uncomfortable and self-conscious. They have no idea that she is part African American, nor does Andrew, and the secretive narrator has no desire to tell them, especially after she witnesses Andrew's friends making racially derogatory comments about African Americans during a Scrabble game that they play. At first, one of Andrew's friends impersonates a "cleaning lady" they all had hired while at Andover for their apartments. They have absolutely no sympathy for this woman's somewhat legitimate but angry complaints about how messy and unsanitary they were, nor does it occur to them that part of her anger towards them might be a result of having such a dismal job. They take pleasure in mimicking her accent as a way to belittle her.

They continue to exhibit not so subtle racist behavior when they subsequently discuss how African Americans sometimes give their children unusual
names such as LaVonne that are often spelled unexpectedly. The most outspoken and racist of Andrew's friends, Sophie, asks, "Are those names supposed to
be creative, or is it all just kind of an epic spelling mistake? Like dyslexia on a
mass scale?" (2004, 13). Yet another of Andrew's friends ridicules a "big fat lady"
on *The Newlywed Show* who is African American for unconsciously making a
lewd comment (2004, 14). Only in the presence of other whites then, do these
individuals feel comfortable enough to reveal their own prejudicial and racist
attitudes towards African Americans. Had they known that the narrator was
African American, they probably would never have revealed themselves in this
way. Through these characters and this scene, Senna reveals buried and implicit
prejudice and racism that still affect the hip-hop generation. The narrator,
unable to take anymore, rushes to the bathroom, feeling insulted and isolated:
"I thought of things I could do or say—things I'd already said and done," but
she does not speak because she does not want to reveal her secret of being of
being part African American (2004, 15). To do so would not only reveal her
deception but also force her to forsake her state of relative blissful ethnic ignorance. Instead, on the fogged-up bathroom mirror, the narrator draws a portrait
of someone who looks like herself, which, we discover, is a defense mechanism
she uses when she is in situation in which she feels ostracized because of her
ethnicity. The narrator longs for someone like herself, especially at times like
this at which she becomes painfully aware of her mixed ethnicity and her perceived differences from others around her.

This is the beginning of the end of the narrator's relationship with Andrew.
Even though she never directly tells Andrew or for that matter the reader that
the party and the racial slurs were the real cause of their breakup, the narrator's
attitude towards others the next morning shows in her face in the mirror how
her mood has significantly soured: "I saw disappointment in the deep lines
etched around a mouth. Rage in the cracks between the eyebrows" (2004,
19–20). She now realizes that from now on, she would associate Andrew with
his racist friends, and she would never again feel fully secure in passing as a
white woman. Later she wonders, "Was it possible to fall out of love in a single
moment? Possible for somebody to turn from lover to stranger in the glimpse
of a smile? Maybe" (2004, 42). This is the case for the narrator, but what she
does not confess to is how the precipitating factor is race. Furthermore it is not
so much Andrew who has turned into a stranger, for after all, it was not he who
made the racist comments, but, rather, the narrator has become a stranger onto
herself.

In the narrator's world, race has become rather performative, and while most people seem to ignore its significance, it still carries great weight. For instance the narrator relates how her coworker, Ross, a white Mississippi native, expresses disdain for African Americans: "If only he had been born in a different skin, he might be editor in chief of the magazine by now. And you, he said, if you were born black, who know where you'd be" (2004, 83). Ironically, of course, he is not aware that the narrator is part African American, and indeed it may be a result of comments like Ross's that the narrator has decided to keep her ethnicity a secret and pass for white.

While the narrator tries to deny her ethnicity, she encounters whites who try to emulate African Americans without having to face the negative aftereffects of prejudice. For instance, when she moves out of Andrew's apartment into a transitional neighborhood in Brooklyn on a tip from coworker Greta Hicks, the narrator is shown the place by the occupant's cousin, a white man named Jiminy, who dresses and acts like a conventional hip-hop performer, repeatedly referring to the narrator as "son" or "G" (2004, 32). She describes him as having "platinum blond hair, pale," with a "pugnacious face," wearing "a huge parka with a fur collar, jeans three sizes too large bagged around his legs like empty sacks" (2004, 38). The narrator reveals her implicit disdain for people such as Jiminy, who co-opt a gangster-like persona while leading relatively comfortable middle-class, white lives: "I'd met people like Jiminy before. The childish nickname, the exaggerated slang, the wild defensiveness were all too familiar" (2004, 32). By and large, race relations seem rather poor in this section of Brooklyn and in New York City in general. This same mostly African American neighborhood does not seem very racially inclusive, for as the narrator describes, in addition to African Americans are, "a few nervous white people, too, walking swiftly toward the light of the subway, hunched over as if hiding something in their coats, eyes twitching back and forth, on guard against phantom muggers" (2004, 37).

Clearly the narrator has not yet come to grips with her own identity as a person of mixed ethnicity. In response to Andrew's question "Who are you?" after she tells him she's leaving, she is quiet: "I didn't say anything. I just stared at him in the dark for a moment, thinking of all of the different answers to this question I had already given" (2004, 34–35). The narrator has not established a firm sense of identity because she denies her ethnicity, shown when she takes a bath and describes her breasts, one of which "was small, prepubescent, with a pale pink nipple, the other slightly fuller, with a deeper mauve nipple. Like they belonged to two different people" (2004, 44). However, she does begin to develop a friendship and bond with coworker Greta. They connect because they both are half-white and half–African American. The narrator even thinks they look similar: "Nothing obvious, but yes, we could have been related. We had the same straight brown hair and olive skin, and the same vague look about our features" (2004, 48). At first, finding someone like her has a positive effect upon the narrator, who feels that she has found a kindred soul in Greta: "As soon as Greta told me [that she was mixed], I'd felt an invisible wall fall away between us" (2004, 49). However, as time progresses, Greta is revealed as not mentally stable, possibly in part because of her experiences as a person of mixed ethnicity. When Greta and the narrator go to a color specialist to find out what kind of "season" the narrator is, there is a sense that Greta may be obsessed with the narrator; before the narrator and Greta had really got to know each other, Greta had told the designer a good deal about the narrator (2004, 67). Being ethnically mixed, at least for Greta, creates an overwhelming sense of loneliness and isolation, leading her desperately to seek out someone like herself to counteract her feelings of low self-worth. In large part a result of her issues with race and identity, the narrator has difficulty connecting with anyone else except Greta, until she is asked to write a feature story on a photographer named Ivers Greene. The narrator is somewhat intrigued by his photos in that they show people "in the most unattractive angles possible" (2004, 94). As someone who struggles with self-esteem and identity problems, the narrator is drawn to these photos because they make her feel somewhat better in contrast to them. She is also drawn to how he scrawls a half monkey, half poodle onto each photograph because she feels herself to be half of two different species. However, the narrator is not free from prejudice herself; she holds expectations of African Americans. This is evident in how she is surprised to discover that Ivers is African American, as if his work somehow reflects a white sensibility.

Ivers, however, shows his sensitivity and/or perception by becoming only the second person the narrator has ever met (outside her family, of course) who has been able to guess that she is partly African American (the other was her best friend from college, Lola). Thereby, Ivers's correct guess foreshadows that there is a connection to be made between her and Ivers. However, Ivers's response to the narrator after she admits she is of mixed ethnicity is hardly polite and is presumably one of the reasons why she never chooses to not reveal or confirm her racial status to other African Americans, because of how they can belittle her as Ivers does by asking, "Do you say 'motherfucker' or do you say 'muthafucka'?" (2004, 104). The narrator, clearly upset, walks out on their interview. A couple of days later, an apologetic Ivers returns, and he and the narrator become romantically involved.

In response, Greta becomes more and more clinging and obsessional to the point that she stalks the narrator, even making a pass at her when she suggests they can wax each other's private areas (2004, 150). Greta is, in a way, a future, dark doppelganger of the narrator, a vision of the nightmarish future that the narrator might have in store for her if she continues to subvert her racial identity and does not change her ways. For it would be easy for the narrator to do what Greta does: blame virtually all her problems upon race and upon being of mixed ethnicity. This is evident in a long, angry diatribe in which Greta tells the narrator that she hates whites and African Americans alike because she perceives that neither treats her as an equal and/or as a full human being. Although there may be some truth to Greta's claim, she makes it worse by expecting this kind of behavior from virtually everyone around her. Greta also claims that, though she's not interested in women, she and the narrator can start "a new race" and "a new people" (2004, 151). Isolated herself, the narrator could easily turn into Greta later in life were she not able to come to grips with her own ethnicity.

The extent to which Greta is mentally disturbed does not become completely evident until towards the end of the novel. Greta has steadily deteriorated and lost her job, presumably at least in part a result of the narrator's rejection of her. As it turns out, the apartment that the narrator currently rents belongs to Greta, who is also known as Vera, among other names. Greta/Vera has so latched onto the narrator at this point that she tells her, "Without you I'm nothing" (2004, 194). Greta/Vera then attacks the narrator, in part a result of anger from being rejected but also because of Greta/Vera's self-destructive tendencies. She sees the narrator as a mirror of herself, and since Greta/Vera has come to hate herself, she projects some of that hatred (as well as love) onto the narrator. Greta/Vera believes that all of her actions and problems are a result of being of mixed ethnicity. She tells the narrator of her lifelong longing to have an ethnically mixed friend like herself: "I knew that if we could just come together, everything would be okay" (2004, 202). However, when her desperate pleading fails to move the narrator, who wants only to escape, Greta/Vera keeps the narrator captive and tries to kill both of them by stabbing the narrator and then trying to jump off the roof of her building with the narrator. The narrator manages to escape Greta/Vera's grasp, but Greta/Vera plummets to her death.

The aftereffect of this near-death experience is highly significant for the narrator. The last chapter takes place five years later, after the narrator leaves New York City. Unable or unwilling to deal with reality, she moves from journalism to fiction: "I have given up on nonfiction. I am working toward the most useless of degrees. I study the art of lying" (2004, 211). Fiction writing is an escape for the narrator from dealing with not only her past but also her unresolved ethnic issues. It is questionable whether she has become better adjusted or has just found another way to avoid reality. She has withdrawn into herself to some degree, claiming perhaps half-heartedly, "I live alone but I am not lonely"

(2004, 212). The narrator is still haunted by Greta/Vera in large part because although she does not admit it, she sees herself in Greta/Vera: "Out on the street, in the glare of the afternoon sun, I see her where she is not: in the huddle of day workers waiting for the bus down to the border, or in the cool impervious smile of a Persian housewife coming out of the dry cleaner's (2004, 213). Given her experience with Greta/Vera, she no longer seeks out others like her but, rather, continues to exist in a rather discombobulated in-between state like Birdie in *Caucasia,* although Birdie finds solace in her sister, Cole. The narrator has no one else to lean on.

For Senna, there are no easy answers to how either Birdie or the narrator (and for that matter, other multiethnic hip-hop-generation members) can overcome their feelings of ostracism. They both long to exist in a state of postethnicity, but the world in which they live still categorizes and judges people on the basis of ethnicity. They may choose to ignore ethnicity as the narrator does, but ultimately they do so at the cost of their own personal well-being. Reading Senna's fiction makes one aware that conditions for multiethnic hip-hop-generation members may be even more difficult than it is for African Americans, and given that in future years, the number of multiethnic progeny will increase, these questions and concerns are especially pertinent.

6

Coinciding with the rise in popularity of hip-hop is the rise of slam or spoken word poetry; the two overlap to a large degree. One could, for instance, argue that Kanye West's songs are poetry set to music. What links these art forms is their emphasis on performance. "The spoken word movement recognizes that to be a vital, relevant part of our culture," Mark Eleveld suggests, "poetry must spread beyond the classroom and reach people where they live" (2003, xiii). Not all or even a majority of the work of African American poets of the hip-hop generation can be classified as spoken word. Yet poets of the hip-hop generation tend to blend the academic and the colloquial as well as popular/low culture with academic/high culture and accounts of inner-city/street life with academic/suburban life in Paul Beatty's poetry and also in Allison Joseph and Terrence Hayes.

Allison Joseph, an assistant professor at Southern Illinois University, Carbondale, is a first-generation American, her parents having been born in Jamaica and Carriacou. Despite not being a descendent of African Americans, she speaks through her work to contemporary African American lives, that is, to both impoverished, inner-city lives and to more-privileged, educationally advanced middle- or upper-class lives. This may be in part a result of her upbringing. Raised in the Bronx, Joseph would not only have experienced inner-city life but also would have been aware of the very beginnings of hip-hop music and culture, which originated in the Bronx in the 1970s, when she was a child. Still, Joseph moved in an almost opposite direction when she decided to attend Kenyon College, a small, liberal arts school in Ohio. She chose Kenyon because of its "literary reputation," but the school did not live up to her expectations: "Little did I know that reputation was pretty exclusively white and male. . . . [It was an] incredible culture shock to go from the most diverse city in the world . . . to go to the middle of Ohio where you could, my senior year, count the number of black people enrolled on two hands" (Hamilton 1996,

464). This exposure to two almost diametrically opposed regions of America helped inform Joseph's writings. She explores race in some but not all of her poems, which she does not want to be considered race specific or race poetry. Her goal is to produce "work that people of all backgrounds, people of all colors, people of all persuasions could read and say that there was something there in your work that stopped or struck me and I wanted to read it again" (Hamilton 1996, 465).

In Joseph's collection of poems entitled *Soul Train* (1997) is an intriguing mix of low and high culture, as well as her autobiographical accounts of inner-city life and adolescence. In these poems, Joseph counteracts stereotypes of African American lives, such as equating inner city life with desperation and violence. Although Joseph makes it clear that those exist in the inner city to some degree, it is not the entire story of the inner city. To consider the inner city in only insidious terms is a narrow, one-dimensional perspective (as the media often does), a false stereotype, and leads people to denigrate those who are raised in the inner city as Joseph herself was.

Joseph's poem "Good Humor" reflects her purpose in counteracting conceptions of the inner city as wholly dismal. The first two lines seem like a typical indictment of inner-city life.

> In our neighborhood of run-down houses,
> of abandoned lots and corner groceries
> (*Soul Train,* 1997, 9)

However, then the poem turns to

> nothing tasted better than ice cream's
> sweet delight: the delicate peaks
> and swirls of vanilla soft-serve,
> cold chill of Italian ices
> (*Soul Train,* 1997, 9)

Certainly, eating ice cream purchased from an ice-cream truck is not specific to the inner city; it is more associated with the predominately white suburbs. That is exactly Joseph's point: to demonstrate the commonalties between communities and children, regardless of race or class. There is no violence, no shame, or anger in Joseph's depictions of the inner city. Even though there is a sense that the children are poor, having to

> wrangle dollars
> and quarters from parents,
> grandparents
> (*Soul Train,* 1997, 10)

They are not desperate. Their poverty seems to have created a stronger passion and desire within them, a

> longing to lick and swallow everything
> that melted beneath the summer sun.
> (*Soul Train*, 1997, 10)

Taken in the wrong direction, this seeming inexhaustible hunger could, of course, lead to anger, violence, and destruction as the children age (which it does for many members of the hip-hop generation), but it could also turn into a productive or creative drive. These children then, like presumably Joseph herself, are at a crossroads, one road that could lead them astray and the other that could lead them to greater success, or at least a means out of the inner city. The emphasis on individualism and materialism in hip-hop culture can help encourage socially, ethnically, and self-destructive behavior, and it is this behavior that Joseph wishes to counteract through her poetry.

Similarly, in the poem "Big Shots," Joseph begins by counteracting negative stereotypes of the inner city.

> Not much violence when you lived
> in the Castle Hill projects, just
> broken elevators, odors of piss
> rising from graffiti-sprayed stairs.
> (*Soul Train*, 1997, 13)

The young, teen-age speaker and her best friend seem relatively untouched by their poverty, gleefully singing pop music out loud.

> We owned
> Henry Hudson Junior High
> (*Soul Train*, 1997, 13)

In another collection of Joseph's poetry, *In Every Seam* (1997), more poems portray children in inner-city environments in almost ecstatic terms as they ride their bikes, play tag, ride skateboards, or play with water. For instance the poem "Summers on Screvin" celebrates the often-denigrated street life that children often experience growing up in the inner city.

> Open fire hydrants
> poured rivers into the streets
> and we danced in rushing water
> until someone turned it off,

told us to do something better
with ourselves, so we stirred
up mud at curbs, digging
rich silt with Popsicle sticks
(*In Every Seam*, 1997, 2)

By necessity the inner city and/or impoverishment develop their imaginations and creative facilities when they play games. Having little or no money to purchase equipment for games, they

jumped on a rank soggy mattress, as if it were a trampoline,
and not some sorry piece of garbage
someone had dumped among bushes
(*In Every Seam*, 1997, 2)

Similarly, community and solidarity are seen within the inner city in the poem, "On Sidewalks, on Street Corners, as Girls."

No one would dare take away
our homemade street-corner music
so we'd spend every afternoon after school
and every shred of summer daylight
riffing, scatting, improvising,
unafraid to tell each other
shake it to the east,
shake it to the west,
shake it to the one
you love best.
(*In Every Seam*, 1997, 5)

In her poems, Joseph does not completely portray an inner-city childhood as idyllic, and the harsh reality of prejudice and racism becomes clear to her from an early age. The poem title "Traitor" indicates either how the speaker is made to feel frightened and ostracized by another African American girl for not acting "black" enough or directed at the accusatory girl for subtly attacking her own people. The speaker of this poem wonders,

What did the girl on the playground mean
when she hissed *you ain't black* at me
(*In Every Seam*, 1997, 6)

The speaker describes this girl as staring

at me with such contempt
that I wanted to hide in my mother's
skirts
(*In Every Seam*, 1997, 6)

What is seen here is divisiveness within the African American community. Feeling disempowered herself, the taunting African American girl can only pick on a less-powerful girl, in this case, the more cultivated speaker, in order to make herself feel better about herself. The only way that the taunting girl believes (at least subconsciously) that she can feel better about herself is by acting superior to other African Americans.

> *You talk funny,* she said,
> *all proper,* as if pronunciation
> was a sin, a scandal, a strike
> against the race only a traitor
> would perform, an Uncle Tom sellout.
> Somehow I'd let her down by not
> slurring, I'd failed her by not
> letting language laze on its own,
> its sound unhurried, I'd said
> *isn't* rather than *ain't,*
> called my mother *mom* instead
> of *momma,* pronounced *th* distinctly
> so no one would confuse them
> with *dem, those* with *dose.*
> (*In Every Seam*, 1997, 6–7)

The taunting girl transfers her internalized anger towards the speaker, laughing when the speaker shows weakness and pushing her down, even though Joseph mentions they are the "the same rough brown" (*In Every Seam,* 1997, 7). Although the poem does not explain what happens to the speaker after this incident, it is easy to see how she could end up rather like Gunnar Kaufman in Paul Beatty's *White Boy Shuffle,* adopting a false, ignorant persona in order to fit in with hip-hop-generation peers.

Similarly, in the poem "Who You Calling Ugly? or When Black Ceased to Be Beautiful" in Joseph's collection *Imitation of Life* (2003), a vicious, presumably African American man insults an African American woman because she has pronounced African features.

> Liver-lips, nappy head,
> you so ugly no one wants

> to be seen with you,
> much less talk to you
> on these streets.
> You so damn dark
> no one can see you,
> lights off or on!
> (*Imitation of Life*, 2003, 38)

She is not desirable to the speaker because she does not or cannot have desirable, conventionally Caucasian features and does not seem feminine enough to the speaker, who although he does not state so directly, really wants an African American woman who looks white or simply wants a white woman. Indeed many of the most popular African American celebrities, for example, Beyonce, Halle Berry, and Tyra Banks, tend to be lighter skinned (often they are multi-ethnic) with conventional white features such as straightened hair.

In other Joseph poems exists a vicious circle of violence possibly engendered by implicit, subverted racism. In "Urban Games" the speaker, possibly the same abused speaker in "Traitor," describes a childhood game—run, catch, and kiss—that she played as a child, but how she

> preferred the more
> violent variation—run, catch
> and *kill*,
> that game's object
> direct, brutal—simply run
> as fast as possible with fists
> ready to pummel
>
> . . .
>
> In summertime playgrounds
> and parks, away from adults
> and school, this cruelty
> sustained us all day long,
> this game far more intricate
> than freeze tag, hopscotch.
> Raggedy boys and girls,
> we loved to see each other
> suffer, unable to leave someone
> on the sidewalk to nurse
> sore arms, bruised thighs,
> unable to resist one last punch.
> (*In Every Seam*, 1997, 10)

Their brusque behavior towards others can also be seen in "Caroline," in which Joseph recollects the harsh manner in which she and her fellow classmates treated a white student.

> In eighth grade, we teased that girl [Caroline]
> as much as anyone could, mocking
> her clothes, her stringy hair,
> her flat, pallid face that revealed
> little protest. Used to being
> the one white girl in our class
> of blacks, Hispanics, she endured
> our taunts on her lack of rhythm,
> on her stiff, flat-butted walk.
> (*Worldly Pleasures*, 2004, 59)

It is easy but frightening to consider how these somewhat-innocent childhood games could turn much more violent or even deadly later in life.

Still, Joseph's hip-hop-generation women are proud and strong, feminine yet independent. For instance, in "Home Girl Steps Out," the narrator prepares to go out dancing and places high standards upon a male partner for whom she searches there, feeling no need to have just any man.

> But if no one appears,
> if no man is real enough
> to dance with the woman
> in the slick leather skirt
> and red pumps, I'll still
> keep stepping, lights playing
> off my white silk shirt
> head aloft. Moment by moment
> I'll learn myself, the woman I am
> set loose, apart, free.
> (*Soul Train*, 1997, 30–31)

Similarly, in "Home Girl Dreams a Dance Partner," the speaker seeks a male partner who is agile and sensitive, yet masculine, but she feels secure enough in her own identity.

> Even if I never find him, I am not
> content to sit home, music within
> too strong for a night of television
> in a dark room.
> (*Soul Train*, 1997, 35)

"Soul Suite" similarly celebrates female independence as the speaker describes how she dances by herself at night,

> grateful for
> solitude
> (*Soul Train*, 1997, 49)

For Joseph, dancing and music provide an enviable space beyond race. It is in that state that many of the speakers of her poems long to be.

> When I'm moving
> I don't have to speak,
> and no language
> can tell my story
> anyways—no words
> can move me like
> a strong single note
> sung over piano
> riffs
> (*Soul Train*, 1997, 48)

In this case, music, or popular culture, helps efface the boundaries between the races. In Joseph's poems, she displays not only the influence and importance of music but also the importance and influence of television. Both mediums help to break down boundaries between the races and help to provide her with a positive self-image. For instance, in the title poem of the collection *Soul Train,* Joseph refers to the music/dance television program of the same name. She explains how empowering the show was for her.

> the shapely
> and self-knowing brownskinned
> women who dared stare straight
> at the camera, the men strong,
> athletically gifted as they
> leaped in full splits.
> (*Soul Train*, 1997, 11)

It was this show that first gave Joseph or the speaker some measure of confidence as she yearns, "to move like those dancers" (*Soul Train*, 1997, 13).

Still, as Joseph or the speaker ages, she finds herself confronting prejudice and racism, even in the multiethnic borough of the Bronx, which she does not portray as a place of cultural and racial acceptance but rather a site of interethnic racism. In one poem "In the Bookstore," the speaker describes a bookstore and the implicit racial hostility she often encounters in non–African American establishments.

> Here I find refuge, though the woman
> behind the counter looks at me
> as if I can't read, regarding me
> as just another colored girl
> who might steal her store
> out from under her
> (*Soul Train,* 1997, 28)

She buys something.

> so when this woman hands me my change
> I hiss a whispered *thank you,*
> make sure my eyes catch hers
> for one second of indictment,
> one moment where I'm right, she's wrong,
> and there are still dollars in my palm.
> (*Soul Train,* 1997, 29)

Similarly, in "Five and Dime," the suspicions are aimed at African Americans from store owners; in this case, it a Hispanic store owner, another minority, who targets African Americans. This owner of a "discount variety store" would

> snarl at all the tan and brown bodies
> that came in and out of his glass doors every day
> (*In Every Seam,* 1997, 14)

His hatred is supposedly due to

> those people always asking their questions,
> touching every items for sale, leaving
> fingerprints on the makeup, the school supplies,
> stains on the ill-fitting clothes.
> (*In Every Seam,* 1997, 14)

In all fairness, the speaker does

> open giant bottles
> of watery shampoo or bubble bath,
> sniffing to tell if they really
> smelled of strawberries or bubble gum.
> (*In Every Seam,* 1997, 15)

However, she may do this because she doesn't have any money or as a response to the owner's suspicions. Indeed she responds to the store manager's not-so-subtle racism.

> I
> didn't care what he thought,
> I touched whatever I wanted to touch,
> ran sticky fingers over wrinkled
> corduroy pants and no-name jeans
> (*In Every Seam*, 1997, 15)

The owner shows no sympathy or understanding for impoverished African American children, even though they all live in an equally dilapidated area, and both are minorities, subject to discrimination, prejudice, and racism.

Despite being born after the civil rights movement and being a member of the hip-hop generation, Joseph, in some of her poems, describes the not-so-subtle ways whites still tend to be valued over African Americans. In "The Black Santa," Joseph makes it clear that this is learned behavior; the speaker recalls sitting on the lap of a drunken, less-than-cheery African American Santa Claus.

> No one could
> have told met that a pink-cheeked
> pale-skinned Santa was the only Santa
> to worship, to beg for toys and candy.
> I wouldn't have believed them,
> wouldn't have believed anyone
> who'd tell me Santa couldn't look
> like me: brown eyes, face, and skin
> (*Imitation of Life*, 2003, 16)

However, as she ages, her illusions are shattered, and she comes to subconsciously, if not consciously, associate whites with major religious and/or magical figures. In addition she comes to associate being white with being attractive. In "Notes from Childhood," Joseph describes how she was virtually brainwashed into equating white features with being attractive.

> No one ever told me
> about alternatives to Nancy Drew
> and Teen Dream Malibu Barbie,
> whose molded plastic features never changed
> from one year to the next
> . . .

And no one let me know
that *Charlie's Angels* weren't
the be-all and end-all in
female beauty
(*Worldly Pleasures*, 2004, 20)

In the poem "Frying Hair," Joseph describes the painful process of straightening her hair, a process she was taught by her mother, who likewise consciously or subconsciously equates white features with physical attractiveness.

I want to ask my mother
what's so great about straight hair,
and why the woman on the jar
of Dax pressing grease looks
like a white woman, a lady
who'd never end up with burn marks
on ears or neck or forehead.
I want to ask why she
and every other black mother I know
insists on filling their homes
with this peculiar scent, this aroma
of mangled and burnt hair.
(*Imitation of Life*, 2003, 24–25)

Ironically Joseph's parents are rather Afrocentric; however, even they can't escape the social pressures to look or act white to some degree. Still, Joseph's father tries to counteract the racial inequality he sees in American society, as shown in the poem, "Numbers."

My father taught me to measure
the worth of any good thing
by the number of black people
involved. Without sufficient numbers,
he wouldn't root for a team,
wouldn't eat in a restaurant,
wouldn't turn on his television
to watch a local newscast
that didn't have a black anchor
(*Imitation of Life*, 2003, 70)

However, Joseph implicitly criticizes this kind of racial exclusivity, because in her family's case, it appears to backfire. Joseph does not embrace her father's ideology as noted by her choice of college: the mostly white Kenyon College. Joseph describes her father's reaction to Kenyon when he first arrives there.

> He thought I was crazy to live
> so close to them, the white people
> who'd conspired so long against him,
> the numbers on that campus
> far too low for him, my scholarship
> bleaching me, making me
> less black, less daughter
> (*Imitation of Life*, 2003, 72)

Indeed her father turns out to be somewhat correct, not in so much as the experiences at Kenyon bleaching Joseph but of her eventual feelings of social and intellectual isolation due to being an African American in a less-than-inclusive, mostly white college and geographical area.

At the mostly white environment of Kenyon College, Joseph is objectified and made to feel overwhelmingly self-conscious, as told in "Higher Education."

> Some people here look at me
> as if I'm not actually a person,
> but a walking statistic instead,
> one of those aliens admitted
> to keep the quotas up,
> liberals happy.
> (*In Every Seam*, 1997, 71)

This environment, though purportedly inclusive, turns out to be rather insular and not welcoming to minorities. The speaker claims that when other white college students and/or townspeople see her, they fear

> another one just like me
> will be admitted soon, upsetting
> delicate tradition.
> (*In Every Seam*, 1997, 71)

The speaker also finds other white students to be rather ignorant and patronizing. These people

> want to know all about me:
> what those funny little braids I wear
> are called, whether
> or not I know

> the only black person in New York
> they know, whether or not a white person
> could walk safely in my neighborhood
> (*In Every Seam*, 1997, 71)

Similar to what happens to Gunnar Kaufman in Beatty's *White Boy Shuffle,* they assume that she knows something about how to save the inner city because she is African American, and their attitude towards her evinces subverted racism.

> Others ask why blacks need a whole month
> devoted to their history
>
> . . .
>
> One girl raised her hand in Sociology,
> said, *I'm not prejudiced, but*
> *why do all their neighborhoods*
> *smell so bad?,* looking at me,
> expecting an answer.
> (*In Every Seam*, 1997, 71–72)

Joseph suggests that, because of her race, she's nearly always expected to be an expert about racial issues. At Kenyon she does not really receive an education as much as she's the one expected to educate others.

> I find myself teaching, educating,
> explaining why my hair is different,
> why I feel no need to sunbathe,
> why it's possible for me to love
> both Aretha Franklin and Kate Bush,
> Janis Joplin and Billie Holiday
>
> . . .

One student even asks,

> *"don't*
> *you think you'd be better off*
> *at a school where there are more*
> *people like you*
>
> . . .
>
> I wince,
> but don't cry, I smile to cover
> my sigh, say *more people like me*
> *know just how to take care of people*
> *like you,* my brown hand stroking

> his white shoulder, making certain
> he flinches, sure that he squirms
> (*In Every Seam*, 1997, 73)

One can only imagine how much worse race relations could be at an institution that is not as liberal as Kenyon. However, for Joseph, the subverted prejudice and unequal treatment extend beyond the student body to include the faculty. In "College Tour," for instance, she describes talking to an English professor who tells her she could

> be
> the next Gwendolyn Brooks
> as long as I studied with him
> (*Imitation of Life*, 2003, 69)

But his comments are disingenuous, given that he makes a pass at her, presumably because he is drawn to her racial exoticism.

Beyond college Joseph discovers that the publishing industry holds a double standard about African American writers and writing. On the one hand, some encourage African Americans to write poems about race, and react negatively if they do not, while others think that the market has been oversaturated with such poetry. In "Academic Instructions," Joseph discusses racial expectations or lack thereof for African American poetry. The unnamed speaker, presumably a publisher or editor, proclaims,

> Don't write
> about being black.
> All that racial jive
> is passe anyway;
> no one wants to hear
> how waitresses won't
> serve you, how plainclothes
> detectives follow you
> in up-scale shops
> (*In Every Seam*, 1997, 74)

The speaker continues in a rather demeaning manner to exclude racial themes.

> We're tired
> of it, tired of your constant
> ancestor worship—your love
> of strong brown women,
> mothers who tilled fields

and birthed babies,
clothed and fed and loved
the sick, insane, and poor,
who made churchgoing clothes
from some rich lady's scraps.
No one wants to hear
what you call your history;
its naïve and mundane,
full of scandalous blame
for everyone but yourself.
Come back when you are ready
to learn how to write
like the rest of us,
when you're ready to admit
all the beauty in the world
around you, finally wise enough
to know nothing you say clearly
can ever really matter.
(*In Every Seam*, 1997, 76)

Like virtually all writers of the hip-hop generation, Joseph defies expectations and demands placed on African American writers, insisting that she can write about whatever she chooses regardless of race or class.

In that is Terrence Hayes, an associate professor in creative writing at Carnegie Mellon University. Born in South Carolina in 1971, Hayes attended Coker College in South Carolina on a basketball scholarship. It was not easy, as he explains, to decide to be a full-time poet, because, as with the situation Gunnar Kaufman faced, poetry, to people around Hayes, was not considered to be a career choice, let alone a manly choice (whereas basketball was). "One could argue," Hayes says, "that people—Southern black people—believe in the kind of work you see, they believe the kind of work that requires tangible action. To my friends and family, my playing basketball was closer to work than any of my art was" (Rowell 2004, 1074). Still, Hayes decided to follow his interests by enrolling in a creative writing program at the University of Pittsburgh, where he received an MFA in 1997.

Hayes has thus far published three books of poetry and has been awarded numerous awards and prizes for his writings. His first collection, *Muscular Music* (1999), "won two awards—the Kate Tufts Discovery Award and the Whiting Writers Award"; his second collection, *Hip Logic* (2002), "was a National Poetry Series winner" (Rowell 2004, 1068). His most recent collection of poetry is entitled *Wind in a Box* (2006). In an interview, Hayes lists his many poetic influences from Amiri Baraka to Phillip Levine, but he describes *Muscular Music* as reflect-ing "someone who is exploring his cultural identity and experiences with very little concern, or awareness, of the constraints of style and subject matter" (Rowell 2004, 1073). He explains the title of the collection, "The idea of muscle and music reflects what is masculine and tender in us; what is corporeal (mus-cle) and what is artistic (music); what is exterior and what is interior" (Rowell 2004, 1075). In *Muscular Music,* Hayes explores masculinity and, like Allison Joseph, blends high/academic and popular/mass cultures. Hayes also investi-gates what it means or should mean to be African American as a member of the hip-hop generation.

Identity is first and forefront in many of Hayes's poems, indicating that he believes one of the main issues facing contemporary, especially younger African Americans is how to best define themselves, whether or not to do so racially and, if so, to what extent. In "What I Am," the speaker, presumably a member of the hip-hop generation, implicitly suggests that consumer products deter-mine much of his perceived identity. The speaker tells us that when he's at a supermarket,

> about to *buy Head & Shoulders*
> the white people shampoo, no one knows
> what I am.
>
> . . .
>
> When I stop
> by McDonalds for a cheeseburger, no one
> suspects what I am.
> (*Muscular Music,* 1999, 15)

In an anonymous society, he is treated as an object and has no sense of what it means to be African American or no concerns but rather, vapidly floats from one idea to another. He may also believe that he is discriminated against or ignored precisely because of his race and appearance. Thereby, people who see him assume that he is a thug or criminal, or they completely ignore him. The speaker says, rather apathetically,

> I never say, *Niggaz*
> in my poems.
> My ancestors leave
> their native land? I'm thinking about shooting
> some hoop later on. I'll dunk on everyone
> of those niggaz.
> (*Muscular Music,* 1999, 15)

However, in all fairness, the people with whom the speaker plays basketball are no better informed or motivated: "They don't know if Toni Morrison is a woman or a man" (*Muscular Music*, 1999, 15). Rather, the speaker and his friends are only concerned with themselves and the immediate present. The speaker plans to buy drugs, "a dimebag," after the game. Even the speaker's friend, Jody, who rants about white people is hardly a real friend to the blasé speaker, who states,

> He's cool, but he don't know
> what I am, & so what.
> (*Muscular Music*, 1999, 16)

The speaker does not care that other people do not really understand him, because he does not really care to understand himself, being satiated by the comforts and pleasures of consumer culture and by the chimera that racial equality exists.

> I got the dandruff-free head
> & shoulders of white people & a cheeseburger
> belly & a Thriller CD & Nike high tops
> & slavery's dead & the TV's my daddy—
> (*Muscular Music*, 1999, 16)

Hayes implicates popular culture in this instance for producing such socially and intellectually apathetic or deadened hip-hop-generation members as the speaker, whom Hayes portrays as nothing more than a vapid consumer.

Similarly, the aimlessness of another young African American speaker is revealed in "Derrick Poem (The Lost World)." The poem begins with the rather-careless speaker buying basketball shoes with "the dough I was suppose to use to pay the light bill & worse, use the change to buy an Ella Fitzgerald CD" (*Muscular Music*, 1999, 21). Presumably he buys these shoes because he has come to associate basketball shoes with prestige, an association fostered by advertisers, marketers, television, and music (as this association is in *The White Boy Shuffle*). When the speaker sees his friend Derrick, they can't really communicate anymore, both having tough masculine façades. Derrick is seeing a white woman, but they do not talk about that; they talk instead about the movie he's about to see, presumably *Jurassic Park*. The speaker describes their situation.

> how we used to talk about black women
> & desire & how I was betraying him then creeping out
> after sundown with a girl in my shorts & white skin
> (*Muscular Music*, 1999, 21)

However, now Derrick now talks

> not about black girls, but dinosaurs which if I was listening
> could have been talk about loneliness, but I wasn't,
> even when he said, "We should go to the movies sometime,"
> and stopped.
> (*Muscular Music*, 1999, 22)

The significance of the poem's title, "The Lost World," is that it represents their lost friendship or lost concern for one another, both having become very self-involved, in lines with hip-hop cultural authenticity for men. Once again, Hayes does not blame the speaker of his poem but popular culture and the ultimately detrimental standards of conduct for African Americans (especially the hip-hop generation) that disallow people, specifically African American men, from being emotionally vulnerable or demonstrative.

Along similar lines, in "Goliath Poem," Hayes displays the tragedy of being a tough man in a society (especially in the African American community) that holds such men in high esteem. The speaker is "always sorry" for people

> all muscle and hands weeping on the shoulder
> of regret, which is a kind of blindness, a recognition come too late.
> (*Muscular Music*, 1999, 51)

Unable or unwilling to express emotions and/or to communicate, these men become extremely isolated and alienated from others, leading them to act in extreme, even violent ways. For instance, in the poem, the speaker refers to his six-foot, eight-inch friend, Rick, who hurls

> stones through the window
> of another woman who's turned him away.
> (*Muscular Music*, 1999, 51)

Rick is unable to communicate or display a full range of emotions; he can only lash out in an angry, atavistic manner, and he appears to be close to self-destruction. The speaker describes how once he found Rick seemingly on the verge of committing suicide,

> Nintendo cords roped
> his shoes, a bottle of pills between his thighs.
> (*Muscular Music*, 1999, 51)

The speaker seems to see himself as similar to Rick: "In the darkness we could have been the same" (*Muscular Music*, 1999, 52). The speaker thinks of comforting Rick, but the codes for male authenticity are such that the two cannot talk because they cannot reveal their vulnerabilities, and they have lost their ability to trust one another. Instead,

> We said nothing.
> We listened to the rain like the sound of a big man's tears.
> (*Muscular Music*, 1999, 52)

It should go without saying that neither Rick nor the speaker of the poem actually cries.

While "Goliath Poem" is more objective, "Tenderness" is more the laments of a tough man who has failed to make any significant emotional or physical connections with others.

> It does not stop. It does not stop until you are safely home,
> smoking the cigarette you will not finish and watching snow
> Which does not stop parade outside the window.
> (*Muscular Music*, 1999, 59)

The *it* the speaker refers to could be regret, loneliness, and/or emotional pain, but that the speaker never says what "it" is indicates that he's not only repressing the pain he feels, he is even unwilling to name "it." When thinking about his failed relationship with Nancy, he thinks of how it might be a result of his failure to communicate and be emotionally intimate. Only when the speaker is alone and reading poetry can he admit his vulnerabilities. Hayes describes the speaker reading poetry.

> Even now, as you read it to yourself, it tells
> you tenderness
> is possible, is in the world, though earlier you said otherwise.
> (*Muscular Music*, 1999, 60)

When thinking over his failed relationship, the speaker claims, "There was tenderness," but then reveals his regrets.

> You should have held that woman. A brief embrace,
> That would have been tenderness.
> (*Muscular Music*, 1999, 60)

By the end of the poem, the speaker surrenders to his submerged and repressed emotions, which overtake him.

> I know one of the rings of Hell is for men who refuse to weep.
> So I let it come. And it does not move from me.
> (*Muscular Music*, 1999, 61)

need not be completely realistic as it could "show people not only as they actually were but also as they wished to be" (Hay 1994, 3). On the other hand, his contemporary Alan Locke promoted drama that was realistic. To Locke, drama need not necessarily be racial or political in topic or scope; it could focus upon the average or lower-class African American (Hay 1994, 4–5).

Throughout African American drama of the twentieth century, from the drama of the Harlem Renaissance to the drama of the hip-hop generation, this debate is still ongoing, all the way to the plays of Suzan-Lori Parks, in which is a combination of the DuBois and Locke ethos. On the one hand, keeping with DuBois's praxis, Parks directly confronts racial issues in a serious manner. Furthermore her plays often contain metaphorical and allegorical representations of how African Americans are often categorized, such as the characters Black Man with Watermelon and Black Woman with Fried Drumstick in the play *The Death of the Last Black Man in the World* (1992). However, her plays are not always tragedies in the DuBois school of drama, nor are they satires or comedies that would fit more in the Locke school of drama. Rather, the result is a combination of both schools with Parks's plays more often tragicomedies poking fun at stereotypes and at the same time attempting to demolish them. She also uses satire and comedy about serious racial issues as Locke does in order to debunk prejudice and stereotypes (Hay 1994, 28).

African American theater continued after the Harlem Renaissance, but it did not return to regain its critically and commercial importance until the late 1950s when Lorraine Hansberry's *A Raisin in the Sun* first opened on Broadway. "Black Theatre reinvented itself in 1959," Woodie King Jr. explains. "It was that year that *A Raisin in the Sun* opened on Broadway. *A Raisin in the Sun* was the first play to appear on Broadway by a Black female author, Lorraine Hansberry; it was also the first drama to be directed by a Black director, Lloyd Richards. Although many Black plays had been presented in New York as well as around the USA, *A Raisin in the Sun* ushered in the New Black Theatre Movement" (2003, 96).

Following the success of *A Raisin in the Sun,* during the period of the new black theater, playwrights such as Amiri Baraka directly challenged racial stereotypes and prejudice in works such as *Dutchman* (1964) and *The Slave* (1964). According to Hay, the years of the late 1960s and 1970s were "the last period of Black experience theatre, The Bridge, which combined ideas from the DuBois and the Locke schools" (1994, 42). However, this period was also marked by a downward turn in theater attendance: "Beginning in the middle seventies, African American theater organizations closed in unprecedented numbers" (Hay 1994, 134). This continued throughout the 1980s, and it was the climate in which Parks and other hip-hop-generation playwrights first began to emerge.

In other poems are men who get these unrealizable standards of authenticity and machismo that ultimately damage them more than help them: from television, film, and music. In "Shafro,"

> Now that my afro's as big as Shaft's
> I feel a little better about myself.
> (*Muscular Music,* 1999, 19)

John Shaft, the tough-talking, no nonsense detective in the 1970s film bearing his name, first became somewhat of an icon to African Americans in the 1970s (as well as to some whites). Shaft became known as the epitome of masculinity, a kind of precursor to hip-hop moguls such as Tupak Shakur, the Notorious B.I.G., and 50 Cent. The speaker of the poem emulates Shaft's power and fearlessness.

> His afro was a crown.
> Bullet after barreling bullet,
> fist-fights & car-chases,
> three movies & a brief TV series,
> never one muffled strand,
> never dampened by sweat.
> (*Muscular Music,* 1999, 19)

However, in contrast to Shaft, the speaker feels inadequate because "I sweat in the least heroic of situations" (*Muscular Music,* 1999, 19). Still, the speaker tries, rather unsuccessfully, to act like Shaft, whom he sees as the epitome of an African American masculinity but admits his failure to succeed.

> I'm sure you won't believe this,
> but if a policeman walks behind me, I tremble:
> *What would Shaft do? What would Shaft do?*
> Bits of my courage flake away like dandruff
> I'm sweating even as I tell you this,
> I'm not cool,
> I keep the real me tucked beneath a wig.
> (*Muscular Music,* 1999, 20)

Only when the speaker sees films, in the darkness, does he feel better about himself. Thus the poem concludes, "I grow beautiful as the theatre dims" (*Muscular Music,* 1999, 20). However, when the lights go on and the movie ends, one can only assume that the speaker reverts to being insecure and doubtful, and the movie stars he emulates, like Shaft, only serve to exacerbate his feelings of inadequacy.

In a similar way, the desire to be tough and fearless can become absurd if taken to its il/logical conclusions in the poem "I Want to Be Fat." The speaker begins,

> I want to be fat,
> I want a belly big enough to hold
> A refrigerator stuffed with trout,
> Big enough to house a husband with a beer gut,
> A wife with a baby in her belly.
> (*Muscular Music*, 1999, 28)

The speaker really just desires power and feels that being physically large will make him seem more important in the eyes of others as well as to himself.

> When I am fat,
> Ladies sipping diet colas will whisper:
> Look at him. My God how'd he get so big?
> And beneath those questions they'll think,
> *I wonder if he still makes love?*
> *I wonder what he looks like naked?*
> (*Muscular Music*, 1999, 28)

Just as the speaker of the poem "Shafro," emulates Shaft, this speaker looks up to cartoon character Fat Albert, claiming that he will "never forget" him (*Muscular Music*, 1999, 29). Being obese, he believes, will allow him to intimidate others. Consequently the speaker yells out,

> You motherfuckers will have to give me
> My own seat on the bus!
> (*Muscular Music*, 1999, 29)

However, just as the speaker in the poem "Shafro" latches onto Shaft to cover over his own manifold insecurities, so does the speaker of this poem. His desire to be obese only serves to enhance his own feelings of powerlessness. The poem ends on a rather pessimistic note.

> I want to be buried in an ocean of dirt,
> This ocean of flesh, this heart
> Like a fish flopping at the center of it.
> (*Muscular Music*, 1999, 30)

The heart as a "skinny man" indicates how the speaker wants to be fat in order to extinguish his own emotions and pain, as well as to cover up his vulnerabilities.

In *Muscular Music,* Hayes shows how socially accepted, even encouraged masculine toughness can become incredibly violent and destructive, affecting even children, especially those who grow up in violent, urban environments. In this collection, Hayes includes a series of poems that he calls "The Yummy Suite," which he describes as being "inspired by events in Chicago the summer of 1994. Eleven year old Robert 'Yummy' Sandifer murdered fourteen year old Shavon Dean while firing on a rival gang" (*Muscular Music,* 1999, 33). The poem that serves as preface to the Suite is called "The Ballad of Bullethead." Bullethead is a stand-in for desensitized, impoverished youth like Yummy, both products of violent environments, who have been emotionally deadened by all that surrounds them. Hayes writes, from Bullethead's perspective, "I was born in metal," and explains how his father left, leaving his mother and himself to try to survive (*Muscular Music,* 1999, 35). Hayes describes these two.

> Metal child & mother of stone
> Another story of moans
> Bank loans Shut off telephones.
> (*Muscular Music,* 1999, 35)

The angry speaker definitively claims,

> I'll beat uncle sam
> & I won't give a dime or a damn
> (*Muscular Music,* 1999, 35)

In this case, it is the environment and poverty that produce the anger and toughness.

Other poems in "The Yummy Suite" are written from the perspective of people who knew Yummy or the person he killed, Shavon. These people speculate on what caused this tragedy to occur. In the poem "Blues for Shavon," Shavon "lived around the corner from Yummy and had known him growing up" (*Muscular Music,* 1999, 38). Yet the two do not become friends, which is indicative of the nonsupportive nature of their community. A never-named speaker subtly blames a lack of parenting and the pressures to fit in as contributing to Shavon's death.

> Shouldna been playin
> On that corner anyway
> Pavement was hot,
> Potholes everywhere
> Bottles everywhere.
> Those streetlights flickered on

> And your little ass should have been home,
> Steada tryin to be so grown.
> (*Muscular Music*, 1999, 38)

Another poem in the suite is from Yummy's mother, Lorena, or Reen, for short. Yummy had a horrific family environment, unloved and uncared for by his mother. The speaker in the poem, presumably Lorena, claims Yummy was

> drivin me out my fuckin mind
> I'm tired of talkin to you
> Nigga, you just won't listen
> Bought me eleven years trouble
> Eleven years grief
> When they find your ass dead,
> Hope they don't call me.
> (*Muscular Music*, 1999, 39)

Other members of Yummy's family seem emotionally deadened by the amount of tragedy they have experienced in their lives. In "Janie Fields" is the perspective of Yummy's grandmother.

> When she gets the news
> she does not fall down. She does not tremble
> returning his shirt to the drawer.
> (*Muscular Music*, 1999, 40)

Presumably, she responds this way because she has already seen or experienced similar tragedies and has come to expect them.

Not only does Yummy's family seem unaffected by his actions and subsequent death, so does his entire neighborhood. Another of Yummy's "friends," Micaiah, says,

> Nothings changed since Yummy died,
> People still bullshit on the corners
> Sunset to sunrise.
> (*Muscular Music*, 1999, 41)

There also is not any real sympathy for Yummy, even at his funeral. According to Little Ron, another of Yummy's "friends," a lady at Yummy's funeral shouts out, "They need to bury him in that sewer" (*Muscular Music*, 1999, 43). Little Ron insists, "I wasn't crying if that's what you want to know" (*Muscular Music*, 1999, 43). With no attempt to understand why this tragedy happened and with no real sympathy for those involved, it is likely that violence and destruction will continue in impoverished urban, largely African American areas like this one, in large part a result of an emotional deadening caused by poverty and destructive social codes that insist on hiding or extinguishing emotions and vulnerabilities.

Hayes's next collection of poetry, *Hip Logic* (2002), continues in the tradition of *Muscular Music* by uncovering and counteracting stereotypes and destructive codes of behaviors for the hip-hop generation. In an interview, he explains the meaning of the title: "In the physical sense the body's 'hips are the cradle of logic' as the title poem says. Which is to say, our understanding of the world and ourselves begins at our center and radiates outward. And then in a cultural sense, the hip logic implies a new and maybe strange way of taking in the world. A logic that is immediate, but not conventional or regular" (Rowell 2004, 1075). However, *Hip Logic* is not merely a continuation of *Muscular Music*. Rather, in his second collection, Hayes tackles subject matter that is more diverse. One of his main interests still is physicality and the body as noted by the subjects of his poems in both collections. Whereas in *Muscular Music*, he mainly examined impoverished youth and hypermasculine men, in "Emcee" he brings in hip-hop artists as a factor in establishing an atmosphere of tough machismo. He calls "explicit lyrics,"

> the pied piper
> Sending children into jerk patterns and grunts
> Into tunnels of smoke—
> I had to get high to write this.
> (*Hip Logic*, 2002, 5)

This is not to suggest that Hayes's poem is a complete critique of hip-hop for it ends,

> You want the exit code from the tenement, the penitentiary—
> You want [beatbox beatbox beatbox]
> Breathlessness.
> (*Hip Logic*, 2002, 6)

Hayes's use of *[beatbox]* indicates that it is not clear exactly what this emcee wants, and breathlessness could be a kind of death, but at the same time, it could be a desire to have listeners awed or shocked, in other words, leaving them breathless.

In the title poem "Hip Logic," Hayes writes about the physicality emphasized in the African American community. This poem contains vivid, aggressive, and violent imagery, beginning with

> Some shoot the soft bloodless
> heads of basketballs.
> (*Hip Logic*, 2002, 12)

In these two lines, Hayes uses a metaphor comparing violent gangsters to basketball players, each seeming to use their preferred activity to take out their aggression. He emphasizes, "No standing still," in that this is an environment in which physical actions represent an entire person (*Hip Logic*, 2002, 12).

> Some leave their car windows
> cracked & a boomboomboom
> rustles the neighborhood.
> No standing still.
> (*Hip Logic*, 2002, 12)

This is another aggressive act, born from a desire to assert one's self in an impoverished environment that thwarts the individual and in a country that still devalues African Americans. The result for the hip-hop generation is instability and desire to be almost in perpetual motion.

> Trying to catch
> the soul here? Like trying
> to slow light down to a trot.
> (*Hip Logic*, 2002, 12)

Slowing light down is, of course, impossible, as, Hayes suggests, is the ability to firmly define or categorize contemporary African Americans or stop the people he describes from acting so aggressively. Ultimately in this environment, "hips are the cradle of logic," in that all thoughts and perceptions originate from the body. It is a purely physical environment in which actions, appearances, and attitudes speak louder than any words could.

Previously Hayes and other hip-hop-generation writers suggest that rampant physicality and aggression can originate and be reinforced by hip-hop culture. In the poem "Touch," Hayes suggests that it can also come from years of prejudice and unfair practices. The speaker describes how he and other children or teenagers were playing innocently when they are stopped by the police. Sarcastically Hayes writes,

> It's true, we could have been mistaken
> For animals in the dark,
> But of all our possible crimes,
> Blackness was the first.
> (*Hip Logic*, 2002, 7–8)

The police officers arrest the speaker for no legitimate reason without asking any questions. From this traumatic experience, one can imagine that the children or teenagers Hayes describes will grow up to not only be suspicious of the police and other authority figures but also, with further experiences like this one, they will become emotionally hardened and even deadened, if not violent as well.

As with *Muscular Music,* Hayes in *Hip Logic* shows how certain celebrities can also provide the inspiration for the tough façade he sees as endemic in the African American community. In the poem "Shaft & the Enchanted Shoe Factory," he once again writes from the perspective of Shaft,

> *Man I'm about to walk from Chicago to Mississippi*
> *Kicking the ass of every redneck & Republican that moves.*
> (*Hip Logic,* 2002, 15)

In "Mr. T," Hayes explores the 1980s television icon. He begins by describing him.

> a man made of scrap muscle & the steam
> engine's imagination.
> (*Hip Logic,* 2002, 14)

Mr. T is emulated only because of his machine-like physique and aggression and not for any other reason. In that sense, he is not much more than a contemporary noble savage, at best. Hayes calls him

> Half Step 'N Fetchit
> half John Henry.
> (*Hip Logic,* 2002, 14)

In one sense, Mr. T was nothing more than a tool of his more-intelligent white "friends"/criminals in his most popular television show *The A-Team* (hence "Half Step 'N Fetchit"), and yet, he could be viewed as an admirable, even heroic figure to African Americans through his fierce, independent style (hence, the John Henry reference). Still, Hayes wonders,

> What were we, the skinny B-boys,
> to learn from him? How to hulk through Chicago
> in a hedgerow afro, an ox-grunt kicking dust
> behind the teeth; those eighteen glammering
> gold chains around the throat of pity,
> that fat hollow medallion like the sun on a leash.
> (*Hip Logic,* 2002, 14)

The answer to this question is they would learn the importance of being tough, of being muscular, and come to believe that physical prowess, not intelligence, is the best way (at least for African Americans) to become admired and successful. This is the sort of lesson that Hayes suggests, through his first two collections of poetry, that has been so detrimental if not destructive to African Americans.

Hayes's most recent collection of poetry is entitled *Wind in a Box* (2006). In these poems, Hayes explores broader issues of race in America as well as the existing state of the African American community. For instance, in the poem "Woofer (When I Consider the African-American)," he counteracts the stereotypes engendered by the label of African American. When he considers "the much discussed the dilemma / of the African American," he does not think of what most people might consider the epitome of African American culture, but rather

> the diasporic
> middle passing, unchained, juke, jock, and jiving
> sons and daughters of what sleek dashikied poets
> and tether fisted Nationalists commonly call Mother
> Africa.
> (*Wind in a Box*, 2006, 3)

Presumably, Hayes does not consider these people, because he finds them to be rather phony, overblown, and superficial. Rather, Hayes tells us that he thinks of an "ex-girlfriend who was the child of a black-skinned Ghanaian beauty and Jewish-American, globetrotting ethnomusicologist" (*Wind in a Box*, 2006, 3). For Hayes, like Danzy Senna, multiethnic African Americans are the ones who truly understand what it means to be African American because they are situated on racial boundaries. Furthermore Hayes thinks of this ex-girlfriend because he knows her, whereas so-called African American traditions are foreign and remote to him. When he thinks of the so-called African American, he can only think of making love to the same biracial woman he described as,

> among the fresh blood and axe
> and chicken feathers left after the Thanksgiving slaughter
> executed by a 3–D witchdoctor houseguest (his face
> was starred by tribal markings) and her ruddy American
> poppa while drums drummed upstairs from his hi-fi woofers.
> (*Wind in a Box*, 2006, 3)

Hayes claims,

> that's the closest I've ever come to anything
> remotely ritualistic or African, for that matter.
> (*Wind in a Box*, 2006, 3–4)

For Hayes then, what is African American is individual and personal, but, at the same time,

> I think of a string of people connected one to another
> and including the two of us there in the basement
> linked by a hyphen filled with blood;
> linked by a blood filled baton in one great historical relay.
> (*Wind in a Box*, 2006, 4)

That Hayes uses the word *string* indicates that the connection is somewhat tenuous and can be broken with relative ease.

In other poems, Hayes explores the often-tenuous connections between whites and African Americans. In "Talk," for instance, the speaker recalls a friendship he once had with a white boy before racial issues interfered. This "friend" feels comfortable enough with the speaker that he tells him to "talk like a nigger," after the speaker's impersonation of Martin Luther King Jr. (*Wind in a Box*, 2006, 5). His friend did not mean anything malicious by saying "nigger," the speaker admits, realizing that his friend was

> thinking I was so far from that word
> that he could say it to me.
> (*Wind in a Box*, 2006, 6)

Still, the speaker is deeply hurt and affected by his friend's comment, but he does not say anything to him, in part because he wants to maintain their friendship, but in hindsight, he realizes that he was in an almost-impossible dilemma. If he had said something or even hit his friend for what he said, the speaker wonders,

> if he would have grown
> up to be the kind of white man who believes
> all blacks are thugs or if he would have learned
> to bite his tongue or let his belly be filled
> by shame.
> (*Wind in a Box*, 2006, 5–6)

As for himself, the speaker wonders if he would then become,

> the kind of black man who believes silence
> is worth more than talk or that it can be

> a kind of grace, though I'm not sure
> that's the kind of black man I've become.
> (*Wind in a Box*, 2006, 5)

There is no easy answer to this dilemma, the narrator realizes, especially in the contemporary age in which there is an increasing amount of subtle, unconscious racism, such as that exhibited by his friend.

One way this racism may exhibit itself is through the hip-hop generation's seeming forsaking of African American cultural traditions. This shows in the poem "Black History," in which the speaker and his roommate sing the classic African American poem/song, "Lift Every Voice and Sing," which became a kind of anthem for the civil rights movement as well as being known as the unofficial African American anthem. However, they lose to two people reciting Run DMC. The speaker claims,

> I know now it makes sense since
> Black Cool seemed worth more than Black Pride,
> rap worth more than gospel.
> (*Wind in a Box*, 2006, 7)

Hayes, like Joseph, appears conflicted about the hip-hop generation. On the one hand, he sees popular culture as helping to efface the divisions between the races, but at the same time, he sees popular culture as helping to create new stereotypes for African Americans, unreal expectations, and shading over the still-existing institutional racism in America.

7

SUZAN-LORI PARKS

Hip-hop can and has been considered to be many things, but one thing most critics agree upon is that it has important performative aspects. Whether it is projecting the tough façade of a gangster or the bravado of a superconfident woman or man, those involved in hip-hop tend to be extremely cognizant of the importance of image and spectacle as a storyteller or actor/actress often can be. Spectacle is important because it brings attention to the performer and his/her message as well as capturing the attention of the audience. With that consideration, theater is an important venue for writers of the hip-hop generation. The drama of the hip-hop generation can be seen in the work of MacArthur- and Pulitzer Prize–winner Suzan-Lori Parks, a celebrated playwright whose works address issues specific to that of the hip-hop generation. Parks and other hip-hop-generation playwrights form a new category of African American drama, distinct but in some ways related to civil rights-era dramatists such as Lorraine Hansberry, Amiri Baraka, and August Wilson. Like Paul Beatty and Colson Whitehead, Parks explores subtle but important race-related issues in contemporary America. She suggests, as Beatty and Whitehead do, that racism and prejudice have not disappeared but have morphed into more easily ignored but still potentially deadly forms.

Historically theater has played an important role in the development of African American culture from the performative nature of spirituals and gospel music during the times of slavery and afterwards to the serious drama of the Harlem Renaissance that rebelled against the debasing stereotypical productions of vaudeville and minstrel shows in early twentieth-century America. Yet, even during the Harlem Renaissance, there was no clear agreement as to what African American playwrights should or should not ideally showcase. On the one hand, W. E. B. DuBois promoted political theater that directly challenged racism of the time. DuBois argued that valuable art and theater needed to have direct social utility (Hay 1994, 3). Furthermore DuBois's ideal dramatic work need not be completely realistic as it could "show people not only as they actually were but also as they wished to be" (Hay 1994, 3). On the other hand, his contemporary Alan Locke promoted drama that was realistic. To Locke, drama need not necessarily be racial or political in topic or scope; it could focus upon the average or lower-class African American (Hay 1994, 4–5).

Throughout African American drama of the twentieth century, from the drama of the Harlem Renaissance to the drama of the hip-hop generation, this debate is still ongoing, all the way to the plays of Suzan-Lori Parks, in which is a combination of the DuBois and Locke ethos. On the one hand, keeping with DuBois's praxis, Parks directly confronts racial issues in a serious manner. Furthermore her plays often contain metaphorical and allegorical representations of how African Americans are often categorized, such as the characters Black Man with Watermelon and Black Woman with Fried Drumstick in the play *The Death of the Last Black Man in the World* (1992). However, her plays are not always tragedies in the DuBois school of drama, nor are they satires or comedies that would fit more in the Locke school of drama. Rather, the result is a combination of both schools with Parks's plays more often tragicomedies poking fun at stereotypes and at the same time attempting to demolish them. She also uses satire and comedy about serious racial issues as Locke does in order to debunk prejudice and stereotypes (Hay 1994, 28).

African American theater continued after the Harlem Renaissance, but it did not return to regain its critically and commercial importance until the late 1950s when Lorraine Hansberry's *A Raisin in the Sun* first opened on Broadway. "Black Theatre reinvented itself in 1959," Woodie King Jr. explains. "It was that year that *A Raisin in the Sun* opened on Broadway. *A Raisin in the Sun* was the first play to appear on Broadway by a Black female author, Lorraine Hansberry; it was also the first drama to be directed by a Black director, Lloyd Richards. Although many Black plays had been presented in New York as well as around the USA, *A Raisin in the Sun* ushered in the New Black Theatre Movement" (2003, 96).

Following the success of *A Raisin in the Sun,* during the period of the new black theater, playwrights such as Amiri Baraka directly challenged racial stereotypes and prejudice in works such as *Dutchman* (1964) and *The Slave* (1964). According to Hay, the years of the late 1960s and 1970s were "the last period of Black experience theatre, The Bridge, which combined ideas from the DuBois and the Locke schools" (1994, 42). However, this period was also marked by a downward turn in theater attendance: "Beginning in the middle seventies, African American theater organizations closed in unprecedented numbers" (Hay 1994, 134). This continued throughout the 1980s, and it was the climate in which Parks and other hip-hop-generation playwrights first began to emerge.

Shawn-Marie Garrett explains, "The American theater, at the moment Parks emerged, found itself smack in the middle of so-called 'culture wars' and the battle over the reconfiguration of the National Endowment for the Arts. Within the theater, debates raged (and still rage) about how multiculturalism should work, not just in theory but in practice" (2000, 25).

These debates hindered African American drama to the point that, according to Hay, African American theater people, as he calls them, are "on their deathbeds, however, because there are too few young people willing to brave the uncertainty of the theatre profession and the racial prejudice in the preparation" (1994, 2). Along similar lines, Parks, writing in the mid-1990s, suggests that there is "a real crisis in American dramatic literature," in danger of becoming the "Theatre of Schmaltz." She thinks this kind of writing is overdone, transparent, "trying so hard to be so hip" or important (1995, 6). Garrett further explains the problems facing hip-hop-generation playwrights: "Despite the increasing diversification of the American repertoire in the decade since then, there persists in many quarters a mentality, however well-meaning, that ghettoizes African-American drama, and in so doing oversimplifies its formal variety and implies that white and black theatre (and by extension white and black history) have nothing to do with each other: they remain separate but unequal" (2000, 23).

Despite its good intentions, hip-hop theater can sometimes pigeonhole contemporary African American theater as a theater of, by, and about the ghetto or inner city. It is this ghettoization and racial segregation of the theater that Parks and other members of the hip-hop generation rebel against. Similar to Trey Ellis, Parks insists that white people do not have to always be in black drama, nor does it have to concern racial issues (Als 2006, 79): "We are not an impoverished people, but a wealthy people fallen on hard times" (1995, 21).

However, it was in this cultural climate during the 1990s and 2000s that hip-hop-generation playwrights such as Parks emerged and flourished. Their impact has been significant enough to spark another dramatic renaissance of sorts. Consequently, as Robert Alexander and Harry Elam argue in the preface to the collection *The Fire This Time* (2004), which contains the writings by and about the hip-hop-generation dramatists, "The theatre remains a site in which to question, to challenge and to probe. For African American theatre in particular this has meant continued contestations with the definitions of blackness and with the social dynamics of race in America. . . . As we enter the new millennium, the American theater has been more receptive to issues of race than ever before, and consequently we have witnessed a de-centering of the established norms, a more inclusive canon of plays, increased opportunities for black playwrights and performers" (xii–xiii).

Some of this has come about because of the writings of the hip-hop genera-tion. Just as in fiction there arose a bifurcation between more low-brow hip-hop fiction and the more serious literature of the hip-hop generation, a bifurcation also developed in drama between hip-hop theater and the drama of the hip-hop generation, the latter being more literary and the former being more aimed to entertain than to instruct or probe. Examples of hip-hop theater include *Slan-guage* by the Universes and *Rhyme Deferred* by Kamilah Forbes and Hip-Hop Theatre Junction. According to Alexander and Elam, hip-hop plays "are works informed by and infused with the sensibilities of hip-hop music and culture. The thumping bass beats, the syncopated poetry and the driving rhythmic pat-terns of rap music find expression within this new theatre. . . . Yet hip-hop the-atre, like hip-hop itself, is not easily defined. Born out of a creative urgency on urban streets (with self-produced rap tapes sold out of the trunks of cars, and graffiti artworks sprayed on brick city walls), hip-hop exudes a politics of sur-vival and celebrates the 'realness' of its underground roots" (2004, xxii).

Elements of hip-hop theater are in the works of Parks; however, her work does not exude "a politics of survival," nor does it necessarily celebrate "the realness of its underground roots," as Elam and Alexander claim hip-hop the-ater does. Furthermore, while Parks does explore machismo and bravado as Elam and Alexander claim that hip-hop theater does, her work is not focused upon spectacle or image. Unlike hip-hop playwrights, Parks does not "exalt in the expression of the singular virtuosity, the bravado, the machismo and verbal dexterity of the solo rapper rocking the mike" (2004, xxii). However, Parks's plays do contain a few elements that can typically be found in hip-hop theater. Parks's plays and those of hip-hop dramatists involve historical revisionism (Alexander and Elam 2004, xii). In Park's own words: "A play is a blueprint of an even: a way of creating and rewriting history through the medium of litera-ture. Since history is a recorded or remembered event, theatre, for me, is the perfect place to 'make' history—that is, because so much of African American history has been unrecorded, dismembered, washed out, one of my tasks as playwright is to—through literature and the special strange relationship between theatre and real-life—locate the ancestral burial ground, dig for bones, find bones, hear the bones sing, write it down" (1995, 4). Both Parks and writ-ers of hip-hop theater also recycle "these elements from the past, creating a new spirit of possibility and an urgency that speaks to the racial and cultural hybrid-ity of today" (Alexander and Elam 2004, xxii). However, Parks does not include live rap music in her plays as most works of hip-hop theater do (Alexander and Elam 2004, xxii).

Without a doubt, Parks has become one of the most critically acclaimed young, contemporary African American playwrights. She received her first major critical acclaim with an Obie award for *Imperceptible Mutabilities in the Third Kingdom* (1989) (Hay 1994, 133). Parks is also the "first black woman to win a Pulitzer Prize for drama—for her 2001 play *Topdog-Underdog*" (Als 2006, 74). Like many writers of the hip-hop generation, Parks's works are hybrid, combining different elements of previous generations such as the modernistic Harlem Renaissance as well as naturalism, realism, and postmodernism. On the one hand, her work displays African and African American rituals in a realistic fashion, but at the same time her plays often have an absurdist/fantasy element to them (Hay 1994, 131). For Parks it is important to embrace all forms of literature, regardless of whether they are currently in vogue or not: "Most playwrights who consider themselves avant-garde spend a lot of time badmouthing the more traditional forms. The naturalism of, say, Lorraine Hansberry is beautiful and should not be dismissed simply because it's naturalism" (1995, 8). According to Garrett, Parks's plays often focus upon "the most painful aspects of the black experience: Middle Passage, slavery, urban poverty, institutionalized discrimination, racist ethnographies" (2000, 22).

At the same time, Parks wants to break away from racial tropes. Similar to other writers of the hip-hop generation, she thinks the main questions her drama addresses are: "Can a White person be present onstage and not be an oppressor? Can a Black person be onstage and be other than an oppressor? For the Black writer, are there Dramas other than race dramas? Does Black life consist of issues other than race issues" (1995, 21). The result can be almost contradictory plays that can be "both horrific and comic—irresistibly or disrespectfully so, depending on your point of view" (Garrett 2000, 22). Parks describes her plays as being "like complex carbohydrates, nourishing but difficult to digest, and for some, even to watch" (Garrett 2000, 26). There is certainly a social importance to her work. As S. E. Wilmer claims, Parks shows how African Americans "remain alienated in the modern American metropolis" (2000, 442). Though still young, with many years and publications ahead of her, Parks has already made "a noticeable impact on a new generation of African American writers" (Vorlickly 276).

The following is an analysis of a few of Parks's major plays, beginning with *The Death of the Last Black Man in the Entire World*. As Hay argues, this play "is not only a significant watershed in African American theatre, it is also one of the most sophisticated plays in contemporary American theatre" (1994, 133). From the title it is immediately apparent that the play is an extended hyperbole or extended metaphor; however, it also conveys the dire situation that Parks believes African Americans, specifically hip-hop-generation men, to be in. The title and play refer more to rampant ethnic stereotyping, which, Parks suggests, still greatly affects African Americans and prevents them from becoming individuals, let alone fully rounded human beings. This is apparent in the names of the two major characters in the play: Black Man with Watermelon and Black Woman with Fried Drumstick. The play is concurrently realistic and absurdist in nature with characters such as Lots of Grease and Lots of Pork and Ham, who both have speaking lines. According to Hay, "Parks's striking originality was in her naming of characters after these traditional foods. African American theater had never seen "the likes of it" (1994, 130). Parks uses these foods to demonstrate how they have come to overshadow the identity of African Americans. While this might seem like material for an absurdist play, Hay also makes a compelling case for the play's realism, demonstrated by "Parks's complete grasp of the southern African American idioms, lifestyles, and obsessions" (1994, 129–30).

In homage to the Harlem Renaissance, Parks uses what she calls "a jazz system of repetition or rep and rev" in this play, as well as in many of her other plays (1995, 8). She uses this repetition for emphasis and effect, as hip-hop artists might, but also to portray how her characters are caught in a narrow frame, if not prison of identity, because of racial stereotypes, forcing them to act in stereotypical/socially accepted ways rather than allowing them to develop their own individual identities. At the very beginning of the play, this is shown in how the Black Man with Watermelon says, "The black man moves his hands" (1995, 101). Parks's use of the third person indicates how not only has the Black Man's identity been stripped away from him, most noticeable by his lack of a name, but it makes his actions seem hollow and rehearsed. The Black Man with Watermelon seems like he is a performer in a minstrel show. Towards the beginning of the play, he also appears to be caught in one of Parks's systems of repetition as he keeps stating that he's moving his hands, which suggests that he is incapable of doing anything else. At one point in the play, he states that he cannot even move his hands.

As the play progresses, the Black Man with Watermelon slowly tries to remove himself from his stereotypical caricature. At first he states, "The black man bursts into flames. The black man bursts into blames. Whose fault is it?" (1995, 103). The first two sentences are presumably a reference to the Black Man with Watermelon's execution, for the audience finds out later that he was killed for a never-specified reason by a group of racist whites. Gradually the Black Man with Watermelon starts questioning his stereotypes and caricatures. He later insists that, in reference to his name, "Saint mines. Saint mines. Iduhnt it. Nope: iduhnt. Saint mines cause everythin I calls mines got uh print uh me someway on it in it dont got uh print uh me someway on it so saint mines" (1995, 105). In reference to his name and current situation, he also questions,

"Who give birth tuh this I wonder" (1995, 105). However, he never comes up with an answer to this question.

The Black Man with Watermelon, a posthumous character, seems related in some way to the so-called Last Black Man in the Entire World, who is both a singular person and a person who collectively stands for virtually all African Americans (especially men); they, Parks suggests, have become homogenized, debased, and severely limited by racial stereotypes. At one point, it is revealed that the Black Man with Watermelon is wearing a noose from a tree branch where whites attempted unsuccessfully to hang him. Similarly the Voice on Thuh Tee V announces, "A small sliver of uh tree branch has been found in The Death of the Last Black Man" (1995, 120). Also, the Black Woman with Fried Drumstick claims that the death of the last man in the entire world is continual and repetitive: "Yesterday today next summer tomorrow just uh moment" that he died, but she also claims that "it was painless" (1995, 102). In doing so, she suggests that the death of a black man is equivalent to the death of all black men because black men have been stereotyped and homogenized by society and the media and for the most part disallowed from becoming individuals. Therefore the event is both all meaningful and meaningless at the same time. Indeed the Black Woman with Fried Drumstick says that the Last Black Man "have uh head he been keeping under thuh Tee V. On his bottom pantry shelf. He have uh head that hurts. Dont fit right" (1995, 102). By this comment one can surmise that the Last Black Man has been effectively brainwashed by the media; his mind is metaphorically detachable, unimportant, and kept directly below the television, which is seemingly shaping it.

That this black man committed suicide by jumping off a building is indicative of the devastation that loss of identity can cause. In this play and through these characters, Parks sets up a kind of alternative or rival version of history, one that uncovers seemingly invisible or covered-over levels of prejudice and racism. The character "Yes and Greens Black-Eyed Peas Cornbread" frequently commands to the other characters, "You should write that down and you should hide it under a rock" (1995, 102). On the one hand is the belief that society and history deem the lives and deaths of African Americans to be insignificant, but there is also a suspicion, even paranoia about how history is being recorded and kept. That there is a desire to keep this rival history under a rock indicates a need to safeguard it from those who may want to literally and metaphorically whitewash history.

Not only are the stereotypical names of the main characters inaccurate but their empty, stereotypical names also ridicule the characters and in some ways are in complete opposition to who the characters really are. The seemingly posthumous Black Man with Watermelon, for instance, claims that he has not eaten in years despite what his name suggests (1995, 106). He also struggles to move his hands at all. This suggests that he is only afforded the most limited amount of volition, and if he does move his hands, it is unclear whether he is doing it himself or whether someone else is controlling him.

Along similar lines, the so-called Last Black Man in the Entire World, Gamble Major, has a symbolic name in the sense that we learn he was or at least tried to be more of an individual; hence his name can be looked at as how much of a gamble it can be to try to break away from the stereotypes of being African American and to challenge society. Gamble Major's attempt to be an individual and break away from stereotypes seems to have failed because he appears to have become homogenized and brainwashed by the media just before he commits suicide. According to The Voice on Thuh Tee V, Gamble Major was "born a slave taught himself the rudiments of education to become a spearhead in the civil rights movement. He was 38 years old" (1995, 110). Historically speaking, it would be impossible to be thirty-eight years old as Gamble Major is, be born a slave, and be involved in the civil rights movement. In that, he represents all African Americans from the mid-nineteenth century (if not earlier) to the mid-twentieth century. Indeed the Queen and then Pharaoh Hatshepsut says that Gamble fell "23 floors from uh passin ship from space tuh splat on thuh pavement" (1995, 111). His death is also important in that it signifies the death or lack of feasibility of the civil rights-era goal of a raceless utopia, which is a typical criticism of them made by the hip-hop generation. That his death "sparked controlled displays of jubilation in all corners of the world" also indicates that the civil rights movement has been mostly meaningless (1995, 110). However, this is not to suggest that Parks celebrates the advancements made during and by the hip-hop generation, for it is during this time that Gamble Major appears to be the most brainwashed and homogenized by the media, which provides stock caricatures of African Americans (especially hip-hop performers). It is also during this time period, after all, that Gamble ends up committing suicide.

Furthermore the Last Black Man seems to have so deteriorated by the time of his death that, right before he died, according to the character Old Man River Jordan, "He spoked uh speech spoked himself uh chatter-tooth babble 'ya-oh-may/chuh-naw' dribbling down his lips tuh puddle in his lap. Dribblin by droppletts" (1995, 112). At the same time, the seeming homogeneity Parks uncovers is not a completely negative manifestation of racism and prejudice. As he becomes increasingly aware, the Black Man with Watermelon states, "In you all theres kin. You all kin. Kin gave thuh permission kin be givin it now still. Some things is all thuh ways gonna be uh continuin sort of uh some thing. Some things go on and on till they dont stop" (1995, 112). His gradual awakening seems to affect others around him, as noted by how Black Woman with Fried Drumstick contemplates and even seems to begin to question her stereotype: "Feathers sprouted from thuh fried hens—dont ask me how. Somethins out uh whack" (1995, 125). By this, Parks seems to suggest that there can be great importance in the power of just one individual who can help to awaken and change others.

While this potential for gradual enlightenment may seem optimistic, the ending of the play seems more pessimistic. Despite Yes and Green's continual admonishments that the ideas and history of African Americans need to be irreversibly recorded, either kept underneath a rock for safekeeping or actually carved on a rock, the character Ham pronounces, "In thuh roc, I wrote: ha ha ha" (1995, 131). It is this refusal to take the issues seriously that endangers the characters, just as it endangers the hip-hop generation with its general emphasis on the individual above the larger society or African American community. Indeed the play ends in a virtual circle with the Black Woman with Fried Drumstick describing the Black Man with Watermelon moving his hands. If there is a note of optimism, it is that all the characters end the play by repeatedly stating, "Hold it" (1995, 131). Through this ending, Parks suggests that they are pleading to end the seemingly endless cycle of meaninglessness, racism, and violence directed towards and within the African American community.

With *The Death of the Last Black Man in the Entire World,* Parks blends fantasy with reality, rituals get mixed with stereotypes, and the focus is upon the macroscopic. With her play *In the Blood* (1999), Parks focuses more on the microscopic. *In the Blood* is essentially a retelling of Hawthorne's *The Scarlet Letter,* with the name of the major character Hester Prynne changed to Hester Jones. Parks also uses elements of Greek drama in this play. She explains that "The Greeks understood distance and journey; their plays often include events that happen offstage and are retold to us later. In *In the Blood,* I use the confessions, the characters' interior monologues, to describe events that happen offstage. As we hear confession after confession, it occurs to us that so much is happening offstage that we must ask, 'What is going to happen in front of us?'" (Sova 2000, 32).

Parks makes most of Greek dramatic tropes through her use of a chorus, which appears at the beginning of *In the Blood* and appears at other crucial points in the play. This chorus represents society's condemnation of the main character, Hester Jones, who in this play is ostracized and shunned by society (like Hester Prynne) because of supposed sexual transgression. In many ways Hester Jones's situation is much more dire than that of Hester Prynne, with the former being an illiterate, homeless single mother with five children by five different fathers. The Greek-like chorus condemns her at the beginning of the play with the following:

> SHE DONT GOT NO SKILLS
>
> CEPT ONE
>
> CANT READ CANT WRITE
>
> SHE MARRIED?
>
> WHAT DO YOU THINK?
>
> SHE OUGHTA BE MARRIED
>
> THATS WHY THINGS ARE BAD LIKE THEY ARE
>
> CAUSE OF
>
> GIRLS LIKE THAT
>
> (1995, 5)

However, part of Parks's purpose in this play is to overturn stereotypes of the impoverished and those who rely on welfare in order to survive. While this play is not as overtly about race as *The Death of the Last Black Man in the Entire World,* Jones does explore a segment of society—the impoverished—a group that contains an inordinate number of African Americans. Parks also emphasizes Hester's ethnicity at the very beginning of the play by calling her La Negrita. Also, Parks portrays Hester as a warm-hearted, selfless woman who is a casualty of her own good intentions and who is manipulated by those around her. Indeed we first see Hester, after the chorus has summarily debased her, lifting her child "towards the sky," calling her "my treasure, my joy" (1995, 7). Later, she also calls her children, "My 5 treasures. My 5 joys" (1995, 21). This is not the kind of action or behavior one would expect from an impoverished single mother of five. Rather, one would expect, because of media caricatures, that Hester would be a vicious, embittered woman who treats her children horribly and is out to take advantage of government services as much as she can. Contrary to that, Hester genuinely loves her children and sacrifices as much for them as possible. For meals she cobbles together soups but rarely has any herself. Despite that she is illiterate, Hester tells her children uplifting bedtime stories such as one about five siblings who all stick together (*America Play*, 1995, 19). Hester also seeks employment and frequently describes how she attempts, unsuccessfully, to "get a leg up" (22).

In this play Parks suggests that one of the root causes for Hester and her family's impoverishment is institutional and subtle but powerful forms of racism and sexism. As an African American and a woman, Hester is subject to prejudice and discrimination from several different fronts. After time she comes to interiorize feelings of inferiority projected upon her by those around her and society itself (in this play that is manifested through the chorus). Feeling increasingly insecure and unloved, Hester gives herself to virtually any man who is interested in her. When those relationships do not work out, as they inevitably do not, Hester latches onto the only thing left to her: her children. At one point, Hester tells another character, "My kids is mine. I get rid of em what do I got? Nothing. I got nothing now, but if I lose them I got less than nothing" (1995, 28).

As an African American woman, Hester is subject to sexism by men, who have more power. Most notably this occurs with the character, Reverend D, who corresponds to Reverend Dimmensdale in *The Scarlet Letter.* Whereas Dimmensdale is a tormented character who battles with this guilty conscience, Parks's Reverend D seems to have no guilt whatsoever for his disparaging treatment of Hester, but, rather, after getting what he wants from her (sexual favors), he repeatedly deceives Hester in order to get her out of his life and/or keep her quiet. In that Parks suggests that Hester Jones's life and post–civil rights society is much worse than Hester Prynne's repressive colonial New England Puritan society. Reverend D is the quintessential deadbeat dad, rarely ever giving Hester any money and never giving her anything substantial. Beyond that, he also represents American idealism as well as the ideology that allows society to dismiss racism, sexism, and poverty and, along with these things, the downtrodden like Hester. Reverend D preaches individualism and self-reliance when he preaches, for, after all, he was previously homeless, but then, at least according to his account, Reverend D pulled himself up by his bootstraps and became a gainfully employed and respected member of society. However, he is a vicious liar, notable by his treatment of Hester, whom he repeatedly lures with money he rarely ever provides. He is also a token African American success story, allowed to succeed because he preaches the frequently unrealizable rhetoric of individualism and self-reliance that allows wealthier people as well as the bulk of society to assuage their guilt and not feel compelled to take responsibility for the most impoverished ones in society (who are often African American) like Hester and her children.

Hester is summarily disregarded and debased by society through the character Welfare. That Parks never names Welfare is indicative of how impersonal Welfare and, consequently, welfare workers can be. The unsympathetic character Welfare argues, "We at Welfare are at the end of our rope with you. We put you in a job and you quit. We put you in a shelter and you walk. We put you in school and you drop out. Yr children are also truant. . . . We build bridges you burn them" (1995, 54). Yet, if anything, the play shows Hester trying her hardest to fight her way up the economic ladder, and she receives virtually no help whatsoever while she attempts this. Furthermore Welfare takes advantage of Hester by giving her sewing work under the counter, for which Welfare may not adequately pay her. Welfare also compels Hester to engage in a ménage à trois with Welfare and her husband in order to please the latter.

Welfare also confirms Reverend D's particularly American and idealistic philosophy of individualism and self-reliance: "The world is not here to help us, Hester. The world is simply here. We must help ourselves" (1995, 59). However, Hester points out that the reality of her situation is at odds with the idealistic notion that she can merely go out and get a job and stay at the homeless shelter. Her illiteracy and need to take care of her small children make keeping any sort of job difficult to say the least, and the homeless shelters are a little-better alternative to being homeless. As Hester tells Welfare, "The shelter hassles me. Always prying in my business. Stealing my shit. Touching my kids" (1995, 55).

To add insult to injury, the character Welfare, like Reverend D, is African American, and she, like him, creates divisions within her race. Indeed this racial infighting is an element within hip-hop music and culture along with the hip-hop generation itself. Welfare says, "I walk the line between us and them between our kind and their kind" (1995, 60). Welfare has internalized the ethos of the wealthier, mostly white elite and does their dirty work for them. Indeed the existence of impoverished persons like Hester and her family helps make working-class African Americans like Welfare feel better about their own less-than-glamorous lives, as they can consider themselves to be above people like Hester and whom Welfare also considers to be "a low-class person" (1995, 62).

Hester is so ostracized and condemned by society that she has learned to not assert herself and to acquiesce to others. Reverend D also takes advantage of Hester when she is at her weakest and desperate for money by compelling her to perform a sexual act on him. In a confession Reverend D says that he was and remains attracted to Hester's suffering. In this Parks displays a disturbing, sadistic side to the wealthier in that they can get pleasure through witnessing the misfortunes of others. Furthermore Reverend D has no sense of allegiance or camaraderie with his fellow African Americans since he treats Hester so poorly. The reverend is hardly a charitable Christian, despite his title. Parks, like other members of the hip-hop generation, appears skeptical towards organized religion. Not only is the reverend corrupt, but instead of helping the poor like Hester, he is determined to build a new church, and he also seems to be pilfering money from his churchgoing audience as well.

If that was not enough, Hester is also debased by the character called simply The Doctor. Unlike Reverend D, The Doctor seems to have relatively good intentions towards Hester, but he is not much more than a puppet of the government, whose sole concern is that Hester no longer be a burden to society and that she no longer have any more children. Instead of treating Hester's medical problems and borderline starvation, The Doctor merely gives her a pill and confesses that he has been asked to "spay" Hester (1995, 42). To the government then, Hester is more animal than human. The Doctor pleads that he has no power to help Hester, which may or may not be true, but he, like the other men in the play, takes sexual advantage of her. He explains that he had a sexual encounter with Hester when he "was lonesome and she gave herself to me in a way that I had never experienced with women Ive [sic] paid" (1995, 44). However, he, like the other men in the play, never takes responsibility for his actions, leaving Hester to carry all the blame and responsibility herself.

Still, despite her treatment by men, Hester continues to sacrifice herself for them, not only by giving her body to them but also by not revealing to Welfare the identities of the fathers of her children. It has been said that the hip-hop generation is suspicious of any and all governmental entities, and this play demonstrates the rational basis for such suspicions. After all, neither Welfare nor The Doctor has Hester's well-being in mind, so why should she trust in them?

With no social or emotional support and the being the recipient of little more than disregard as an impoverished African American single mother, Hester moves towards a breaking point. She is devastated when Chilli, the father of her first child, Jabber, comes looking to marry her, claiming he is in love with her, only to seemingly change his mind when he sees that Hester has other children. The reverend also deceives Hester by claiming to take up a collection for her at his church, only to keep the money for himself, while calling Hester a slut. Lastly Hester gets the same treatment from her Jabber, who repeatedly calls her a slut.

Hester, experiencing hatred on all sides, even from her children who seem to be the only source of love for her, can no longer contain her own wild devastation. The fury that she had been forced to internalize bursts forth, and in an impulsive, irrational act, she bludgeons Jabber to death with a club. Hester only has power over her children, and she uses them in this one moment as a scapegoat for all of the abuse that has been heaped upon her by more-powerful others. She shouts out, "Never should had him. Never shoulda had none of em. Never was nothing but a pain to me: 5 *Mistakes!*" (1995, 106). Yet when she looks at Jabber's broken body, Hester comes to her senses, realizing that she has destroyed the only meager love she has left in her life. She cries out, "No: I shoulda had a hundred a hundred I should had a hundred-thousand A hundred thousand a whole army full I shoulda!" (1995, 107). The play ends with a newly spayed Hester in prison, no doubt to be punished for the murder of her son. With this ending, Parks, like other writers of the hip-hop generation, suggests that the greatest threat to the African American community comes from within, as well as from subverted but filtered-down institutional racism. After all, no one had to destroy Hester and her children. The climate of racism and neglect surrounding Hester helped lead her to self-destruct, taking her family with her.

Of all of Parks's plays, none has been so critically acclaimed as *Topdog/Underdog* (2001), which won the Pulitzer Prize. Aaron Bryant claims, "Not since Lorraine Hansberry's 1958 *A Raisin in the Sun* or Ntozake Shange's *for colored girls who have considered suicide, when the rainbow is enuf* in the late 1970s has Broadway seen such thought-provoking drama written by a Black woman" (2002, 43). *Topdog/Underdog* details the lives of two brothers, Lincoln and Booth, ironically named by their father and their egoistic attempts to outdo one another and to con others. Just as in hip-hop culture, the criminal life is enticing to both brothers who, having virtually nothing, want to have as much wealth and respect as possible. However, their selfish individualism comes at a devastating cost.

Their names, Lincoln and Booth, are important in several regards. Lincoln, the sixteenth U.S. president, holds an important but contradictory position in African American culture. On the one hand, he is revered for helping to free the slaves and for becoming a martyr in so doing (at least in the eyes of others). However, upon closer look, Lincoln was not a fervent abolitionist, certainly not in the John Brown mold (a person who definitely gave his life in an attempt to help end slavery). After all, in the early days of the Civil War, Lincoln claimed that if he could end the war by not freeing any of the slaves, he would (and, conversely, if he could end the war by feeing all the slaves, he said he would). In the end Lincoln chose the latter as much, if not more, from a military necessity rather than a moral act. Although the emancipation of the slaves produced some immediate gains in civil rights for African Americans over the next decade or so, racial separatism and prejudice returned in full force after the North left the South in 1877, making Lincoln's act somewhat of a hollow victory. Perhaps for these reasons, Lincoln in the play calls the historical Lincoln a "fool" (*Topdog/Underdog*, 2001, 20). African Americans were no longer slaves, but they were not much better off than that in late nineteenth- and early twentieth-century Southern America. On the other hand, there is John Wilkes Booth, one of the most despised figures in American history, who may have inadvertently helped nullify the path towards civil rights and equality for African Americans, for if Lincoln had lived, it is possible that there might have been much greater and quicker advances in civil rights for African Americans.

By this coupling Parks suggests that among the most accepted roles for African American men are being the killer and the killed. In a way this keeps with the most hard-edged elements of hip-hop music and culture: an almost-obsessive focus on murder and death. Furthermore, symbolically, African Americans are placed in the role of Booth in how according to Parks's praxis as well as other writers of the hip-hop generation, they tend to do the most damage to the advancements of African Americans themselves. One can tell from the names of these two major characters that one is destined to destroy the other and that the surviving other will eventually be destroyed himself. That their father, presumably a member of the civil rights generation, named them supposedly as a joke also displays the hip-hop generation's ongoing criticism and suspicion of their parents' generation. Here they seem to be directly implicated in the eventual destruction of these two characters. The "joke" ends up backfiring upon Lincoln and Booth, and in a larger sense, upon the hip-hop generation.

In the play, both Lincoln and Booth seem to be mostly immoral, shady characters. Previous to the present time of the play, Lincoln used to make a living as a con man/card shark in a rigged card game, and his younger brother, Booth, now wants to follow in his seemingly redeemed brother's footsteps by becoming a con man/card shark himself. It is important to point out that Lincoln does not stop being a shady con man/card shark because he develops a moral conscience but more because of safety reasons. He explains to Booth that one of his confederates was killed during one of their cons, and he became concerned for his own well-being (*Topdog/Underdog*, 2001, 33). Along similar lines, Lincoln explains that after the murder of his friend he "didnt have the taste for it no more. Like something in you knew—. Like something in you knew it was time to quit. Quit while you was still ahead" (*Topdog/Underdog*, 2001, 54). Consequently he quits his racket and pursues gainful employment, which he finds as a Lincoln impersonator.

Both Lincoln and Booth are actively dishonest characters and are so in order to appear hyperstrong or hypertough. Booth proudly shoplifts with no guilt whatsoever, while a good deal of both their lies and bravado concern sexual exploits. Throughout the play, Booth brags about his sexual conquests with women (which is, of course, a frequent trope in hip-hop music) and claims that one woman, Grace, is especially in love with him, when Grace either does not exist or does not really want him. Booth also boasts about having unprotected sex with Grace, and when Lincoln and Booth fight, each questions the other's virility. For them, having little or no power in their lives, the only real opportunity to feel confident and secure (in other words, the top dog) is through their sexuality. When Lincoln ridicules Booth for masturbating, Booth retaliates by telling him, "You a limp dick jealous whiteface motherfucker whose wife dumped him cause he couldnt get it up and she told me so. Came crawling to me cause she needed a man" (*Topdog/Underdog*, 2001, 43). Later in the play, Booth also claims that he had sex with Lincoln's ex-wife Cookie in order to wound Lincoln and to become the top dog.

Still, the two brothers are not one and the same, and their difference are significant in the sense of highlighting the distinctions between the harder-edged elements of the hip-hop generation, as represented by Booth as a virtual sociopath and Lincoln as a reformed man who is trying to morally raise himself above his previous life of crime and deceit. Unlike Booth, Lincoln has tried to turn his life around by becoming gainfully employed as a Lincoln impersonator at a place that allows guests to play the role of Booth and mock-shoot Lincoln. To play this role, Lincoln not only dresses up as his historical namesake but he also dresses up in whiteface, and by so doing, his act becomes a kind of minstrel show in reverse. Ironically he is allowed to impersonate a white man only in this circumstance: that this white man, Lincoln, will be killed. To Booth, Lincoln's job is debasing and nothing more than a con just like Lincoln's previous card games. It may be Lincoln himself who is getting conned, Booth believes, because he is apparently getting paid less than he would were he white (*Topdog/Underdog*, 2001, 27). Possibly sensing this, when seeing Lincoln in historical costume, Booth tells him, "I don't like you wearing that bullshit, that shit that bull that disguise that getup that motherdisfuckinguise anywhere in the vicinity of my humble abode" (*Topdog/Underdog*, 2001, 7). Booth claims, "Dressing up like some crackerass white man, some dead president and letting people shoot at you sounds like a hustle to me" (*Topdog/Underdog*, 2001, 20). For Lincoln, however, the job is more meaningful and important. He claims that it is honest work: "I like the job. This is sit down, you know, easy work. I just gotta sit there all day. Folks come in kill phony Honest Abe with the phony pistol. I can sit there and let my mind travel" (*Topdog/Underdog*, 2001, 31).

Lincoln says that he has customers who come frequently in order to "kill" him, and one of his most frequent customers is African American as well. This is symbolically important in the sense that one of the reasons this individual may keep coming back to shoot Lincoln is that he has the opportunity to shoot a white man. However, while he thinks he is shooting a white man, he is actually shooting another African American man—Lincoln. This represents how misguided animosity towards oppressive whites can manifest itself in violence by and upon other African Americans, a common theme in the literature of the hip-hop generation.

As with *The Death of the Last Black Man in the Entire World,* Parks also deconstructs dominant historical narratives in this play. Lincoln fears that he may lose his job, and Booth suggests that he act out the murder scene with more panache. Booth realizes that what Lincoln is doing in his job is entertainment and that he could strive to entertain them more. However, Lincoln does not entirely agree: "People are funny about they Lincoln shit. Its historical. People like they historical shit in a certain way. They like it to unfold the way they folded it up. Neatly like a book. Not raggedy and bloody and screaming" (*Topdog/Underdog*, 2001, 50). Along these same lines, one of the biggest criticisms that members of the hip-hop generation level against contemporary American society is how institutional, subtle racism tends to be ignored or dismissed. Rather, the common societal belief is that we now live in an egalitarian or nearly egalitarian society. To Booth, though, historical accuracy does not matter. He is content to give the audience what they want (in his own words, by adding some "spicy shit" [*Topdog/Underdog*, 48]) in order to get what he wants: more money. His selfishness is what will ultimately undo the two brothers, just as selfish individualism, taken to an extreme, can help lead towards implosion of the hip-hop generation and the African American community.

While Lincoln claims to have reformed his previous criminal ways, he is not the bastion of honesty by any means. Towards the beginning of the play, he tells Booth about how a rich-looking boy asked for his autograph when Lincoln was in historical costume while on the bus. Lincoln not only extorts ten dollars from the boy, but when the boy gives him a twenty-dollar bill, Lincoln keeps the change and lies to the boy, falsely claiming that he already gave the boy his change back. While Lincoln seems more settled and more moral than Booth, he may only appear so. He, like Booth, also has no real ties to his heritage or culture as an African American man. Although Lincoln does, at one point, sing and play an old-fashioned blues song on his guitar, it has no deeper significance to him as a response to racial oppression by his forebears. Furthermore, when Booth advises his brother to possibly change his name to something else, Lincoln responds, "You gonna call yrself something african? That be cool. Only pick something thats easy to spell and pronounce, man, cause you know, some of them african names, I mean, ok, Im down with the power to the people thing, but, no ones gonna hire you if they cant say yr name" (*Topdog/Underdog*, 2001, 12). Lincoln's advice shows how little his heritage means to him. It also shows how cynical he is (and perhaps, understandably so) towards the powers that be. Lincoln's belief is that the celebration of African heritage is a social liability more than an asset.

Part of the play concerns Lincoln and Booth's upbringing, which seems to be at least partially responsible for their subsequently dysfunctional adulthood. Not only did their father give them their names that will indirectly or directly lead to their eventual destruction but both parents also abandoned them when they are children. According to Booth, "What he [their father] didnt spend on booze he spent on women" (*Topdog/Underdog*, 2001, 27). Booth and Lincoln's subsequent dishonesty may stem from their desire to not confront their past. This is apparent in how Lincoln generates and even seems to believe in false, happy memories of their childhood. For instance Lincoln remembers them "selling lemonade on the corner, thuh treehouse in the back," but Booth reminds him that it never happened (*Topdog/Underdog,* 2001, 64). It is important to acknowledge that Parks does not display their parents as aberrant but rather as typical civil-rights-era members. Lincoln explains to Booth, "I think there was something out there that they liked more than they liked us and for years they was struggling against moving towards that more liked something. Each of them had a special something that they was struggling against. Moms had hers. Pops had his. And they was struggling" (*Topdog/Underdog,* 2001, 66).

In their struggle to achieve a middle-class existence and in their fight against racism and discrimination, their parents gradually ignore Lincoln and Booth and eventually abandon them. The parents end up leaving within two years of one another, providing Lincoln and Booth each five hundred dollars (a total of one thousand dollars each). Booth claims, "Theyd been scheming together all along. They left separately but they was in agreement" (*Topdog/Underdog,* 2001, 69). Given how they both leave identically, it is hard to disagree with Booth's analysis. In one sense their abandonment brings the two brothers closer together. Booth explains, "I didnt mind them leaving cause you was there. Thats why Im hooked on us working together. . . . It was you and me against the world, Link. It could be like that again" (*Topdog/Underdog,* 2001, 69). Yet the two keep battling for dominance because they have no other method to assert themselves and develop confidence and a sense of self-worth.

These battles between the two brothers escalate when Lincoln loses his job as a historical reenactor and goes back to being a con man/card shark. Now they are both competing for the same thing, and the stakes to outdo one another become greater as their livelihoods depend in it; both brothers are too selfish and egotistical to work together and/or help the other one out. The animosity and competition between the two brothers reach a boiling point as Lincoln purportedly teaches Booth how to conduct his card con game, only to cheat Booth out of his so-called inheritance, the money that was left him by his parents.

That each brother's only inheritance is money indicates how culturally devoid these two are. They were provided with no heritage or culture through their parents, let alone love, only money. Because of that, Lincoln and especially Booth come to regard money as their culture and heritage and, most significantly, the money left to them by their parents. When Lincoln tries to cheat Booth out of his inheritance, it is too much for Booth to stand because it would be essentially robbing him of his heritage. Even when Lincoln has a change of heart and tells Booth to take back his inheritance, Booth encourages Lincoln to take it, for it gives Booth the opportunity to act upon his thwarted and now-raging anger by shooting and killing Lincoln, thus getting rid of his older brother, who has become the top dog. The play ends similarly to *In the Blood,* with Booth initially cursing Lincoln just like Hester curses Jabber (whom she also kills). However, when Booth gets closer to Lincoln's body to get the money/inheritance (just like when Hester gets closer to Jabber's body), the stage directions state, "He just crumples. As he sits beside Lincolns body, the money-stocking falls away. Booth holds Lincolns body, hugging him close. He sobs"; the play ends with Booth screaming, "AAAAAAAAAH" (*Topdog/Underdog*, 2001, 109). Just like *In the Blood*, these characters self-destruct because of the structure of their institutional and implicitly racist society.

With these three plays, Parks suggests that the greatest threat to African Americans comes from themselves. Without a clear-cut common cause or goals but still suffering the ill effects of racism, members of the hip-hop generation are, to some extent, in a worse situation that the members of the civil rights generation were in the 1950s and 1960s. In absence of a distinct adversary and of clear and common goals, their anger and frustration get misdirected upon themselves, threatening the very fabric of the African American community. Parks's plays are miles away from the hedonistic and individually focused, popular hip-hop of today. Furthermore her plays help to overturn the individually focused ethos of hip-hop and demonstrate how it is this very ethos, a product of contemporary institutional and subtle racism and prejudice, that can help further undo, if not completely destroy the African American community.

CONCLUSION

When most people hear the words *hip-hop*, literature is probably furthest from their minds, because hip-hop, due in large part to the media, is now commonly associated with physicality, violence, and sexuality, whereby the body is not only placed above the mind but also may be all there is to develop, display, and promote. This, according to Kai Wright, a member of the hip-hop generation, "is the hip-hop my dad and his generation have no patience for" (2004, 40). However, this is not a true representation of the hip-hop generation. When Wright hears the word *hip-hop*, she, like many members of the hip-hop generation, has more positive, constructive connotations. She thinks of a twenty-five-year-old poet named Baron who is "everything hip-hop is not supposed to be: a tall, thin, and unapologetically gay brother, with a quick wit drawn from both the classroom and the street" (2004, 41). Her point is that there is an important, intellectually rich, and socially engaged hip-hop generation who defies contemporary stereotypes about hip-hop.

Along similar lines, in the article "Making Some Noise: The Academy's Hip Hop Generation" (2004), Kendra Hamilton suggests that in recent years, a new field of hip-hop studies in academia has emerged. Corroborating her claim is Scott Heath, an assistant professor of English at Georgetown University, who sees hip-hop studies not only as "a vital mode of African American cultural expression" but also one that allows the combination of "theory and practice" (35). Similarly I feel that the academic study of the literature of the hip-hop generation is an important intersection point between academics and street life as well as literature and sociology. As with Generation X, members of the hip-hop generation have been debased by the media as anti-intellectual hedonists or slackers, but this demeaning picture is far from accurate or comprehensive.

It has been suggested that literature is losing relevance for the younger generation, who tend to view reading as a dull, academic chore. However, one way for students to become engaged with contemporary racial issues and encourage them to read literature is by including works written by members of the hip-hop generation. Doing this could have broader, real-world implications that go beyond the classroom. Many contemporary Americans have been lulled into a false sense of security in their belief that racial issues are passé or that American society is egalitarian. However, it has been estimated that "one black men in three will go to jail at some point during his life—more than five times the rate for white men" ("Free to Succeed or Fail," 2000, 21). Furthermore a vicious circle of poverty has developed in the inner city: "legitimate businesses tend to shun the ghetto. And since they do, ghetto youths often grow up without positive adult role models—only dreams that they will one day be a drug boss, drinking Cristal with a bevy of mistresses" ("Free to Succeed or Fail," 2000, 21).

The writers of the hip-hop generation refuse to believe that this discrepancy in the quality of life between whites and African Americans is a result of genetic differences or a lack of motivation on the part of African Americans. Rather, the writers of the hip-hop generation suggest that as much as we might wish otherwise, America still has a long road ahead before approaching anything like racial egalitarianism. It has been suggested that the hip-hop generation shuns education and academia. I submit that if this is correct, it is because the material assigned in college courses is not speaking to them and their passions. The gifted writers of the hip-hop generation are completely deserving of further academic study and inclusion in academic courses. Sociological and cultural-studies courses on the hip-hop generation are important, but literature provides a comprehensive, humanistic, and holistic approach to issues that can further engage readers and students alike. Statistics and theories are important, but so are the stories that put human faces on issues. It is my deepest hope that the writers of the hip-hop generation are given further scholarly attention and incorporated into college curriculums, for their primary goals are among the most noble and valuable aspirations an artist can ever have: to counteract inequalities, prejudice, and racism.

Notes

Introduction

1. To my knowledge there has yet to be a full-scale, legitimate survey to determine the most famous and widely respected African American man. Prior to the emergence of Barack Obama as a presidential candidate in 2008, if it was not Cosby, he would be close in the running to such individuals as Colin Powell, Michael Jordan, Magic Johnson, and Denzel Washington.

2. Loosely speaking, the civil rights generation is equivalent to African American baby boomers. If the *Brown* decision in 1954 is considered as the beginning of the civil rights movement, this generation includes African Americans such as Cosby who were born in the late 1930s to the middle to late 1950s.

3. Essentially the hip-hop generation is African American Generation X and similar to Generation X. There is some debate as to what years frame this generation. The birth-year range of 1960–79 for the hip-hop generation is used in this volume. Those born in the early 1960s should be considered part of the post–civil rights generation, as the hip-hop generation is often called, not the civil rights generation, as they would have been too young to participate in the civil rights movement and, for that matter, would have little or no memories of segregation. To my knowledge no one has yet come up with a name to describe African Americans born after the early 1980s, whereas a number of names were coined and are used to describe the entire American generation born in the 1980s and 1990s, such as Generation Y, Generation Next, and the millennials.

4. One class responded particularly vehemently to an essay arguing in favor of giving Native Americans back some of their sacred spaces. Ironically many students against the idea were part Native American. Only one brave student, a Native American who had grown up on a reservation, spoke out in support of the author, and after class she said that the rest of the class was "a bunch of racists." I did not share that sentiment, but her comment helped solidify my perception of the still-lingering racial divide in this country and even in the ranks of American youth.

5. This analysis is somewhat simplified, as when hip-hop was started in the 1970s in the Bronx, it was not strongly socially engaged music but rather more dance and party oriented. In the early 1980s, there were politically active hip-hop songs such as Grandmaster Flash's "The Message."

6. Some exceptions to this rule are Sister Souljah's novel *The Coldest Winter Ever*, in which the protagonist ends up in jail, and some of Omar Tyree's novels.

7. The exception to this might be Turner's Mercy in *Riding Dirty on I-95,* who improbably becomes a wealthy screenwriter.

Chapter 1: Trey Ellis

1. A direct link between Spike Lee and hip-hop-generation writers is Suzan-Lori Parks (see chapter 7), who wrote the screenplay for Lee's film *Girl 6* (1996).

2. Like Coupland, Ellis has moved away from being categorized as a generational spokesperson in recent years. Whereas Coupland continued writing novels, Ellis has moved into journalism and the film industry. He is a regular blogger on Arianna Huffington's popular political Web site www.huffingtonpost.com. He has also cowritten the film *The Inkwell* (1994) and the made-for-TV movie *The Tuskegee Airmen* (1995).

3. I am not suggesting that rock 'n' roll was a white invention, for rock music has its origins in the African American forms of rhythm and blues, and to be certain, one germinal rock musician was Chuck Berry. In that sense bands such as Fishbone and In Living Color reclaim rock music for African Americans. As far as punk music goes, although white musicians primarily created it, it has its origins in rock 'n' roll and thereby can be traced back to rhythm and blues as well.

4. For instance Diddy's homage to the Notorious B.I.G., "I'll Be Missing You," is an adaptation of the Police song "Every Breath You Take."

5. In this way Ellis and other writers of the hip-hop generation have much in common with Caucasian Generation X writers such as David Foster Wallace, Douglas Coupland, and Dave Eggers, who both embrace and reject certain aspects of postmodern fiction. Specifically they tend to embrace the textual and form experimentation but reject what they perceive to be an emotional and social disconnect in postmodern fiction.

6. Ashton believes it to be an authentic religious experience, but since because the rest of the novel is realistic and straightforward, I do not believe Ellis intends for the reader to believe that Ashton had really seen a spirit. Furthermore, that he drank cough syrup before seeing this spirit makes it hard to believe he actually saw anything.

7. It is my belief that Ashton is still alive, and the final vision in the novel is a hallucination, as once again, the novel is otherwise realistic.

Chapter 2: Jake Lamar

1. I do not feel that Lamar is being anti-Semitic with Seth because no character in *The Last Integrationist* is wholly sympathetic, and the true villain of the novel turns out to be President McCracken, who is not Jewish.

2. They thought it was Trudy's dog until they unexpectedly catch Trudy in the act one night.

Chapter 3: Colson Whitehead

1. Because Whitehead describes Quincy as the third-oldest university in the United States and as extremely well endowed, I believe it is a fictional version of Yale University.

2. Presumably Admiral Java is Starbucks coffee; the sneaker chain could be Foot Locker. It is hard to determine what the computer chain could be, although it may represent Best Buy.

3. The protagonist does not limp because he has to, though, which suggests that Whitehead believes that the protagonist's pain and isolation are largely self-imposed.

Chapter 4: Paul Beatty

1. To be fair, there has been some debate about the number of Jewish American slaveholders and the extent to which they played a part in the slave trade. In October 1991 the Nation of Islam's Historical Research Department anonymously published *The Secret Relationship between Blacks and Jews,* a book claiming to use "the most respected Jewish authorities" to charge Jews with "monumental culpability" in the slave trade. However, other sources dispute this information. For instance, Rabbi Sholomo Ben Levy claims, "The number of Jewish slave owners is known to have been small and proselytizing by Jews was not common." Furthermore, as Rabbi Perry Raphael Rank explains, "A Charleston record of the day (in the 1850s) points to the presence of 19,532 slaves, of which 300 were owned by Jews."

2. Considering Manischewitz is a Jewish name for a brand of wine typically used during Passover, this may be a subtle criticism of Judaism. Beatty may be implicating Jews for the denigration of the educational system or just realistically reflecting how African Americans have taken over the impoverished areas that used to be predominately Jewish.

3. All of the recruiters are African American, indicating not only that the colleges believe African Americans will only truly trust one of their own but also these same recruiters seem to be mostly amoral, for the most part ready to capitalize on Gunnar however they can.

Chapter 5: Danzy Senna

1. Birdie's and Cole's experience seems based on Senna's own. She describes that her sister and she "attended an Afrocentric school in the late 1970s, where I got teased and on occasion roughed up for looking so 'light, bright, and damn near white.' My sister, being braver, and more visibly black than me, became my protector. There I witnessed the hypocrisy of black nationalism. While the school preached the Kwanzaa value of community, I was not invited to perform in it with the rest of my classmates" (1998, 76).

2. Deck's book is probably a response to Henry Louis Gates Jr.'s *Signifying Monkey: A Theory of African-American Literary Criticism* (1989) in which Gates explores the relationship between the African and African American vernacular traditions and literature.

Works Cited

Alexander, Robert, and Harry Elam, eds. 2004. *The Fire This Time*. New York: Theatre Communications Group.

Als, Hilton. 2006. "The Show-Woman." *New Yorker* 82(35):74–81.

Arias, Claudia Millian. 2002. "An Interview with Danzy Senna." *Callaloo: A Journal of African American and African Arts and Letters* 25(2): 447–52.

Beatty, Paul. 1991. *Big Bank Take Little Bank*. New York: Nuyorican Poets Café.

———. 1994. *Joker, Joker, Deuce*. New York: Penguin.

———. 1996. *The White Boy Shuffle*. New York: Picador.

———. 2000. *Tuff*. New York: Anchor.

Boucher, Geoff. 2002. "A Politician Who Runs on Hip-Hop." *Los Angeles Times,* May 11. Available at http://www.daveyd.com/newsdetroitmayorhiphop.html (accessed June 23, 2006).

Boyd, Todd. 2003. *Young, Black, Rich and Famous*. New York: Doubleday.

Bryant, Aaron. 2002. "Broadway, Her Way." *New Crisis* 109(2): 43–45.

Bynoe, Yvonne. 2004. *Stand and Deliver*. Brooklyn, N.Y.: Soft Skull.

Carroll, Mary. 1995. "The Last Integrationist." *Booklist* 92(5): 454.

Chang, Jeff. 2005. *Can't Stop, Won't Stop: A History of the Hip-Hop Generation*. New York: St. Martin's.

Childress, Sarah, Ellis Cose, and Lisa Helem. 2004. "Does Cosby Help?" *Newsweek* 145(1): 66–69.

Cosby, Bill. 2004. "Pound Cake Speech." Address at the NAACP on the Fiftieth Anniversary of *Brown versus Board of Education,* Constitution Hall, Washington, D.C., May 17, 2004. http://www.americanrhetoric.com/speeches/billcosbypoundcakespeech.htm (accessed June 15, 2008).

"Cosby Cries Foul." 2004. *People* 62(3): 75.

DaCosta, Kimberly, and Rebecca King. 1996. "Changing Face, Changing Race." In *The Multiracial Experience,* edited by Maria P. P. Root, 227–44. Thousand Oaks, Calif.: Sage.

Dais, Risasi. 2004. "Bill Cosby's 'Tough Love' Message Electrifies Newark." *New York Amsterdam News* 95(38): 5–6.

Dubey, Madhu. 2003. "Postmodernism as Postnationalism? Racial Representation in U.S. Black Cultural Studies." *Black Scholar* 33(1): 2–18.

———. 2003. *Signs and Cities: Black Literary Postmodernism*. Chicago: University of Chicago Press.

Dyson, Michael Eric. 2005. *Is Bill Cosby Right? (Or Has the Black Middle Class Lost Its Mind?)* New York: Basic Civitas Books.

Eleveld, Mark, ed. 2003. *The Spoken Word Revolution.* Naperville, Ill.: Sourcebooks.

Ellis, Trey. 1988. *Platitudes.* Boston: Northeastern University Press.

———. 1989. "The New Black Aesthetic." *Callaloo: A Journal of African American and African Arts and Letters* 12(1): 233–43.

———. 1994. *Home Repairs.* New York: Washington Square.

———. 1999. *Right Here, Right Now.* New York: Simon and Schuster.

Ferguson, Darren, and Marjorie Fields Harris. 2006. "Who's Pimpin' Who: The Hip-Hop Generation's Need to Rename (Reclaim) Itself." *New York Amsterdam News* 97(13): 13–35.

"Free to Succeed or Fail." 2005. *Economist* 376(8438): 20–22.

Fulwood, Sam, III. 2005. "Is Bill Cosby Right? Or Has the Black Middle Class Lost Its Mind?" *Black Issues Book Review* 7(4): 75.

"Funnyman's Serious Message." 2006. *USA Today,* May 22: 12A.

Furman, Andrew. 2003. "Revisiting Literary Blacks and Jews." *Midwest Quarterly* 44(2): 131–49.

Garrett, Shawn-Marie. 2000. "The Possession of Suzan-Lori Parks." *American Theatre* 17(8): 22–29.

Gates, Henry Louis, and Cornel West. 1996. *The Future of the Race.* New York: Alfred Knopf.

Gilmore, Brian. 2002. "Fear of a Hip-Hop Planet." *Progressive* 66(7): 41–42.

Ginwright, Shawn A. 2004. *Black in School.* New York: Teachers College Press.

"The Halloween Fallout Continues." November 22, 2002. *Critical Mass.* http://www.erinoconnor.org/archives/2002/11/the_halloween_f.html (accessed June 23, 2006).

Hamilton, Kendra. 1996. "An Interview with Allison Joseph." *Callaloo: A Journal of African American and African Arts and Letters* 19(2): 461–72.

———. 2004. "Making Some Noise: The Academy's Hip-Hop Generation." *Black Issues in Higher Education* 21(5): 34–35.

Hay, Samuel. 1994. *African American Theatre.* Cambridge: Cambridge University Press.

Hayes, Terrence. 1999. *Muscular Music.* Chicago: Tia Chucha.

———. 2002. *Hip Logic.* New York: Penguin.

———. 2006. *Wind in a Box.* New York: Penguin.

Historical Research Department of the Nation of Islam. 1991. *The Secret Relationship between Blacks and Jews.* Chicago: Nation of Islam.

Hollinger, David. 1995. *Postethnic America.* New York: Basic Books.

Jones, Steve. 2006. "Cosby Gives a 'Call Out.'" *USA Today,* May 17: 1D.

Joseph, Allison. 1997. *In Every Seam.* Pittsburgh, Penn.: University of Pittsburgh Press.

———. 1997. *Soul Train.* Pittsburgh, Penn.: Carnegie Mellon University Press.

———. 2003. *Imitation of Life.* Pittsburgh, Penn.: Carnegie Mellon University Press.

———. 2004. *Worldly Pleasures.* Cincinnati: WordTech Communications.

King, Woodie, Jr. 2003. *The Impact of Race.* New York: Applause Theatre and Cinema Books.

Kitwana, Bakari. 2002. *The Hip Hop Generation.* New York: Basic Books.

Lamar, Jake. 1992. *Bourgeois Blues.* New York: Plume.

———. 1996. *The Last Integrationist.* New York: Crown.

———. 1998. *Close to the Bone.* New York: Crown.

———. 2001. *If Six Were Nine.* New York: Crown.

———. 2003. *The Eighteenth Arrondissement.* New York: St. Martin's Minotaur.

Levy, Sholomo Ben. "The Black Jewish or Hebrew Israelite Community. The Jewish Virtual Library." http://www.jewishvirtuallibrary.org/jsource/Judaism/blackjews .html (accessed September 2, 2006).

Lewis, Joel. 1991–92. Review of *Big Bank Take Little Bank. American Book Review* 13: 6.

Lott, Eric. 1989. "Response to Trey Ellis's 'The New Black Aesthetic.'" *Callaloo: A Journal of African American and African Arts and Letters* 12(1): 244–46.

McQuillar, Tayannah, Yvette Mingo, and Malcolm Venable. 2004. "It's Urban, It's Real, but Is This Literature?" *Black Issues Book Review,* 6(5): 24–25.

Miller, Laura. 1999. "Colson Whitehead: The Salon Interview." *Salon,* January 12. http://www.salon.com/books/int/1999/01/cov_si_12int.html (accessed March 27, 2006).

Molette, Carlton, and Barbara Molette. 1992. *Black Theatre.* Bristol, Ill.: Wyndham Hall.

Neal, Mark Anthony. 1998. "'It Be's That Way Sometimes 'Cause I Can't Control the Rhyme': Notes from the Post-Soul Intelligentsia." *Black Renaissance/Renaissance Noire* 1(3): 8.

———. 2002. *Soul Babies: Black Popular Culture and the Post-Soul Aesthetic.* New York: Routledge.

New York State Writers Institute. 2006. "Colson Whitehead," April 2. http://www .albany.edu/writers-inst/webpages4/archives/whitehead_colson.html (accessed June 15, 2008).

Parks, Suzan-Lori. 1995. *The America Play and Other Works.* New York: Theatre Communications Group.

———. 2001. *The Red Letter Plays.* New York: Theatre Communications Group.

———. 2001. *Topdog/Underdog.* New York: Theatre Communications Group.

Patrick, Diane. 2004. "Book of the Day: *Rendezvous Eighteenth.*" *PWDaily,* September 23. http://www.jakelamar.com/diane-patrick.html (accessed April 22, 2006).

Peterson, V. R. 1992. "Jake Lamar." *Essence* 22(12): 67.

Pinckney, Darryl. 1993. Review of *Home Repairs.* "Home Repairs." *New York Review of Books* 40: 33.

Pough, Gwendolyn. 2004. *Check It While I Wreck It.* Boston: Northeastern University Press.

Poulson-Bryant, Scott. 1991. Review of *Big Bank Take Little Bank. Voice Literary Supplement* 93: 5.

Powell, Kevin. 1997. *Keepin' It Real: Post-MTV Reflections on Race, Sex, and Politics.* New York: Ballantine.

———, ed. 2000. *Step into a World.* New York: John Wiley.

Rank, Perry Raphael. 2004. "Celebrating 350 Years of American Jewry." *Midway Cybershul,* September 16–17. http://www.mjc.org/cyber%20shul/Cyb092504.htm (accessed September 2, 2006).

Rowell, Charles Henry. 2004. "The Poet in the Enchanted Shoe Factory: An Interview with Terrence Hayes." *Callaloo: A Journal of African American and African Arts and Letters* 27(4): 1068–81.

Schmidt, Alvin. 1997. *The Menace of Multiculturalism.* Westport, Conn.: Prager.

Seaman, Donna. 1998. Review of *Caucasia. Booklist* 94(12): 985.

Senna, Danzy. 1998. *Caucasia.* New York: Riverhead Books.

———. 1998. "Passing and the Problematic of Multiracial Pride." *Black Renaissance/Renaissance Noire* 2(1): 76.

———. 2004. *Symptomatic.* New York: Riverhead Books.

Sollors, Werner. 1997. *Neither Black nor White Yet Both.* Oxford: Oxford University Press.

Souljah, Sister. 2000. *The Coldest Winter Ever.* New York: Pocket Books.

Sova, Kathy. 2000. "A Better Mirror." *American Theatre* 17(3): 32.

Svobaba, Terese. 1995. Review of *Joker, Joker, Deuce. Kenyon Review* 17(2): 154–60.

Tammaro, Thom. 1991. Review of *Big Bank Take Little Bank. Library Journal* 116: 107.

Turner, Nikki. 2004. *A Project Chick.* Columbus, Ohio: Triple Crown.

———. 2005. *Riding Dirty on I-95.* Columbus, Ohio: Triple Crown.

Vorlickly, Robert. 2007. "An American Echo: Suzan-Lori Parks's The America Play and James Scruggs's Disposable Men." In *Interrogating America through Theatre and Performance,* edited by William Demastes and Iris Smith Fischer, 271–90. New York: Palgrave Macmillan.

Washington, Robert E. 2001. *The Ideologies of African American Literature.* Oxford: Rowman & Littlefield.

Weber, Rebecca L. 2004. "The Africana QA: Danzy Senna." July 6. http://www.rebecalweber.com/danzy.html (accessed June 7, 2006).

Weich, Dave. 2005. "Reading Along to the Paul Beatty Shuffle." *Powell's Books,* December 13. http://www.powells.com/authors/beatty.html (accessed April 18, 2006).

Wells, Monique. 2004. "The Africana Profile: Novelist Jake Lamar." *Africana: Gateway to the Black World,* September 23. http://archive.blackvoices.com/articles/daily/bk200404271amar.asp (accessed May 2, 2006).

West, Cornel. 1993. *Prophetic Reflections: Notes on Race and Power in America.* Monroe, Maine: Common Courage.

———. 1993. *Prophetic Thought in Postmodern Times.* Monroe, Maine: Common Courage.

Whitehead, Colson. 1999. *The Intuitionist.* New York: Anchor Books.

———. 2001. *John Henry Days.* New York: Anchor Books.

———. 2004. *The Colossus of New York.* New York: Doubleday.

———. 2006. *Apex Hides the Hurt.* New York: Doubleday.

———. 2006. "I Worked at an Ill-Conceived Internet Start-Up and All I Got Was This Lousy Idea for a Novel." April 3. http://www.randomhouse.com/boldtype/0501/whitehead/essay.html (accessed June 15, 2008).

Williams, Brett. 1983. *John Henry: A Bio-bibliography.* Westport, Conn.: Greenwood Press.

Wilmer, S. E. 2000. "Restaging the Nation: The Work of Suzan-Lori Parks." *Modern Drama* 43: 442–52.

Wright, Kai. 2004. "Hip-Hop Kids These Days." *Progressive* 68(10): 40–42.

Young, Kevin, ed. 2000. *Giant Steps: The New Generation of African American Writers.* New York: HarperCollins.

Zack, Naomi. 1996. "On Being and Not-Being Black and Jewish." In *The Multiracial Experience,* edited by Maria P. P. Root, 140–51. Thousand Oaks, Calif.: Sage.

Index

About the Author

DANIEL GRASSIAN is the chair of the Department of Humanities and assistant professor of English at Nevada State College in Henderson. He is the author of *Understanding Sherman Alexie* and *Hybrid Fictions: American Literature and Generation X*. His essays and articles on contemporary American fiction and culture have appeared in the *Midwest Quarterly*, the *Journal of the Fantastic in the Arts*, *Journal X*, *Popular Culture Review*, and several edited collections.